FOLK TALES FROM TIBET

FOLK TALES FROM TIBET

WITH ILLUSTRATIONS BY A TIBETAN ARTIST AND SOME VERSES FROM TIBETAN LOVE-SONGS

COLLECTED AND TRANSLATED

BY

CAPT. W. F. O'CONNOR, C.I.E.

Secretary and Interpreter of the Mission of Lhasa (1904)

GYAN

Published by

Gyan Publishing House
5, Ansari Road
Daryaganj, New Delhi-110002
Phone: 011-47034999, 9811692060
E-mail: books@gyanbooks.com

Distribution Network
gyanbooks.com
India, USA, Canada, UK, Australia, France

ISBN : 978-81-212-2895-4 (PB)
First Published, 1906

2nd Impression 2021

Printed at: Gyan Press, Delhi.

Folk tales From Tibet
Author: CAPT. W. F. O'Connor

FOLK TALES FROM TIBET

WITH ILLUSTRATIONS BY A TIBETAN ARTIST
AND SOME VERSES FROM TIBETAN
LOVE-SONGS

COLLECTED AND TRANSLATED

BY

CAPT. W. F. O'CONNOR, C.I.E.

Secretary and Interpreter of the Mission to Lhasa (1904)

LONDON
HURST AND BLACKETT, LTD.
182, HIGH HOLBORN, W.C.

1906

THE CHAPEL RIVER PRESS
KINGSTON SURREY

PREFACE.

In presenting these little stories to the public, it may perhaps be of interest if I describe how I came by them.

During two years spent in Tibet, at Gyantse, Lhasa, and elsewhere, I have made many friends amongst all classes of Tibetans—high and low, rich and poor—and have conversed with all sorts of persons upon all sorts of topics. In the course of my wanderings I learned that there exists amongst this fascinating and little-known people a wealth of folk-lore, hitherto inaccessible to the outside world, and I made efforts to collect as many of their stories as I could.

For certain special reasons this quest proved more difficult than I had anticipated. In the first place, I found that many of the best known stories had been imported bodily from India* or China, and possess but little of that local colouring which is one of the chief charms of folk-lore. Secondly, some of the very best and most characteristic stories are unfit for publication in such a book as this.† And, thirdly, human nature being much the same all the world over, it was not always

* Compare, for example, "Tibetan Tales derived from Indian Sources," translated from the Tibetan of the Kah Gyur into German by F. Anton von Schiefner. Done into English from the German by R. W. S. Ralston.

† But I am preserving such of these as appear to me to possess any scientific interest.

possible to find a suitable *raconteur* in a suitable mood for story-telling. A story told by a nervous or reluctant narrator loses half its charm. A good story must be natural, and necessitates sympathy on the part both of teller and of hearer. Armed diplomatic missions and an official position, apart from all questions of difference of language and nationality, do not tend to elicit the ideal sentiments necessary for the establishment of complete mutual confidence.

But patience, and the growth of kindly feelings on both sides, helped me to some extent to overcome the shyness and reluctance of the simple folk who have supplied me with my material; and, as time went on, I was able to coax a story from many unlikely sources. Village headmen, monks, servants, local government officials, peasants, traders—these and many others have contributed to my store. Shyly and haltingly at starting, with many bashful apologies and disclaimers, the story-teller will begin his tale. But a Tibetan audience is one of the best imaginable, and their open sympathy and appreciation soon melt the frosts of reserve, and the words flow freely. Presently all sense of constraint is lost, and I have known a story interrupted for ten minutes at a time by the uncontrollable merriment aroused by some comic incident.

Some of the stories, then, I have been obliged, reluctantly enough, to discard altogether for the present; others require further revision or elucidation. But the rest of my little store I give here, and with this one apology: that I have made no attempt to ornament or improve upon them. I have written them down just as I heard them, and have translated them, as accurately as I could, from the Tibetan idiom into ours. As to their origin or scientific bearing I say nothing, and put forward no theories. I leave the Tales to speak for themselves; but would invite, and shall cordially welcome, the criticisms and surmises of all students of folk-lore who are in a position to give an expert opinion upon such points, and to shed a light upon obscure corners into which I have been unable to penetrate.

I have added to the stories a few verses taken at random from popular Tibetan love-songs, as a sample of the wealth of imagery and genuine poetic sentiment which is to be found amongst the inhabitants of this strange country. Owing to the extremely idiomatic form and severe compression of Tibetan metrical compositions, the translation of these songs into anything even distantly resembling poetry, without altogether destroying the characteristics of the original, presents peculiar difficulties; and I must crave indulgence for their crudeness and lack of artistic finish.

The pictures are the maiden effort at book illustration of a Tibetan artist, resident at Gyantse, and are, I fear, somewhat weak in details, as owing to my absence from Gyantse during the time they were in progress I was unable personally to superintend their execution. For the excellent photograph which appears as the frontispiece I am indebted to my friend and companion at Gyantse, Capt. R. Steen, of the Indian Medical Service.

In conclusion, I must express my grateful acknowledgments to Mr. Perceval Landon, to whose suggestion the collection and publication of these Tales, as well as their illustration by a native artist, is in a great measure due; and I must thank him, moreover, for many valuable hints and much kindly sympathy and assistance.

W. F. O'CONNOR, Capt.

CONTENTS.

LIST OF ILLUSTRATIONS.

FOLK TALES FROM TIBET.

STORY No. I.

HOW THE HARE GOT HIS SPLIT LIP.

A HARE was going along a road one day, when suddenly, on turning a corner, he came upon a large Tiger. The Tiger at once seized the Hare, and said that he was going to eat him.

"Please, please, Uncle Tiger," said the Hare, holding up his thumbs in supplication, "please don't eat me, I am only a very small beast, and will make a very insufficient meal for a great big animal like you. And if you will spare my life I will take you to where you can find a much bigger, fatter creature than me for your supper."

"Very well," said the Tiger, "I agree to that. But if you don't show me a much bigger animal than you are, I shall certainly be obliged to eat you."

So he released the Hare, and the two walked off along the road together.

As they went along night began to fall, and when it was quite dark the Hare began smacking his chops and making sounds as if he was eating something very nice.

"What are you eating, Brother Hare?" asked the Tiger.

"I am eating my eye, Uncle Tiger," replied the Hare. "I have taken it out and eaten it; it is very nice, and it soon grows again."

The Tiger was rather surprised at hearing this, but being very hungry he proceeded to scrape out his own eye and eat it up. After going a little further the Hare again began smacking his lips, as if he was eating something.

"What are you eating now, Brother Hare?" asked the Tiger.

"I am eating my other eye, Uncle Tiger," replied the Hare; "it is even better than the first."

The foolish Tiger on hearing this proceeded to scrape out his other eye and eat that.

The Tiger was now quite blind, and the Hare led him along to the brink of a deep gulf, where he advised the Tiger to sit down and rest for a while. And after the Tiger was seated, the Hare said:

"Don't you find it cold, Uncle Tiger? shall I light you a fire?"

"Yes, please, Brother Hare," said the Tiger, "I think a fire would be very pleasant."

So the Hare lighted a fire just in front of the Tiger, and when it was blazing up he kept putting the sticks nearer and nearer the Tiger, so that the Tiger was obliged to keep edging further and further away, when all of a sudden he toppled over backwards into the gulf behind. Now it happened that half-way down the

THE HARE AND THE TIGER

gulf a tree was growing from a cleft in the precipice, and as he passed this the Tiger seized one of the boughs with his teeth, and so arrested his fall. The Hare, peeping over the edge, saw what had happened, and he called out:

"Oh, Uncle Tiger, Uncle Tiger, are you safe?"

The Tiger was afraid to open his mouth to reply, and all he could do was to growl, "M—m—m——"

"Oh, Uncle Tiger," said the Hare, "is that all you can say? I am afraid you must be very badly hurt. Do just say 'Ah!' and I shall know that you are all right."

The Tiger, anxious to please the Hare, opened his mouth to say "Ah!" and was instantly precipitated to the bottom of the gulf, where he fell upon some rocks and was killed.

Next morning the Hare went hopping down the road when he met a Man driving along a lot of Horses.

"Good morning, Father Man," said he to the driver. "Would you like to know where you can find a good Tiger's skin?"

"Yes, please, Brother Hare," said the Man, thinking he would sell the skin and make a lot of money.

So the Hare pointed out to him where the dead Tiger lay in the ravine, and the Man hastened off to skin it, after first asking the Hare to take care of his Horses while he was away.

As soon as he was out of sight the Hare saw two Ravens sitting in a tree overhead. He called out to them:

"Brothers Raven, look here! Here are a lot of Horses

with no one in charge. Why don't you come down and feed on the sores on their backs ?"

The Ravens thought this was a good idea, and flying down, they perched on the Horses' backs, and began to dig their beaks into the sore places. The poor Horses, in fear and pain, soon stampeded, and galloped about all over the country.

The Hare then hopped on a little further down the road and came upon a Boy tending Sheep.

"Good-morning, Brother Boy," said the Hare, "would you like to know where there is a fine Raven's nest, full of eggs ?"

"Yes, please, Brother Hare," said the Boy, thinking he would climb the tree and take the Raven's eggs. So the Hare pointed out to him the tree where the Raven's nest was, and the Boy ran off to get the eggs, after first asking the Hare to take charge of the Sheep for him while he was away.

The Hare soon espied a Wolf on the hill-side not far off, so he went up to him and said :

"Good-morning, Brother Wolf, do you know that there is a fine flock of Sheep quite unguarded down there, and I should advise you to take advantage of this opportunity of killing some of them."

The Wolf at once rushed down the hill into the middle of the flock of Sheep, scattering them all in every direction, and killing as many as he thought he required for his own use.

Meanwhile the Hare proceeded to the top of a high hill whence he could survey the whole country. From there he was able to discern the dead Tiger lying in the ravine, with the Man stripping off its skin; the Horses careering all over the country, with the Ravens pecking at the sores on their backs; the Boy robbing the Raven's nest; and the Sheep, pursued by the Wolf, scattered to the four quarters of the compass.

The sight so amused the Hare that he leaned back on a handy stone, and laughed to such an extent that he actually split his upper lip. And it has remained split to this very day.

STORY No. II.

THE STORY OF THE TIGER AND THE MAN.

ONCE upon a time there were two Tigers who lived in a certain forest and had a family of three children. The Father Tiger grew old and began to fail, and just before his death he sent for his three children and addressed them as follows:

"Remember, my children," said he, "that the Tiger is Lord of the jungle; he roams about at his will and makes a prey of the other animals as he wishes, and none can gainsay him. But there is one animal against whom you must be on your guard. He alone is more powerful and cunning than the Tiger. That animal is Man, and I warn you solemnly before I die to beware of Man, and on no account to try to hunt or to kill him."

So saying, the old Tiger turned on his side and died.

The three young Tigers listened respectfully to the words of their dying parent and promised to obey; and the elder brothers, who were obedient sons, were careful to follow his advice. They confined their attentions to the slaughter of deer, pigs, and other denizens of the forest, and were careful, whenever they came within sight or scent of any human being, to clear off as fast as they could from so dangerous a neighbourhood. But the youngest Tiger was of an independent and inquisitive disposition. As he grew older and stronger he began to chafe against the restriction that had been imposed upon him.

"What, after all," thought he to himself, "can be this creature Man that I should not slay him if I wish. I am told that he is but a defenceless creature, that his strength cannot be compared to mine, and that his claws and teeth are quite contemptible. I can pull down the largest stag or tackle the fiercest boar with impunity. Why, then, should not I be able to kill and eat Man also?"

So after a while, in his conceit and folly, he determined to quit his own part of the forest and to venture forth towards the open country in search of a Man as his prey. His two brothers and his mother tried to reason with him and to persuade him to remember the words of his dying father, but with no avail; and finally, one fine morning, in spite of their prayers and entreaties, he set off alone on his search.

He had not proceeded very far when he met an old, worn-out pack-Bullock, thin and emaciated, and with the marks of many ancient scars on his back. The young Tiger had never seen a Bullock before, and he regarded the creature with some curiosity. Walking up to it he said:

"What sort of animal are you, pray? Are you a Man by any chance?"

"No, indeed," replied the creature; "I am only a poor Bullock."

"Ah!" said the Tiger. "Well, perhaps you can tell me what sort of an animal Man is, for I am just going out to find and kill one."

"Beware of Man, young Tiger," replied the Bullock; "he is a dangerous and a faithless creature. Just look at me for example. From the time when I was very young I was Man's servant. I carried loads for him on my back, as you may see by these scars, and for many years I slaved for him faithfully and well. While I was young and strong he cared for me and valued me highly; but as soon as I became old and weak, and was no longer able to do his work, he turned me out into this wild jungle to seek my food as best I might, and gave no thought for me in my old age. I warn you solemnly to leave him alone and not to try and kill him. He is very cunning and dangerous."

But the young Tiger only laughed at the warning and went on his way. Soon afterwards he came across an ancient Elephant wandering by itself on the outskirts of the forest, and feeding with its trunk on the grasses and foliage which it loves. The old animal had a wrinkled skin and a small and bleary eye, and behind its huge ears were many cuts and ancient scars, showing where the goad had been so frequently applied.

The young Tiger eyed this strange animal with some surprise, and going up to it he said:

"What sort of an animal are you, please? You are not a Man, I suppose?"

"No, indeed," replied the Elephant; "I am only a poor old worn-out Elephant."

"Is that so?" answered the Tiger. "Perhaps you can tell me, however, what sort of a creature Man is, as I am now hunting for one in order to kill and eat him."

"Beware how you hunt Man, young Tiger," replied the old Elephant; "he is a faithless and dangerous animal. Look at my case. Although I am the Lord of the jungle, Man tamed me, and trained me, and made me his servant for many years. He put a saddle on my back and made stirrups of my ears, and he used to strike me over my head with an iron goad. While I was young and strong he valued me highly. Food was brought to me, as much as I could eat every day, and I had a special attendant who used to wash and groom me, and to see to all my wants. But when I became old and too infirm for further work, he turned me out into the jungle to fend for myself as best I could. If you will take my advice you will leave Man alone, or it will be the worse for you in the end."

But the young Tiger laughed contemptuously and went on his way. After proceeding for some little distance he heard the sound of some one chopping wood, and creeping near he saw that it was a Woodcutter engaged in felling a tree. After watching him for some time the Tiger emerged from the jungle, and going up to the Man, he asked what sort of an animal he was. The Woodcutter replied:

"Why, what an ignorant Tiger you are; can't you see that I am a Man?"

"Oh, are you," replied the Tiger, "what a piece of

luck for me. I was just looking for a Man in order to kill and eat him, and you will do nicely."

On hearing this the Woodcutter began to laugh. "Kill and eat *me*," he replied; "why, don't you know that Man is much too clever to be killed and eaten by a Tiger? Just come with me a little way and I will show you some things which only a Man knows, but which will be very useful for you to learn."

The Tiger thought that this was a good idea, so he followed the Man through the jungle until they came to the Man's house, which was strongly built of timber and heavy logs.

"What is that place?" said the Tiger when he saw it.

"That is called a house," replied the Man. "I will show you how we use it."

And so saying he went inside and shut the door.

"Now," said he, speaking from the inside to the Tiger, "you see what a foolish creature a Tiger is compared to a Man. You poor animals live in a hole in the forest, exposed to wind, rain, cold and heat; and all your strength is of no value to make a house like this. Whereas I, although I am so much weaker than you, can build myself a fine house, where I live at my ease, indifferent to the weather and secure from the attacks of wild animals."

On hearing this the young Tiger flew into a violent passion.

"What right," said he, "has an ugly, defenceless creature like you to possess such a lovely house? Look at me, with my beautiful stripes, and my great teeth and claws, and my long tail. I am far more worthy than you of a house. Come out at once, and give your house over to me."

"Oh, very well," said the Man, and he came out of the house leaving the door open, and the Tiger stalked in.

"Now, look at me," called out the conceited young Tiger from inside, "don't I look nice in my fine house?"

"Very nice indeed," replied the Man, and bolting the door outside he walked off with his axe, leaving the Tiger to starve to death.

STORY No. III.

THE STORY OF GOOD FAITH.

THE Tiger soon got tired of sitting in the house and tried to force his way out; but the house was too strongly built for him to be able to make any impression upon the walls, so he gave it up in despair and soon began to suffer severely from hunger and thirst. Two or three days passed away and the Tiger was in a sorry state, when, as he was peering through a chink in the logs he saw a little Musk Deer, which had come down to drink at the stream which was close by. When the Tiger saw the Deer he called out to her:

"Oh, Sister Deer, will you please come and open the door of this house. I am shut up inside, and as I have nothing to eat and drink I am afraid of starving to death."

The Deer was a good deal frightened when she heard the Tiger's voice, but when she understood how matters were she was reassured, and replied:

"Oh, Uncle Tiger, I am very sorry to hear of your misfortune. But I am afraid if I open the door and let you out you will kill and eat me."

"No, no, I won't," replied the Tiger, "you can rely

upon me. I promise you faithfully that if you will release me I will let you go free."

Accordingly, the Deer came up to the house and unbolted the door from the outside, and the Tiger sprang out joyfully. As soon as he got outside he seized upon the Deer and said:

"I am very sorry for you, Sister Deer, but the fact is I am so famished that really I have no alternative but to eat you immediately."

"This is really too bad," replied the Deer; "after promising faithfully that you would not eat me, and after the benefit which I have conferred upon you, you should certainly keep faith with me."

"Faith!" said the Tiger. "What is faith? I don't believe there is any such thing as good faith."

"Is there not?" answered the Deer. "Well now, let us make a bargain. We will ask the first three living things we meet whether or no there is such a thing as good faith. If they say there is not, then you are welcome to kill and eat me; but if they say there is such a thing, then you shall let me go free."

"Very good," said the Tiger, "I agree to that; that is a bargain."

So the two set off together side by side, and after proceeding a short distance down the road they came upon a large Tree growing by the roadside.

"Good-morning, Brother Tree," said the Musk Deer, "we want to refer a question to you for your decision."

The Tree waved its branches in the air and replied in a gentle voice:

"What is your question, Sister Deer? I am ready to do my best to help you."

"The case is this," replied the Musk Deer, "a short while ago I found this Tiger shut up in a Woodcutter's hut in the forest, unable to get out. He called out to me asking me to open the door of the hut, promising me, if I did so, that he would let me go free. So I opened the door and let him out. No sooner was he released than he seized upon me and threatened to kill and eat me; and when I reproached him of breaking his faith, he said he did not believe that there was such a thing as good faith in the world. So we made a bargain that we would ask the first three living things we met whether or no there is such a thing as good faith in this world. If they say there is not, then the Tiger is to kill and eat me; but if they say that there is such a thing, then I am to go free. Will you please give us an opinion as to whether such a thing as good faith exists or not."

On hearing this story the great Tree moved its branches slowly in the breeze and replied as follows:

"I am much interested in your story, Sister Deer, and would gladly help you if I could; but I am bound to answer you honestly in accordance with my own experience of life. Now consider my own case. I grow here by the roadside and spread my branches over the dusty highway ready to give shelter to man and beast in their shade. Travellers passing constantly up and down the road avail themselves of this cool retreat, and they come themselves and they bring their poor beasts of burden to rest in my shadow. And then what happens ? Are they grateful to me for the comfort which I afford them ? Does my example inspire them with any consideration for others ? Far from it. When they have rested and refreshed themselves enough, they proceed on their way, and not only do they not thank me for my hospitality, but they break off my tender branches and use them as whips, further to goad and distress their weary animals. Can such conduct as that be called good faith ? No, I am bound to say that my experience of life leads me to believe that there is no such thing as good faith in this world."

The poor Musk Deer was much cast down on hearing these words, and she and the Tiger moved on together till, a little farther along the road, they caught sight of a Cow Buffalo and her Calf grazing quietly in a field of succulent grass. They noticed that the old Cow contented herself with the driest and smallest patches of grass, whilst showing her Calf where to find the richest and most luxuriant pasture, and that she willingly deprived herself of any comfort in order to afford pleasure to the youngster. The Tiger and the Deer approached the old Cow, and the Deer, addressing her said :

"Good-morning, Aunt Buffalo ! This Tiger and I have a small matter which we wish to refer to you for an opinion."

The Buffalo gazed at them with her big eyes, and after ruminating for a while she replied slowly :

"Say on, Sister Deer, I am ready to give you my opinion for what it is worth."

"Well," said the Deer, "this Tiger was shut up in a hut in the forest, and being unable to open the door, he was in danger of starving to death. I happened to pass by, and he called to me, asking me to let him out, promising that if I did so he would spare my life. So I opened the door and released him. But no sooner was he free than he seized upon me and said that he would kill and eat me; and when I reproached him with his bad faith, he replied that he did not believe that such a thing as good faith existed. So we made a bargain that we would ask the first three living things we met whether or no they believed that there is such a thing as good faith. If they say there is not, then the Tiger is to eat me; but if they say that there is such a thing, I am to go free. Now, will you please give us your opinion on the matter."

On hearing this statement the old Buffalo continued to chew the cud for some minutes, and then replied gravely:

"I would gladly help you in the matter, Sister Deer, if I could; but I must regard it from the point of view of my own experience in life. I am considering the case of myself and my Calf. While the Calf is young and tender, I do all in my power to nourish and care for it. I first give it my milk, and later on, as you see, I encourage it to browse upon the best of the herbage, whilst I gladly stint myself in order that it may have plenty of the best of everything. But what happens later on, when the Calf grows strong and lusty? Does it remember its old mother with gratitude, and fend for her in her old age? Far from it. As soon as it is big enough it will push me away from the places where I am grazing and take the best for itself, and will drive me away altogether from the pastures if it can. Can that be called keeping faith with its mother? No; my experience makes me believe that there is no such thing as good faith in this world."

When the Musk Deer heard this she was much downhearted, and fully expected to be killed and eaten without further delay; but she begged the Tiger to give her one more chance, saying that she was fully prepared to abide by the opinion of the third person whom they met.

The Tiger consented to this, and after going on a little farther together they met a Hare, hopping quietly down the road towards them.

"Good-morning, Brother Hare," called out the Musk Deer; "could you spare us a few moments to give us an opinion upon a point of difference which has arisen between this Tiger and myself?"

"Certainly," replied the Hare, stopping short in the roadway. "I shall be delighted to do the best I can for you."

"Well," replied the Musk Deer, "the facts are as follows: I was drinking just now at a stream in the forest when I noticed this Tiger shut up in a Woodcutter's hut. The door was bolted outside, and he was unable to come out, and was in danger of starving to death, so he called out to me, asking me to release him, promising me, if I did so, that he would spare my life. I accordingly opened the door; but no sooner did the Tiger come out, than he seized upon me, saying that he was so hungry that he had really no alternative but to devour me on the spot. And when I reproached him for his bad faith, he replied that he did not know what good faith was, and, in fact, did not believe that such a thing existed. So we made a bargain that we would ask the first three living creatures we met whether or no there is such a thing as good faith in this world. If they say there is, then I am to go free; but if they say there is not, then the Tiger is at liberty to kill and eat me. We have already consulted two persons in the matter, and they are both of opinion that there is no such thing as good faith. You are the third and last, and on your decision depends my life."

"Dear me," replied the Hare, "this is a very strange story, and before giving an opinion on so momentous a matter it is necessary that I should understand exactly how it all happened. Let me see. You say that you were shut up in the Woodcutter's hut."

"No, no," broke in the Tiger; "it was I who was shut up in the Woodcutter's hut."

"Oh! I see," said the Hare; "then the Musk Deer must have shut you in?"

"Oh! no," interrupted the Musk Deer. "You don't seem to understand at all; that was not how it happened."

"Well," said the Hare, "it is such a complicated story that it is difficult to follow it exactly. So before giving a decision I propose that we all adjourn to the scene of action, and there you can explain to me precisely what occurred."

The Tiger and the Musk Deer agreed to this, and the three set off together until they arrived at the Woodcutter's hut in the forest.

"Now," said the Hare, "will you please explain to me exactly what happened. Where, for instance, were you, Sister Deer, at the time the Tiger spoke to you?"

"I was down here drinking at the stream, so," replied the Deer, going off to the place in question.

"And where were you, Uncle Tiger?" said the Hare.

"Well, I was inside the hut, thus," replied the Tiger, going inside the house.

"And the door, I presume, must have been shut, so?" said the Hare. And so saying he shut the door and bolted it; and he and the Deer went on their way safely, leaving the Tiger shut up inside, where he shortly after starved to death.

STORY No. IV.

THE STORY OF THE TWO NEIGHBOURS.

ONCE upon a time there were two Neighbours living in two houses, side by side, in the same village. One of these was rich, and the other one poor. The rich man, whose name was Tse-ring, was proud, arrogant, and stingy; whilst the poor man, whose name was Cham-ba, was a kind-hearted man, who was generous to all as far as his means allowed.

Now it happened that a pair of Sparrows came and built their nest in the eaves over the doorway of the poor man's house, where, in the course of time, the young birds were hatched out. One day, before the young birds had learnt to fly, the two old Sparrows were away hunting for food, and one of the young ones fell out of its nest on to the poor man's door-step, and broke its leg. Shortly after the poor man coming into his house saw the young Sparrow lying helpless on his door-step, so he picked it up to see what was wrong, and found that its leg was broken. So he carried it into the house, and very carefully bound up its leg with a piece of thread; and then took it up to the roof, and put it back in the nest.

Now this Sparrow, although the poor man did not know it, was really a fairy in disguise, and later on, when it had grown up, it flew out one day and returned with its beak full of grain. The poor man was sitting in his house when the little Sparrow flew in and perched on the table in front of him. It dropped the grain on the table, and after giving one or two chirps it said to the man :

" This grain is in return for your kindness to me. Plant it in your garden and see what comes up," and so saying it flew away.

The poor man was very much surprised at hearing the Sparrow speak, and he thought to himself :

" Well, this is not a very valuable present, but still it shows how grateful even a little bird can be for a kindness done to him ; and any way I will plant the grain in my garden as it directed."

So he planted the grain just in front of his house, and soon forgot all about the incident.

A month or two later the grain grew, and soon attained its full height ; and one day the poor man, going to look at it, was astonished to find that, instead of grain, each ear of corn contained a valuable jewel. He was very much delighted at this discovery, and having collected all the jewels, he carried them away to a neighbouring town, where he was able to sell them for a large sum of money, and thus found himself in a condition of great comfort and prosperity.

Soon after this the rich Neighbour, having observed the change which had taken place in the poor man's circumstances, came over one day in order to try and find out how Cham-ba had become so rich and prosperous. He carried over with him a jug of beer, and, on the pretence of conviviality, he offered his Neighbour a drink, and during the course of the conversation which followed he asked Cham-ba to tell him the secret of his new wealth. Cham-ba, who was of a very unsuspicious nature, related to him the whole story of the Sparrow, the grain, and the jewels, and having learnt the secret the rich man returned to his own house, pondering deeply how he could turn this story to his own advantage.

Now it happened that a Sparrow had hatched out her young in a nest just over his house door also. So next day he went up on to the roof, and leaning out over the parapet he picked out a young Sparrow from the nest with a pair of chop-sticks, and dropped it on to the ground below, where the poor little bird broke its leg. He then went down, picked up the young Sparrow, bound up its leg with a piece of thread, and put it back into its nest, saying as he did so that he hoped it would remember his kindness.

Sure enough, when the Sparrow grew up it flew into his house one day, and perched on the table before him. It dropped some grain from its beak, and after a few preliminary chirps it said:

"This grain is a present in return for your kindness to me. Plant it in your garden and see what grows up."

The rich man was greatly delighted on hearing this,

THE WICKED NEIGHBOUR REMOVING YOUNG SPARROW FROM NEST.

Page 22.

and thought to himself that he would soon be the possessor of beautiful jewels like his Neighbour. He prepared a bed very carefully in his garden, and planted the grain in the richest part of the soil. Every day he used to go and watch the spot, carefully examining the young shoots to see how they were getting on.

The seeds sprouted and grew very fast, and one morning, when he went out as usual to see how his crop was doing, to his astonishment he found that instead of a few stalks of barley, as he had expected, a great fierce-looking man, with a bundle of papers under his arm, was standing in the middle of the bed. The rich man was very frightened at seeing this truculent-looking stranger, and asked who he was.

"I was a creditor of yours in one of your former existences," replied the Apparition. "You were then heavily in my debt, and I have come back here with all the necessary documents to claim what you owed me."

So saying, the Stranger seized upon the rich man's house, his cattle, his sheep, his lands, and all his possessions, and reduced the rich man to the position of a slave in his household.

Some months after, Cham-ba, now rich and prosperous, started off on a journey, and before going he asked Tse-ring to take charge of a bag of gold-dust for him, and to keep it until he returned. Tse-ring undertook the charge of the gold, but in his new state of poverty and dependence he was unable to resist the temptation of spending some of it, and at last he found that the whole of the gold left in his charge was exhausted. Not knowing what to do he filled the bag with sand, and awaited his Neighbour's return with some trepidation.

A few days after Cham-ba came back from his journey, and called upon his Neighbour, and asked for his bag of gold. Tse-ring produced the bag and handed it over to Cham-ba without saying anything, and when Cham-ba opened it to see whether the gold was all right he found that it contained sand instead of gold.

" How is this ? " said he. " I entrusted to you a bag of gold-dust, and you have given me back only sand."

The dishonest Neighbour had no reply to make. He pretended to look very surprised, and all he could say was :

" My friend, it has turned into this ! My friend, it has turned into this ! "

Cham-ba said nothing more, but carried off the bag to his own house.

Soon afterwards Cham-ba announced his intention of starting a school for little boys, where they would be taught free, and Tse-ring, thinking that a free education for his Son was not to be neglected, sent over his young Son to attend the school. A few days later he found it necessary to make a short journey to a neighbouring town, and before starting he entrusted his little Son to his neighbour, Cham-ba, and asked him to look after the boy until his return.

As soon as he was gone Cham-ba procured a tame Monkey and taught it to say the following words .

"WORTHY FATHER, I AM TURNED INTO THIS."

"Worthy father, I am turned into this! Worthy father, I am turned into this!"

When Tse-ring returned from his journey he walked over to the school-house one day to see how his Son was getting on, and he found Cham-ba seated there teaching the boys their lessons. Tse-ring looked round to see his Son, but could not detect him anywhere, but to his surprise he noticed a Monkey seated on one of the benches.

"Where is my son?" asked Tse-ring, "and how is he getting on?"

Cham-ba said nothing, but picked up the Monkey and carried it to him.

"What do you mean by this?" said Tse-ring. "This is not my Son. Where is the boy whom I entrusted to your care?"

Whereupon the Monkey spoke up and said:

"Worthy father, I am turned into this! Worthy father, I am turned into this!"

The father flew into a violent rage and stormed at his neighbour, Cham-ba, for some time, but without producing any impression. Finally, on thinking the matter over, he decided it was better to pay up the gold he had stolen, on condition of having his proper Son restored to him.

STORY No. V.

THE STORY OF THE CAT AND THE MICE.

ONCE upon a time there was a Cat who lived in a large farm-house in which there was a great number of Mice. For many years the Cat found no difficulty in catching as many Mice as she wanted to eat, and she lived a very peaceful and pleasant life. But as time passed on she found that she was growing old and infirm, and that it was becoming more and more difficult for her to catch the same number of Mice as before; so after thinking very carefully what was the best thing to do, she one day called all the Mice together, and after promising not to touch them, she addressed them as follows:

"Oh! Mice," said she, "I have called you together in order to say something to you. The fact is that I have led a very wicked life, and now, in my old age, I repent of having caused you all so much inconvenience and annoyance. So I am going for the future to turn over a new leaf. It is my intention now to give myself up entirely to religious contemplation and no longer to molest you, so henceforth you are at liberty to run about as freely as you will without fear of me. All I ask of you is that twice every day you should all file past me in procession and each one make an obeisance as you pass me by, as a token of your gratitude to me for my kindness."

When the Mice heard this they were greatly pleased, for they thought that now, at last, they would be free from all danger from their former enemy, the Cat. So they very thankfully promised to fulfil the Cat's conditions, and agreed that they would file past her and make a salaam twice every day.

So when evening came the Cat took her seat on a cushion at one end of the room, and the Mice all went by in single file, each one making a profound salaam as it passed.

Now the cunning old Cat had arranged this little plan very carefully with an object of her own; for, as soon as the procession had all passed by with the exception of one little Mouse, she suddenly seized the last Mouse in her claws without anybody else noticing what had happened, and devoured it at her leisure. And so twice every day, she seized the last Mouse of the series, and for a long time lived very comfortably without any trouble at all in catching her Mice, and without any of the Mice realising what was happening.

Now it happened that amongst these Mice there were two friends, whose names were Rambé and Ambé, who were very much attached to one another. Now these two were much cleverer and more cunning than most of the others, and after a few days they noticed that the number of Mice in the house seemed to be decreasing very much, in spite of the fact that the Cat had promised not to kill any more. So they laid their heads together and arranged a little plan for future processions. They agreed that Rambé was always to walk at the very front of the procession of the Mice, and that Ambé was to bring up the rear, and that all the time the procession was passing, Rambé was to call to Ambé, and Ambé to answer Rambé at frequent intervals. So next evening, when the procession started as usual, Rambé marched along in front, and Ambé took up his position last of all. As soon as Rambé had passed the cushion where the Cat was seated and had made his salaam, he called out in a shrill voice.

" Where are you, Brother Ambé ? "

" Here I am, Brother Rambé," squeaked the other from the rear of the procession. And so they went on calling and answering one another until they had all filed past the Cat, who had not dared to touch Ambé as long as his brother kept calling to him.

The Cat was naturally very much annoyed at having to go hungry that evening, and felt very cross all night. But she thought it was only an accident which had brought the two friends, one in front and one in rear of the procession, and she hoped to make up for her enforced abstinence by finding a particularly fat Mouse at the end of the procession next morning. What, then, was her amazement and disgust when she found that on the following morning the very same arrangement had been made, and that Rambé called to Ambé, and Ambé answered Rambé until all the Mice had passed her by, and so, for the second time, she was foiled of her meal. However, she disguised her feelings of anger and decided to give the Mice one more trial; so in the evening she took her seat as usual on the cushion and waited for the Mice to appear.

Meanwhile, Rambé and Ambé had warned the other Mice to be on the lookout, and to be ready to take flight the moment the Cat showed any appearance of anger. At the appointed time the procession started as usual, and as soon as Rambé had passed the Cat he squeaked out:

"Where are you, Brother Ambé?"

"Here I am, Brother Rambé," came the shrill voice from the rear.

This was more than the Cat could stand. She made a fierce leap right into the middle of the Mice, who, however, were thoroughly prepared for her, and in an instant they scuttled off in every direction to their holes. And before the Cat had time to catch a single one the room was empty and not a sign of a Mouse was to be seen anywhere.

After this the Mice were very careful not to put any further trust in the treacherous Cat, who soon after died of starvation owing to her being unable to procure any of her customary food; whilst Rambé and Ambé lived for many years, and were held in high honour and esteem by all the other Mice in the community.

STORY No. VI.

THE STORY OF THE FOOLISH YOUNG MUSSULMAN.

THERE was once a young Mussulman, who lived with his poor mother in a small cottage on the outskirts of a large town. As the Boy grew up, it was found that he was rather weak-minded, and that he was continually getting himself into scrapes, owing to his own folly and carelessness; and the naughty boys of the neighbourhood used to take advantage of the poor young fellow, and were constantly teasing him and telling him all sorts of absurd stories.

It chanced one day that he went for a walk in a large meadow, where there were a number of yellow flowers, and presently sitting down to rest, he began to gather a nosegay, when a young man passing by called out to him:

"Hullo! what are you doing there? Do you know that the soles of your feet are all yellow, and that is a sure sign that you are going to die at once?"

The poor young fellow was greatly frightened at hearing this, and he thought to himself:

"Well, if I am going to die, I had better have a grave ready."

So he set to work, and soon scraped out for himself a shallow grave in the soft soil. As soon as it was ready, he lay down in it and resigned himself to death.

A few minutes later one of the King's Servants, who happened to be passing by carrying an earthen jar full of oil for the King's palace, noticed the Boy lying on his back in the shallow grave, so he stopped and asked him what he was doing. The Boy replied:

"The soles of my feet are turning yellow, and that, as you know, is a sure sign that I am going to die; so I have prepared myself a grave, and am just waiting here till death comes."

"Oh, nonsense!" replied the Servant; "you could not talk like that if you were really dying. Come, get up, and help me to carry this jar of oil for the King, and I will give you a hen for yourself."

So the foolish Boy got up out of his grave, and taking the jar of oil on his back, he walked along the road with the King's Servant towards the palace. As they went along, he kept thinking to himself what he should do with his hen when he got it.

"As soon as I have got some eggs," thought he to himself, "I shall set the hen to hatch them. And then I shall have a nice lot of chickens. And when the chickens grow up into cocks and hens I shall sell them in the market. And with the money I get I shall buy a cow. And presently the cow will have a calf. And when the calf grows big I shall sell both the cow and the calf. And with the money I get I shall buy a nice little house. And when I have settled down in my house I shall marry a wife. And after a time we shall have a child. And as the child grows big I shall have to take its education in hand. And I shall be very firm and judicious with it. And if it is a good child and does what I tell it, I shall be very kind to it. And if it is naughty and does not do what it is told, I shall be very stern and stamp my foot, so!"

And thus thinking he stamped his foot so violently that the jar of oil slipped off his back and was smashed to pieces on the ground. When he saw this, the King's Servant became very angry, and asked him what on earth he meant by stamping his foot like that, and breaking a valuable jar of oil, which was intended for the King. The Boy tried to explain how it occurred, but the Servant would not listen, and dragged him off by force into the King's presence.

When the King saw them coming in together, he asked his Servant what he wanted, and why he was bringing in a strange Boy with him. The Servant replied that he had entrusted the Boy with a jar of oil intended for the King, and as they were walking along the road quite quietly together, the Boy all of a sudden began to stamp his feet like a maniac, and the jar of oil slipped off his back and got broken. The King asked the Boy what he meant by his conduct, and the Boy replied:

"Well, Your Majesty, your Servant said that if I would carry this jar of oil, he would give me a hen, and it seemed to me quite natural to consider within myself what I should do with my hen when I got it. So I soon saw that by selling the chickens I could buy a cow, and that later on by selling the cow and her calf, I could get a wife and set up a house of my own, and that presently we should have a child; and I was thinking to myself how I should keep my child in order, and if it was naughty I should be obliged to stamp my foot very firmly, in order to show it that I was not to be trifled with."

On hearing this ridiculous story the King was much amused, and laughed very heartily; and he gave the foolish Boy a piece of gold, and told him to go home to his Mother.

So the Boy went off towards his own home, and as he got near to the house he saw a strange dog sneaking out of the door, carrying in his mouth a purse full of money, which he had just picked up inside. On seeing this the Boy became very much excited, and began calling aloud to his Mother that a dog was making off with her purse. The Mother, when she found what was up, was afraid that he would attract the attention of the neighbours to the loss of the purse, and that in the excitement some one else would chase the dog and get the money; so hastily running up on to the flat roof of the house she sprinkled some sugar over the roof, and then called to the Boy to come up as quickly as he could.

"Look!" she said, as soon as he arrived; "what a curious thing! It has been raining sugar all over the roof of the house."

Her son, who was very fond of sugar, at once set to work to pick up all that he saw; and while he was so engaged, the good woman slipped away and soon found the dog and recovered her purse.

Some time afterwards the Boy's Mother arranged with a rich family, who lived some miles away, and who were not acquainted with her son's failings, that the Boy should marry the daughter of the house; and that, in accordance with Tibetan custom, he should become a member of the Bride's family. When all the preliminaries had been satisfactorily arranged, a party of horsemen arrived from the Bride's house to greet the Bridegroom and to bring him home. The Boy dressed himself up in his best clothes, and, after feasting the wedding party in the usual manner, he begged them all to go on ahead of him, saying that he would follow as soon as he had said good-bye to his Mother.

Towards evening he set out by himself on horseback. It was a moonlight night, and as he rode down the road he could see his own shadow travelling along beside him. He could not make out what the shadow was, but thought it must be some ghost or demon, which wanted to do him an injury, so he urged his horse into a gallop, in order to try and get away from it. But the faster he galloped the faster went the shadow, and he soon saw that it was no good trying to escape. So in order to frighten the strange object he took off his puggaree and flung it at it. As this produced no effect, he followed up the puggaree with his cloak, and, finally, with all the clothes he had on, but without in any way frightening the shadow, which still continued to follow him closely. So thinking to give it the slip, he jumped

THE YOUNG MUSSULMAN PURSUED BY HIS OWN SHADOW.

Page 35.

off his horse and ran along the road on foot, until he got into the shade of a big poplar-tree growing near the road-side.

Here he stopped to take breath, and he noticed to his great joy that the shadow had disappeared; but on peeping out from the shadow of the tree he was annoyed to find that on whichever side he looked the shadow immediately showed itself also. So thinking that the shade of the tree was the safest place to stay in, he climbed into the upper branches and very soon fell fast asleep.

A short while after a party of travellers happened to be passing by this road from the same direction, and as they came along they were surprised to find a number of garments scattered about the roadway. So they picked them up as they came along, and presently they found a horse grazing beside the road. Him, too, they brought along with them, and when they arrived in the shade of the poplar-tree, they all stopped and sat down on the ground to divide the spoil amongst them.

Just then the Boy woke up, and looking down he saw what was going on below, so he called out in a loud voice:

"I say, I want my share too, you know."

On hearing this voice emerging from the upper branches of the tree, the travellers were greatly alarmed. They thought it must certainly be a demon, who lived in the tree, and who wanted his share of the spoils, so they took to their heels and made off as fast as they could, leaving the horse and all the clothes behind them. The Boy then climbed down from the tree, put on his own clothes, and, mounting his horse, rode off to his Bride's house.

When he arrived at the house the parents of his Bride hurried out to greet him, and after asking him why he was so late, they led him to the room where the wedding feast was laid out. All the friends and neighbours from round about were gathered there ready to share in the feast, and to offer their congratulations to the Bride and Bridegroom.

During the progress of the feast the young Mussulman, who was of a very kindly disposition, and very fond of his Mother, kept thinking to himself how he could save something nice for her to eat from amongst so much plenty. So he picked from the table a narrow-mouthed copper vessel and concealed it in his lap, and whilst eating his food he every now and then dropped into it some particularly succulent dainty, which he thought his Mother would enjoy. Presently, however, he inadvertently thrust his hand right into the vessel, and to his horror he found that he was unable to withdraw it again. In this awkward predicament he was unable to eat anything, and the Bride's parents noticing that he no longer partook of any food, kept pressing him to have a little more. The young Man was still hungry, but was obliged to refuse all their offers, saying that he had already eaten enough.

Towards evening, when the feast was completed, the guests withdrew, and the Boy was left alone with his Bride; and she began asking him what the matter was, and why he had been behaving so strangely during the banquet.

He was at first too shy to tell her what had happened, but after much coaxing she elicited from him the fact that his right hand was confined in the neck of the copper vessel.

"Never mind," said she; "there is a large white stone lying at the foot of the staircase. You had better slip down stairs in the dark, and by beating the vessel against the stone you will soon succeed in freeing yourself."

The young fellow thought this was a good idea, and he went off quietly down the staircase, until he detected what he thought was a white stone lying near the foot of the steps. So, creeping up to it, he raised his arm and brought down the copper vessel with great force upon the white object, shattering the vessel and leaving his hand free. But to his horror the stone, instead of being hard, gave way, and a muffled groan issued from it; and on examining the spot, he found that instead of striking a stone, he had delivered a violent blow upon the grey head of his Bride's father, who, overcome by his potations during the wedding feast, had fallen asleep at the foot of the stairs.

The young Man was terrified at what he had done, and feeling sure that he must have killed the old man, he decided to flee from the house; so he opened the door and ran off into the night. After running for some distance he reached a neighbouring farm, where, as it happened, a large honeycomb had been left lying in the corner of the courtyard. The Boy, not knowing what it was, lay down upon this and fell fast asleep, and soon smeared himself all over with honey. Later in the night he woke up feeling very cold, and creeping into a shed close by, which was used as a storage for wool, he lay down upon the wool and slept until morning.

He woke with the first gleam of dawn, and in the early morning light he saw that he was all white and woolly, and in his simplicity he believed that, as a punishment for his wickedness in killing his father-in-law, he had been turned into a sheep. So under this impression, he ran out of the courtyard and joined a flock of sheep, which were grazing on a neighbouring hillside. He wandered about with the sheep all day, feeling very miserable, and trying to accommodate himself to the manners and customs of his new companions, and when evening came he accompanied them into the fold where they always spent the night.

About midnight some robbers came to the fold, and getting in amongst the sheep felt about for a good fat heavy one; and finally finding that the Boy was the heaviest of them all, they proceeded to carry him off. One of them hoisted him up on to his back, and they carried him along for some distance until they reached the banks of a small stream. Here they halted, and, laying him down upon the ground, they began to make preparations for cutting his throat. This trial proved rather too much for the nerves of the young Man, and forgetting his *rôle* of sheep, he called out in a shrill voice :

"Please don't kill me, kind robbers."

On hearing this the robbers were very much frightened, and ran off as fast as they could; and the Boy, thankful to have escaped from this danger, and being thoroughly worn out by the exertions and exposure of the last twenty-four hours, returned to his Bride's house. There he found that the old man, though sorely hurt, was not dead, and having explained all the circumstances of the case, he was freely forgiven, and taken back into the household.

After living for some years very happily with his Bride, he thought that he would like to make a little money for himself by trading, so having procured a good stock of merchandise he set off for India, in the hope of making a good profit on his goods. On the way he halted one evening at a large house. The Landlord received him very hospitably, and made him quite comfortable, and during the conversation which followed their evening meal the Master of the house began telling some very tall stories. Some of these stories being rather too wonderful for belief, the young Man bluntly said that he could not believe them. Thereupon the Landlord replied:

"I can prove to you that I am telling the truth by showing you a stranger thing than anything which I have hitherto related. I will bet you that when night falls a lantern will be carried into this room by a cat instead of by a servant."

The young Man was amused at his Host's boasting, and he said:

"Very well, I am prepared to bet you anything you like that this will not happen."

"Very good," said the Landlord. "If this does not happen, I will hand you over my house, my merchandise, and everything I possess; but if it does, you will forfeit all your baggage, animals and merchandise to me." And so the bet was arranged.

Now this was a regular trick of the Landlord's, who had a tame cat which had been taught to carry in a lantern in her mouth every evening just at dusk, and he was accustomed to practise this deceit upon unwary travellers, and by this means to secure their goods and whatever property they possessed.

Sure enough, just at dusk a large white cat entered the sitting-room, holding a lighted lantern in its mouth, and the unfortunate young Man was obliged to hand over to his Host everything he possessed in the world; and finding himself without money or goods he decided to stay on in the house as a servant.

After the lapse of one or two months his Wife grew anxious about him, and knowing that from the infirmity of his mind he was likely to get himself into some scrape or another, she decided to set out herself to see what had become of him. So she disguised herself as a man, and taking with her a few ponies laden with wool, she started off to follow in the tracks of her Husband.

After several days she arrived at the house where her Husband was now employed as a servant, and, meeting him in the courtyard, she learnt from him all that had happened. So she bade him hold his tongue, and she herself entered the inn, and asked for a night's lodging. During the evening the Host got talking, and in the course of the conversation he made her the same wager as he had done to her Husband some time before.

"Well," said she, "that sounds a very strange story. I can scarcely believe it possible you can have a cat so well trained as to be able to carry in a lantern. But I will think over what you say to-night, and we will see about making the bet to-morrow morning."

Next morning at breakfast she said to her Host:

"I have thought over what you said to me yesterday, and I am now prepared to make a bet with you that the cat will *not* carry a lantern into this room at dusk this evening."

So the bet was concluded upon the same terms as before, and the Lady privately told her Husband what he was to do. So in accordance with the instructions she had given him, he caught three mice, and concealed them in a little box, which he placed in the bosom of his robe. When evening approached, the Landlord and the Lady seated themselves in the supper room, waiting to see whether or no the cat would appear as expected, whilst the Husband hid himself in a corner of the courtyard, just outside the door near where the cat was accustomed to pass.

Just at dusk the cat, carrying the lantern in its mouth, began to cross the courtyard towards the door of the room where it was expected to bring the light, and when about half way across the yard the Husband released one of the mice from the box which he had hidden in his robe. The mouse scampered off across the courtyard, and the cat gave a violent start, and was on the point of pursuing it, when its training overcame its natural instincts, and it allowed the mouse to escape.

It reluctantly continued its way towards the house, and scarcely had it started to go on, when the Husband released a second mouse, which also scampered off right in front of the cat. This time it was all the cat could do to refrain from following so tempting an opportunity. It paused with great indecision, but again, its training standing it in good stead, it pursued its way towards the house.

Just as it was reaching the door of the house the third mouse was released. This was more than the cat could stand. It dropped the lantern upon the threshold, bounded across the courtyard, and seized the mouse just as it was entering its hole.

Meanwhile the Landlord and the Lady having waited until long after dark, the Landlord was reluctantly obliged to own that he had lost his bet. So he handed over to the disguised merchant, not only his own property, but also the merchandise, which he had previously won from her Husband; and the two, carrying their possessions with them, returned to their own home, where they lived happily ever afterwards.

STORY No. VII.

THE KYANG, THE FOX, THE WOLF AND THE HARE.

ONE day a hungry Wolf was roaming about in search of something to eat in the upper part of a Tibetan valley far beyond the level of cultivation,* when he came across a young Kyang† about a year old. The Wolf at once proceeded to stalk the Kyang, thinking that he would make an excellent meal off him, and just as he was about to seize upon him the Kyang, noticing his approach, addressed him as follows :

"Oh! Uncle Wolf," said he, "it is no good your eating me now ; this is the spring time and after the hard winter I am still very thin. If you will wait for a few months until next autumn you will find that I shall be twice as fat as I am now and will make you a much better feast."

"Very well," said the Wolf, "I will wait until then, on condition that you meet me on this very spot in six months' time."

* Such a locality is described in the Tibetan language by a single word—a monosyllable.

† The Kyang is the wild ass of Tibet.

And so saying he galloped off in search of some other prey.

When autumn came the Wolf started off one morning to meet the Kyang at the appointed place, and as he was going across the hills he came across a Fox.

"Good-morning, Brother Wolf," said the Fox. "Where are you going to ?"

"Oh!" replied the Wolf, "I am going into the valley to meet a young Kyang by appointment, as I have arranged to catch him and eat him this very day."

"That is very pleasant for you, Brother Wolf," answered the Fox; "but as a Kyang is such a large animal you will scarcely be able to eat him all by yourself. I hope you will allow me to come too and share in the spoil."

"Certainly, Brother Fox," replied the Wolf. "I shall be very glad of your company."

And so saying the two went on together. After proceeding a short distance they came across a Hare.

"Good-morning, Brother Wolf and Brother Fox," said the Hare; "where are you two going this fine morning ?"

"Good-morning, Brother Hare," replied the Wolf; "I am just going off to yonder valley to keep an appointment with a fat Kyang, whom I have arranged to kill and eat this very day, and Brother Fox is coming with me to share in the spoil."

"Oh! really, Brother Wolf," said the Hare, "I wish you would allow me to come too. A Kyang is such a large animal that you can scarcely eat him all yourselves, and I am sure you will allow a small creature like me to have a little bit of the spoil."

"Certainly, Brother Hare," replied the Wolf. "We shall be glad if you will accompany us."

And so the three animals went along together towards the appointed spot. When they got near the place they saw the young Kyang waiting for them. During the summer months he had eaten a quantity of grass and had now become very fat and sleek, and was about twice as big as he had been in the spring. When the Wolf caught sight of him he was much pleased and began to lick his chops in anticipation.

"Well, Brother Kyang," said he, "here I am according to agreement, ready to kill and eat you, and I am glad to see you look so plump and well. And here are Brother Fox and Brother Hare who have come along with me to have a bit too."

And so saying the Wolf crouched down ready to spring upon the Kyang and kill him.

"Oh, Brother Wolf," called out the Hare at this moment, "just wait one moment, for I have a suggestion to make to you. Don't you think it would be a pity to kill this fine young Kyang in the ordinary way by seizing his throat, for if you do so a great deal of his blood will be wasted? I would suggest to you, instead, that it would be a very much better plan if you would strangle him, as in that case no blood would be lost, and we should derive the full benefit from his carcase."

The Wolf thought this was a good idea and he said to the Hare:

"Very well, Brother Hare, I think that is an excellent idea of yours, but how is it to be done?"

"Oh! easily enough," answered the Hare. "There is a shepherd's encampment over there where we can borrow a rope, and then all we have to do is to make a slip-knot in the rope, put it over the Kyang's neck, and pull as hard as we can."

So they agreed that this should be done, and the Fox went off to the encampment near by and borrowed a rope from the shepherd, which he carried back to where the three other animals were standing.

"Now," said the Hare, "leave it all to me; I will show you exactly how it is to be done."

So he took the rope and made a large slip-knot at one end and two smaller slip-knots at the other end.

"Now," said he, "this is the way we must proceed: we will put this large slip-knot over the Kyang's neck, and as he is such a large heavy animal the only way to strangle him will be for us three to pull together at the other end of the rope. So you, Brother Wolf, and you, Brother Fox, can put your heads through these smaller loops, and I will seize the loose end of the rope with my teeth, and when I give the signal we will all pull together."

The other two thought this was a very good plan, and so they threw the slip-knot over the Kyang's neck, and the Wolf and the Fox put their heads through the smaller loops. When they were all ready the Hare took up his position at the end of the rope and caught hold of it with his teeth.

"Now," said he, "are you all ready?"

"Yes, quite ready," replied the Wolf and the Fox.

"Well, then, pull," said the Hare.

So they began to pull as hard as they could.

When the Kyang felt the pull on the rope he walked forward a few paces, much to the surprise of the Wolf and the Fox, who found themselves being dragged along the ground.

"Pull, can't you!" shrieked the Wolf, as the rope began to tighten round his neck.

"Pull yourself!" shrieked the Fox, who was now beginning to feel very uncomfortable.

"Pull, all of you," called out the Hare, and so saying he let go of the end of the rope and the Kyang galloped off dragging the Wolf and the Fox after him. In a few minutes they were both strangled, and the Kyang, shaking off the rope from his neck, proceeded to graze quietly on his usual pastures, and the Hare scampered off home, feeling that he had done a good day's work.

STORY No. VIII.

THE FROG AND THE CROW.

A Crow once caught a fine fat Frog, and taking him in her bill she flew with him to the roof of a neighbouring house in order to devour him at her leisure. As she alighted on the roof of the house the Frog gave an audible chuckle.

"What are you laughing at, Brother Frog?" said the Crow.

"Oh, nothing, Sister Crow," said the Frog; "never mind me. I was just thinking to myself that, as it fortunately happens, my Father lives close by here, on this very roof, and as he is an exceedingly fierce, strong man, he will certainly avenge my death if anyone injures me."

The Crow did not quite like this, and thinking it as well to be on the safe side she hopped off to another corner of the roof near to where a gutter led away the rain water by means of a small hole in the parapet and a wooden spout. She paused here for a moment and was just about to begin to swallow the Frog when the Frog gave another chuckle.

"What are you laughing at this time, Brother Frog?" asked the Crow.

"Oh, it's only a small matter, Sister Crow, hardly worth mentioning," replied the Frog, "but it just occurred to me that my Uncle, who is even a stronger and fiercer man than my Father, lives in this very gutter, and that if anybody was to do me an injury here they would have a very small chance of escaping from his clutches."

The Crow was somewhat alarmed at hearing this, and she thought that, on the whole, it would be safer to leave the roof altogether; so again picking up the Frog in her bill she flew off to the ground below, and alighted near the edge of a well. Here she placed the Frog upon the ground and was just about to eat him when the Frog said:

"Oh, Sister Crow, I notice your bill seems rather blunt. Before you begin to eat me don't you think it would be a good thing to sharpen it a little. You can strop it very nicely on that flat stone over there."

The Crow, thinking this was a good idea, took two or three hops towards the stone, and began sharpening her bill. As soon as she had turned her back the Frog gave one desperate jump, and dived into the well.

As soon as the Crow had made her bill nice and sharp she returned from the stone, and looked about for the Frog. Not finding him where she had left him she hopped to the edge of the well and peeped over, craning her head from side to side. Presently she spied the Frog in the water, and called out to him:

"Oh, Brother Frog, I was afraid you were lost. My

bill is quite nice and sharp now, so come along up and be eaten."

"I am so sorry, Sister Crow," replied the Frog, "but the fact is, I cannot get up the sides of this well. The best thing would be for you to come down here to eat me."

And so saying he dived to the bottom of the well.

STORY No. IX.

THE HARE AND THE LIONS.

ONCE upon a time there lived a Lion and a Lioness who inhabited a den amongst some rocks on the slopes of a mountain. They were both very fine, well-grown animals, and they used to prey upon all the smaller beasts in that part of the country; until at last they became so powerful that no other animal was safe from their clutches, and the wild beasts of the neighbourhood lived in a continual state of terror.

It chanced one day that while the Lion was hunting for something to eat, he came across a Hare sleeping behind a boulder; and seizing the Hare in his great paws he was just about to devour him, when the Hare spoke as follows:

"Oh! Uncle Lion," said he, "before eating me I just want to tell you about another animal who lives in that pond down there in the valley. He is very big and fierce, and I think he must be even stronger than you are. But if you will allow me to do so I will show you where he lives, and if you can succeed in killing him he will make a very much better meal for you than a poor little beast like me."

On hearing this the Lion was very indignant.

"What!" said he, "do you mean to tell me that there is any animal in this country stronger and more powerful than I am? Don't you know that I am the Lord of this district, and that I should never allow anyone else to dispute the mastery with me. Show me at once where this creature lives, and I will show you how I shall deal with him."

"Oh! Uncle Lion," said the Hare, "let me beg you to be careful. You have no idea what a big, strong creature this is; you must on no account allow yourself to be injured by fighting with him. Think what a grief it would be to us all if you were to come to any harm."

This remark of the Hare's made the Lion more angry than before, and he insisted that the Hare should at once lead him down and show him where the other animal lived. So the Hare, after again begging him to be careful of himself, preceded him down the hill until they arrived at the edge of a square-built stone tank, which was nearly full of water.

"Now, Uncle Lion," said the Hare, "if you will go to the edge of that tank and look down into the water you will see the animal I speak of."

So saying he moved on one side, and the Lion, stalking to the edge, peered down into the tank. The water was very smooth, and on the clear surface he saw his own head reflected.

"There he is," called out the Hare from the background; "there he is, Uncle Lion, I can see him quite plainly in the water. You see how fierce he is looking; please be careful not to start fighting with him."

These remarks made the Lion more angry than ever, and he moved up and down on the brink of the tank, glaring fiercely at his own reflection in the water, and growling and showing his teeth at it.

"That's right, Uncle Lion," called out the Hare; "I am so glad you are taking good care of yourself. Don't on any account come to grips with that beast in the water or he might do you an injury. You are certainly much safer on the bank, and no doubt you will frighten him if you continue to growl and show your teeth."

These last observations of the Hare goaded the Lion to desperation, and with a fierce roar he sprang straight at the image in the water. Once in the tank he was unable to get out, for its sides were built of masonry, and it was impossible for him to climb them. So he swam about for some time in the tank, whilst the Hare, sitting on the bank, threw stones at him and made nasty remarks; and finally, when quite wearied out, he sank to the bottom and was drowned.

The Hare was very pleased at having accomplished the destruction of the Lion, and he now turned his attention to the Lioness. It happened that near by there was a thick wall standing, which was part of the remains of a ruined castle; and in one portion of the wall there was a hole, very large at one end and tapering down to quite a small opening at the other. The Hare, having studied his ground, went off next morning to find the Lioness. He soon came across her stalking up and down near her den, very much perturbed at the disappearance of her lord and master.

"Good-morning, Aunt Lioness," said the Hare, going up cautiously towards her; "what is the matter with you this morning? How is it I find you pacing here in front of your den instead of hunting your prey as usual on the hillside?"

The Lioness took no notice of the Hare, except to growl at him in an angry manner, and to lash her sides with her tail.

"I suppose," went on the Hare, "you are anxious about Mr. Lion, but I am sorry to tell you that you are not likely to see him again for some time. The fact is, he and I had a little argument yesterday, in which we both lost our tempers. It ended in our having a free fight, and I regret to say that I was obliged to injure Mr. Lion rather severely before I could make him see reason, and he is now lying in a dying state in the valley below."

This impudence so enraged the Lioness that she sprang towards the Hare and endeavoured to seize him; but he eluded her and galloped off down the hill hotly pursued by the angry beast. The Hare made straight for the ruined wall, and entering the breach in the wall at the large end he emerged safely at the other side by the smaller recess, which was just large enough for him to pass through. The Lioness, following closely at his heels, was so blind with rage that she did not see that she was being led into a trap; so she rushed head-foremost into the opening in the wall, and before she had time to stop herself was wedged tightly in the tapering hole. She struggled violently, trying to extricate herself, but all in vain.

Meanwhile the Hare, having cantered round to the other side, took up its position in rear of the Lioness, and began pelting her with stones and calling her all the bad names he could think of. When he was tired of this he went off home very pleased with himself, and the Lioness, being unable to free herself from the trap she was in, shortly afterwards starved to death.

STORY No. X.

THE SHEEP, THE LAMB, THE WOLF AND THE HARE.

ONCE upon a time there lived an old Sheep in a low-lying valley of Tibet, and every year she, with her Lamb,* were in the habit of leaving the valley during the early months of summer, and going up on to the great northern plateau, where grass is plentiful, and where many Sheep and Goats graze throughout the summer.

One spring the Sheep, in accordance with her annual custom, set out for the north, and one day, as she was strolling sedately along the path, while her little Lamb skipped about beside her, she suddenly came face to face with a large, fierce-looking Wolf.

"Good-morning, Aunty Sheep," said the Wolf; "where are you going to?"

"Oh! Uncle Wolf," replied the trembling Sheep, "we are doing no harm; I am just taking my Lamb to graze on the rich grass of the great northern plateau."

"Well," said the Wolf, "I am really very sorry for you; but the fact is, I am hungry, and it will be necessary for me to eat you both on the spot."

* This story is also told of a Sheep and a Goat, instead of a Sheep and a Lamb. See accompanying illustration.

"Please, please, Uncle Wolf, don't do that," replied the Sheep. "Please don't eat us now; but if you will wait till the autumn, when we shall both be very much fatter than we are now, you can eat us with much more benefit to yourself on our return journey."

The Wolf thought this was a good idea.

"Very well, Aunty Sheep," said he, "that is a bargain. I will spare your lives now, but only on condition that you meet me at this very spot on your return journey from the north in the autumn."

So saying, he galloped off, and the Sheep and the Lamb continued on their way towards the north, and soon forgot all about their encounter with the Wolf.

All the summer they grazed about on the succulent grass of the great plateau, and when autumn was approaching both were as fat as fat could be, and the little Lamb had grown into a fine young Sheep.

When the time came for returning to the south, the Sheep remembered her bargain with the Wolf, and every day as they drew farther and farther south she grew more and more downhearted.

One day, as they were approaching the place where they had met the Wolf, it chanced that a Hare came hopping along the road towards them. The Hare stopped to say good-morning to the Sheep, and noticing that she was looking very sad, he said:

"Good-morning, Sister Sheep, how is it that you, who are so fat and have so fine a Lamb, are looking so sad this morning?"

"Oh! Brother Hare," replied the Sheep, "mine is a very sad story. The fact is that last spring, as I and my Lamb were coming up this very road, we met an ugly-looking Wolf, who said he was going to eat us; but I begged him to spare our lives, explaining to him that we should both be much larger and fatter in the autumn, and that he would get much better value from us if he waited till then. The Wolf agreed to this, and said that we must meet him at the same spot in the autumn. We are now very near the appointed place, and I very much fear that in another day or two we shall both be killed by the Wolf."

So saying, the poor Sheep broke down altogether and burst into tears.

"Dear me! dear me!" replied the Hare; "this is indeed a sad story; but cheer up, Sister Sheep, you may leave it to me, and I think I can answer for it that I know how to manage the Wolf."

So saying, the Hare made the following arrangements. He dressed himself up in his very best clothes, in a new robe of woollen cloth, with a long ear-ring in his left ear, and a fashionable hat on his head, and strapped a small saddle on to the back of the Sheep. He then prepared two small bundles, which he slung across the Lamb, and tied them on with a rope. When these preparations were complete, he took a large sheet of paper in his hand, and, with a pen thrust behind his ear, he mounted upon the back of the Sheep, and the little procession started off down the path.

Soon after, they arrived at the place where they were

THE HARE CONVERSING WITH THE WOLF.

to meet the Wolf, and sure enough there was the Wolf waiting for them at the appointed spot.

As soon as they came within earshot of where the Wolf was standing the Hare called out in a sharp tone of authority:

"Who are you, and what are you doing there?"

"I am the Wolf," was the reply; "and I have come here to eat this Sheep and its Lamb, in accordance with a regular arrangement. Who may you be, pray?"

"I am Lomden, the Hare," that animal replied, "and I have been deputed to India on a special mission by the Emperor of China. And, by the way, I have a commission to bring ten Wolf skins as a present to the King of India. What a fortunate thing it is that I should have met you here! Your skin will do for one, anyway."

So saying, the Hare produced his sheet of paper, and, taking his pen in his hand, he wrote down the figure "1" very large.

The Wolf was so frightened on hearing this that he turned tail and fled away ignominiously; while the Sheep and the Lamb, after thanking the Hare heartily for his kind offices, continued their journey safely to their own home.

[This story is a satire on the assumption and arrogance of Tibetan and Chinese officials, and the timidity and submissiveness of the Tibetan peasants. It illustrates how the meanest Government clerk, more especially when armed with pen and paper, can strike terror into the heart of the boldest and strongest countryman.]

STORY No. XI.

THE STORY OF HOW THE HARE MADE A FOOL OF THE WOLF.

[This story is really the continuation of Number X., which is sometimes told of "the Sheep and the Goat," instead of "the Sheep and the Lamb." The first part of the story is exactly the same as Number X. They experience the same adventures with the Wolf and are extricated in exactly the same manner by the aid of the Hare. But the end of the story is different.]

When the Wolf ran away, Da-gye the Sheep and Pen-dzong the Goat were so elated that they could not refrain from vaingloriously galloping after him until they saw him dive hastily into his earth some distance away; they then sat themselves down at the mouth of the hole and remained there for some time chaffing the Wolf and telling him to hurry up and come out to be skinned, whilst the foolish Wolf lay cowering and trembling within.

Presently the Sheep grew rather hungry and thirsty, so she went off to eat and drink, leaving the Goat to watch the earth. After sitting for a short while the

Goat began rubbing his horns on a stone, and the Wolf hearing the grating sound squeaked out very humbly:

"Oh! Brother Goat, what are you doing now?"

"Sharpening a knife to kill you with," replied the Goat.

And the Wolf cowered into the furthest recesses of his den trembling with fear.

A few minutes later some rain began to fall, and the Wolf hearing the sound of the pattering raindrops called out:

"What is happening now, pray, Brother Goat?"

"I am collecting the water to cook you in," answered the Goat gruffly.

Presently the Goat began to scrape the earth with one hoof and the Wolf asked:

"What is that scraping noise, Brother Goat?"

"I am preparing a fireplace to boil the water at," answered the Goat. "It will soon be time to finish you off."

Just then the Sheep came back from grazing and said to the Goat:

"Now, Brother Goat, it is time for you to go and refresh yourself. I will stay here and look after the Wolf while you are away."

The Goat thanked the Sheep for her offer and told her how he had been acting during her absence, and after advising her to behave in the same manner and on no account to show any signs of fear, he went off to get something to eat and drink.

When the Sheep found herself left alone at the mouth of the Wolf's den, her natural timidity asserted itself, and she began to feel very nervous, but in order to keep up appearances she started to rub her horns against a stone, just as the Goat had advised her to do. As soon as he heard this noise the Wolf called out as before, asking what was happening.

"I am sharpening a knife to kill you with," replied the Sheep, but she was so nervous that the Wolf at once noticed the terrified sound of her voice and began to suspect that he had been made a fool of.

"Is that you, Sister Sheep?" said the Wolf; "I thought it was Brother Goat."

"No, Brother Wolf, it is me," replied the Sheep. "Brother Goat has gone away to get himself something to eat and drink."

"And are you all alone, Sister Sheep?" asked the Wolf.

"Yes, Brother Wolf," replied the Sheep.

On hearing this the Wolf dashed out of his den, and seizing hold of the poor Sheep he quickly slew her.

The Wolf now realised that he had been made game of by the Sheep and the Goat and became very angry. So he started off to hunt for the Goat, vowing vengeance against him. As soon as the Goat caught sight of the Wolf coming along in the distance he guessed what had happened, and fled as fast as he could across the hills with the Wolf after him. They soon came to some rough, rocky ground, and here the Goat missed his footing and fell into a deep, narrow cleft between two rocks, breaking his leg; and the Wolf, who had not seen what had happened, jumped over the crevice and pursued his way, still hunting for the Goat.

For some time the poor Goat lay helpless at the bottom of the crevice, when by chance a Fox, who happened to be passing that way, heard him moaning and came to see what was wrong.

"Good-morning, Brother Goat," said the Fox, peering down into the cleft. "What has happened to you, and why do you lie there moaning?"

"Oh! Brother Fox," replied the Goat, "I have had a terrible misfortune. I am Pen-dzong the Goat, and I and my friend Da-gye the Sheep hunted a Wolf into his lair this morning and tried to frighten him by telling him that we were going to skin him; and while I was away getting myself something to drink and eat the Wolf came out of his den and killed my poor friend Da-gye the Sheep, and then proceeded to chase me. But I, as you see, fell down into this cleft and have broken my leg. I am unable to move, and the Wolf jumped over the crevice as I lay here and has gone right away. I have one dying request to make to you, however. I beg you when I am dead to strip off my skin and to hand it over to my young ones as a mat for them to lie on, and in return for this service you can have my flesh for yourself."

The Fox was much affected on hearing the Goat's tale, and promised to do as he asked. So when the Goat died shortly after the Fox stripped off his skin, and set off with it to hand it over to the Goat's young ones. As he was going along, carrying the skin on his back, he chanced to come across a Hare.

"Good-day, Brother Fox," said the Hare. "Where are you going to, and what is that you have on your back?"

"Good-day, Brother Hare," replied the Fox. "This is the skin of Pen-dzong the Goat, whom I found lying in a cleft between two rocks with a broken leg. He and his friend Da-gye the Sheep have both been killed by a Wolf, and he begged me after his death to strip off his skin and to take it as a last present from him to his young ones.

"Dear me," replied the Hare, "that no doubt must be the same Goat and the same Sheep whom I rescued so recently from that very Wolf. What foolish creatures they are to have got themselves into so much trouble after I had freed them from all their difficulties. But, nevertheless, I am not going to let the Wolf get the best of me like this, and kill my friends with impunity. Come along with me and we will see what we can do to avenge Da-gye and Pen-dzong."

The Fox agreed to this, and he and the Hare set off together to hunt for the Wolf. They travelled a long way without coming across him, but at length, as they were crossing a high pass they found him feeding upon the carcase of a dead Horse.

"Good-day, Uncle Wolf," called out the Hare genially. "I am so glad to have met you. The fact is, there is a wedding feast going on at that big house over yonder, where Brother Fox and I expect to find plenty to eat and drink. If you care to come along with us too we shall be very glad, and I think we can promise you some better refreshment than that old Horse you are devouring here. So come along and see what we can find."

The Wolf was very pleased at this invitation, so he joined the Hare and the Fox, and all three went off together to the big house where the wedding feast was being held. They studied the premises carefully before approaching too near, and they soon ascertained that the whole of the wedding party were busy feasting in the central room, and that the larder, full of good things to eat and drink, was quite unguarded. So they jumped in through a narrow window and began to enjoy themselves thoroughly, eating and drinking anything which took their fancy. When they were as full as could be the Hare said:

"What I advise now is as follows: let us each take some provisions, as much as we can carry, and bring them with us to our own homes, so that we may have something to go on with when we next feel hungry. I myself shall take some cheese; Brother Fox no doubt would like some cold fowl; and I should advise you, Brother Wolf, to carry off that jar of wine."

The Fox and the Wolf both agreed with the Hare's proposals, and they began to load themselves with the provisions they proposed to take with them. The Fox and the Hare had no difficulty in making up a bundle of cheese and cold fowl, but the Wolf found that it would be very difficult for him to carry off the jar of wine. So the Hare explained to him that the best plan would be for him to slip his head through the handle of the jar, in which case it would be quite easy for him to drag the jar along with him. So the Wolf put his head through the handle of the jar, and all three made ready to start.

"Well now, Brother Fox and Brother Wolf," said the Hare in a genial tone of voice, "it is nearly time for us to be off. How are you both feeling? Have you had a good dinner? Are your bellies full?"

"Couldn't be fuller," replied the Wolf, rubbing his stomach with one paw. "I have done very well."

"Well, then," said the Hare, "as we have feasted well and feel happy and contented, let's have a song before starting."

"Certainly, Brother Hare," replied the Wolf. "Will you begin?"

"I would with pleasure," answered the Hare, "but really, the fact is, I can't recollect a single song at this moment. Perhaps Brother Fox will oblige us."

"I am very sorry, Brother Hare," answered the Fox, "but I am afraid I don't know any songs. I am sure Brother Wolf sings beautifully."

"Yes," joined in the Hare. "Pray, Brother Wolf, let us hear you sing?"

"No, no, please," said the Wolf modestly, scratching his ear with one paw. "I am a very poor singer, you really must excuse me."

But the Fox and the Hare pressed him, and presently he began to sing. At the first sound of his voice the men in the next room stopped their feasting, and saying to one another, "There is a Wolf in the house," they rushed towards the larder.

As soon as they heard the disturbance the Hare and the Fox, carrying their provisions with them, hopped quietly out of the window and made off quickly for their homes. The Wolf, too, made a leap towards the window, but the great jar round his neck was too broad to go through the narrow opening, and he fell back into the room below. Again he jumped and again he fell back; and he was still jumping and falling when the people of the house rushed in and soon despatched him with sticks and stones.

STORY No. XII.

THE MOUSE'S THREE CHILDREN.

MANY years ago, in the kingdom of Nepal, there was a little Mouse, who lived with her husband in a snug nest not far from the King's palace.

Finding that she was about to be delivered of a child, the Mouse prayed to the gods that her offspring might be very strong; and when the child was born it appeared in the form of a young Tiger. The Tiger soon grew up, and one day he said to the Mouse :

"Mother, I must now go off into the jungle and live there with my brother Tigers. But if at any time you want my help, all you need do is to go into yonder thicket, and throw a handful of my hair into the air, and call my name three times."

So saying, he gave the Mouse a handful of his hair, and went off into the forest.

Shortly afterwards the Mouse was again with child, and this time she prayed that her offspring might be very beautiful. When the child was born, instead of a young Mouse, she found that she had given birth to a Peacock. The Peacock soon grew into a large and beautiful bird, and when he had reached his full growth he one day said to his mother :

"Mother, it is now time for me to go and seek my own livelihood with my brothers in the forest. But if at any time you should require my assistance, all you have to do is to go to the top of that hill over there, and to throw a handful of my feathers into the air, and call my name three times."

So saying, he gave the little Mouse a handful of his feathers, and flew away into the jungle.

Presently the Mouse found herself a third time with child, and this time she prayed to the gods that her child might become wise, wealthy and powerful; and when the child appeared she saw that it was a young man child. As the Boy grew up the mother was afraid that he, too, like his brothers, would want to leave his nest and go out into the world to live with his fellow-men. So she told him the story of his two elder brothers, and explained to him that he was a man child, and could not wander away into the jungle like they did, but must stay in the nest. The Boy promised to do so, and every day he used to sit and play about at the mouth of the nest.

Now it happened that in that country there lived a Mussulman, who made his living as a barber and by paring people's nails. This man, who was very clever at his work, was often employed in the King's palace, and one day, as he was going to his work in the palace, he passed near to the Mouse's nest. There he saw the Boy seated on the ground, and, going up to him, he asked him whether he would like his hair cut and his nails pared.

The Boy said, "Yes," and the Barber proceeded to cut his hair. To the Barber's astonishment, each hair, as it fell to the ground, immediately turned into diamonds, pearls, and other jewels; and when he proceeded to pare the Boy's nails, each paring, as it touched the ground, became a beautiful turquoise.

The Barber then went on to the palace, and as he was cutting the King's hair, he told him about the miraculous child, whose hair and nails turned into jewels. The King, who was a greedy and unscrupulous man, determined to gain possession of so valuable a Boy, so he sent out some of his servants to bring the Boy up to the palace. When the Boy arrived, he was brought before the King, and the King told him that as he had been found trespassing in the royal forests, he intended to kill the mother, and to keep the Boy as a slave, unless the Boy could furnish him at once with four full-grown Tigers to guard the four gates of the palace, in which case he would marry the Boy to his daughter and would give him half his kingdom.

The poor Boy went in great grief to Mother Mouse, and related to her the whole of his interview with the King. The Mouse told him not to vex himself, and she gave him a handful of Tiger's hair and sent him out into the jungle with full directions as to what he should do.

The Boy went off into the heart of a dense thicket in the jungle, and throwing the Tiger's hair into the air, he called out at the same time:

"Brother Tiger! Brother Tiger! Brother Tiger!"

Scarcely had the words left his lips when he heard a low, deep growl just beside him, and a great Tiger stalked out of the thicket, licking his chops.

"Here I am, Brother," said the Tiger. "What do you want?"

"Oh! Brother Tiger," said the Boy, "the King has said that if I do not immediately provide him with four full-grown Tigers to guard the four gates of his palace he will kill our mother and make me a slave."

On hearing this the Tiger laughed aloud.

"Is that all?" said he. "That is easily arranged. I can get you a hundred Tigers."

So saying, he opened his mouth, and gave forth a series of fearful roars; and in a few minutes the whole jungle seemed to be full of Tigers, hastening up from all directions. When they were all ready, the first Tiger told his brother to mount upon his back, and so, with the Boy leading the way, and the other Tigers following in procession, they all went off in a body to the King's palace.

As they approached the palace great consternation arose; servants ran hither and thither, and the guards were called to arms. And when the King was told what was happening he was greatly alarmed himself, but he seated himself on his throne, and gave orders for the Boy and the Tigers to be admitted.

The Boy rode in on the Tiger's back to the royal presence, followed by all the other Tigers; and halting a few steps from the throne he said:

"Here, oh King! are a number of the best Tigers I could find in the forest. You can take your pick of any four you like."

The King was very much astonished at this, and having

selected four of the finest Tigers, he allowed the others to go away. But he still hankered after the jewels, and in a few days' time he again summoned the Boy before him, and told him that unless he at once furnished four Peacocks to sit one on each of the four golden pinnacles of his palace roof, he should kill his mother and keep the Boy as a slave.

The poor Boy was very down-hearted on hearing this, and went sadly back to his mother with the news; but the little Mouse told him that it was all right, and giving him a handful of Peacock's feathers, she instructed him how to proceed. So the Boy went off to the top of a high hill, and, throwing the feathers into the air, he called aloud:

"Brother Peacock! Brother Peacock! Brother Peacock!"

Immediately a fluttering sound was heard, and a magnificent Peacock dropped to the ground in front of him from the branch of a neighbouring tree.

"Here I am, Brother," said the Peacock. "What do you want with me?"

"Oh! Brother Peacock," said the Boy, "the King says that if I cannot at once provide him with four Peacocks to sit on the four golden pinnacles of his palace, he will kill our mother and make me a slave."

"Never mind," said the Peacock, "we can easily arrange that."

So he fluttered back to the top of a high tree, and called the loud, shrill call of the Peacocks.

In a few moments the air was bright with numbers of fine Peacocks flying in from all directions.

"Now," said the first Peacock, "come along to the palace."

So saying, four of the strongest Peacocks seized the Boy in their claws, and they all flew together over the tops of the trees to the King's palace.

When the courtiers saw the Peacocks coming, they ran to tell the King, and the King seated himself upon his throne in the courtyard all ready to receive them.

The Peacocks placed the Boy upon the ground in front of the King's throne, and arranged themselves in rows behind him, with their tails spread.

"Here, oh King!" said the Boy, "are all the finest Peacocks I could find in the forest. You can have your pick of any four of them."

The King was greatly astonished at what had happened, but he selected the four best Peacocks, and sent away the rest.

But the King still hankered in his heart after the jewels. So, a few days later, he sent for the Boy again, and he told him that unless his Mother Mouse could fight single-handed with the King's state Elephant and destroy it, he would kill the mother and make the Boy a slave.

The Boy was greatly distressed on hearing this, for he did not think it possible that the little Mouse could compete successfully with the King's great Elephant; so he went home very sadly and told his mother the whole story. But the Mouse told him he was not to be alarmed, and she directed him to smear her body all over with poison, and to tie a long string to her tail. As soon as she was ready the Boy placed her in the sleeve of his coat, and carried her along to the palace.

In the courtyard of the palace everything had been made ready for the fight. Seats had been prepared behind a barrier for the King and his nobles, whilst the roofs and the windows were crowded with hundreds of people who had come to see the show. At one end of the enclosure the King's great tusker stood ready, still chained by the leg; and the Boy, with the Mouse in his sleeve, took up his stand at the other end of the arena, face to face with the angry Elephant.

At a given signal the Elephant's chain was loosed, and with a bellow of rage he rushed towards where the Boy was standing. As he came on, holding his trunk high in the air, the little Mouse jumped to the ground and ran to meet him. The Elephant caught sight of this small object, and stopped for a moment to see what it was, and the Mouse hopped on to his foot. The Elephant at once put down his trunk to feel what was there, and in a twinkling the Mouse jumped into the open end of the trunk, and scuttled up it as fast as she could till she reached the head. She soon found herself inside the Elephant's brain, and there she ran round and round, smearing poison all over the brain of the great beast.

The Elephant, not knowing what had happened, rushed round the arena, bellowing with rage and pain, and smashing everything within reach of his trunk. But presently, the poison taking effect, he fell to the ground stone dead, and the Boy, pulling the string which was attached to the Mouse's tail, guided her out of the Elephant's trunk till she reached the open air.

The King could no longer hesitate to fulfil his promise to the Boy, so he gave him his daughter in marriage, and presented him with half his kingdom. And on the King's death the Boy succeeded to the kingdom, and he and his mother lived happily ever afterwards.

STORY No. XIII.

THE JACKALS AND THE TIGER.

Once upon a time there was a family of Jackals, consisting of a Father, Mother, and five young ones. After living for some time very comfortably near a large village, they found that the dogs of the village were becoming so numerous and so troublesome that they considered it necessary to change their place of abode. So one fine evening they started off and travelled away across the country, keeping a sharp look-out for some desirable spot in which they might settle down.

After a while they came to the edge of a forest, and having travelled for some little distance into the thickest part of the wood, they arrived all of a sudden at a Tiger's den. The young Jackals were a good deal frightened at the smell of the Tiger's den, but Father Jackal reassured them, and said that he thoroughly understood Tigers, and knew how to deal with them. So he went forward alone, and, peeping in, he found that the Tiger was out, but that he had left a large quantity of deer's flesh lying in one corner, which apparently he had not had time to consume. So he called Mrs. Jackal and the children, and told them to go inside and to have a good feed, and to make themselves quite comfortable. After making a good meal himself off the deer's flesh, he said to Mrs. Jackal:

"You and the children can now go to sleep; I shall go on to the roof of the den and keep a look-out for the Tiger. When I see him coming I shall rap on the roof, and you must at once wake up the children and make them begin to cry, and when I ask you what they are crying about, you must say that they are getting impatient for their supper."

Accordingly Mr. Jackal went up on the roof, while his family settled down to sleep in the snuggest corner of the Tiger's den. Shortly after Father Jackal heard a slight crackling amongst the dry leaves of the forest; and in the dim morning light he discerned the form of a great Tiger approaching his den through the tree-stems.

According to the arrangement he had made, he rapped with a loose stone upon the roof of the den, and Mrs. Jackal immediately woke up the young Jackals and made them cry.

"What are those children crying about?" called out Father Jackal.

"They are very hungry, and getting impatient for their supper," was the reply.

"Tell them they won't have long to wait now," said Father Jackal; "the Tiger will probably be home very soon, and we shall all be eating hot Tiger's meat before long."

On hearing this the Tiger was very much alarmed, and thought to himself:

"What kind of strange animal can this be which has

entered my den, and is waiting to cook and eat me on my return ; it must certainly be a very fierce and terrible creature."

So without waiting to investigate the matter any further, he turned tail and ran off as fast as he could through the forest. After running some way, he came across an old Baboon, with a great fringe of white hair all round his face.

"Where are you running to, Uncle Tiger ?" asked the Baboon.

"Well," said the Tiger, "the fact is, that a family of strange animals, who call themselves Jackals, are at this moment in occupation of my den. As I was approaching my den, after a long night's hunting, one of the creatures was actually sitting on the roof, looking out for me, and as I got close up I heard him tell his young ones that they were to have hot Tiger's meat for supper. Fortunately for me, he hadn't seen me, so I thought the best thing I could do was to make off as fast as I could, in order to avoid being eaten."

On hearing this the Baboon was very much amused, and set to work to laugh very heartily.

"Why," said he, "what a foolish Tiger you are! Have you never heard of a Jackal before ? Don't you know that it is you should eat the Jackals, and not the Jackals you ? You come along with me, and I will soon show you how to deal with people like that."

The Tiger was somewhat reassured on hearing what the Baboon had to say, but, even so, he was at first very reluctant to return again and to incur the danger of being

THE TIGER AND THE MONKEY APPROACHING THE JACKAL'S DEN.

eaten; but the Monkey encouraged him, and finally they set off together, the Monkey twisting his tail round the Tiger's, in order to give him a feeling of support and confidence.

As they came nearer to the den, the Tiger grew more and more timorous, and would only advance very slowly, ready to take flight at any moment. However, they went on together, tail-in-tail, until presently Father Jackal on the roof of the den caught sight of the pair, and called out:

"That is right, Brother Monkey, bring him along quickly; we are all half starved. But what do you mean by only bringing one of them? I had expected you would bring us at least two or three."

On hearing this, the Tiger at once suspected that the Baboon was in the Jackal's employ, and that he was being led into a trap. Without a moment's hesitation he turned about and fled precipitately into the depths of the forest. The unfortunate Baboon, whose tail was tightly twisted round the Tiger's, was unable to free himself, and was dragged and bumped hither and thither in the Tiger's rush through the thickest and thorniest parts of the jungle. When at length the Tiger paused, many miles away, to take breath, he looked back at his flanks, and all he saw of the Monkey was a bit of its tail which had broken off and was still twisted round his own.

He never again returned to his den, which was occupied henceforth by the Jackals, who lived there for many years in peace and comfort.

STORY No. XIV.

THE STORY OF THE THREE THIEVES.

ONCE upon a time there lived within the dominions of the Emperor of China three very clever Thieves. These men, owing to their skill and cunning, were quite at the head of their profession, and by sleight of hand and dexterity were able to accomplish feats of trickery which the ordinary thieves could not emulate. The first was so clever that he was able to withdraw eggs from under a sitting hen without in any way disturbing her, and without her being aware that the theft had been accomplished. The second was able to cut the soles off a man's boots as he walked along the road without the victim knowing that he had been robbed. And the third was able to eat his fill off a man's plate during dinner without the man who was robbed, or his friend opposite, being able to detect where the victuals had gone to.

Now it happened one day that these three Thieves met together in a country inn, and entering into conversation with one another, began to exchange confidences.

"May I ask what you do for a living?" asked the first Thief of the second.

"Oh, I am a Thief," answered the man who was addressed.

"Very good," replied the other men, "we also are Thieves. Can you tell us, please, if there is any particular line in which you excel?"

"Yes," said the second Thief; "I am able to cut the soles off a man's boots as he walks across the road without his being aware of what has happened. What can you two do, pray?"

"I," replied the first Thief, "can withdraw the eggs from under a sitting hen without disturbing her."

"And I," said the third, "can steal another man's dinner from off his plate, and eat my fill as he sits at table, without the victim, or the man sitting opposite, being able to detect me."

So the three Thieves, having struck up a friendship on the ground of their unusual skill, set off together to the court of the Emperor of China, in order to see whether they could not succeed in making their fortunes there.

On arriving at the court they consulted together and came to the conclusion that in order to make any headway in China it was necessary to attract the attention of the Emperor. So they agreed to separate for twenty-four hours, and to meet next day in the courtyard of the palace, each bringing some gift to the Emperor which would please him, and prove to him that they were men of no usual calibre. Accordingly, they parted in different directions, and the following day at noon, they met together in the courtyard of the palace, and each one proceeded to relate his adventures during the preceding twenty-four hours.

"As soon as I left you yesterday," began the first Thief, "I went into the royal farm adjoining the palace, and there I found one of the Emperor's pea-hens sitting upon her nest, and hatching a clutch of eggs, which was calculated to produce a breed of the very finest peacocks. By the Emperor's orders this nest was watched by an attendant night and day, in order that no one should interfere with the eggs, and the pea-hen herself was so cross that she would not allow anyone to approach her except the man who fed her. But such obstacles as these were nothing to me, and I had no difficulty in evading the watchers and abstracting the eggs from under the hen, without even disturbing her, or her being aware of the loss. Now here they are in my wallet, and when the loss is discovered presently, as it is sure to be, and a reward offered for their discovery, I propose to present them to the Emperor."

The other two Thieves applauded their comrade for his skill and ingenuity, and the second Thief then proceeded to relate his story as follows:

"When we separated yesterday, I at once entered the Emperor's antechamber, and mingled with the nobles and officials who were awaiting an audience with His Majesty, and amongst the others I soon noticed the Prime Minister. He was a very stout man, dressed in his finest robes, and with a new pair of boots on his feet. As he passed to and fro in the crowd, I succeeded in cutting the soles off his new boots without his having any idea of what had happened. Shortly afterwards he was summoned to the Emperor's presence, and when he knelt down to *kow-tow* before His Majesty, it was observed that he had no soles to his boots. The Emperor, thinking that the Minister had committed this serious breach of etiquette on purpose, fell into a violent passion, and ordered him to be imprisoned at once. It was no use for the wretched man to protest his innocence or to plead for mercy. The Emperor's orders are that, unless a satisfactory explanation is given to him before six o'clock this evening and the missing soles produced, the Minister is to be beheaded. Here are the soles of the Prime Minister's boots in my wallet, and I propose to present them to His Majesty this afternoon during his public audience. I shall thus earn the gratitude of the Prime Minister and appease the wrath of the Emperor."

The other two Thieves, on hearing this story, congratulated their comrade on his successful manœuvre, and the third Thief proceeded to relate his adventures as follows:

"When we parted yesterday," said he, "I entered the palace, and after wandering about for some time I found myself in the chamber where the Emperor's dinner was being prepared, and where all the chief officials of the palace were assembled to superintend the arrangements for the royal meal. There were the Head Chamberlain and the Under Chamberlains, the Head Usher and the Under Ushers, the Head Waiter and the Under Waiters, and many other officials of minor degree. I mingled with the servants, who were standing about, without attracting any attention, and remained in the room until the Emperor himself entered and seated himself with great ceremony to partake of his mid-day meal. The Chief Cook and the Chief Chamberlain placed themselves in front of the Emperor, in order to see that the service of his food was properly conducted, whilst the other high officials took their stand on either side of his chair and assisted in bringing in the dishes. In spite of all these precautions, however, I was able by my skill to take the food from each dish as it was placed upon the table, before the Emperor had time to partake of more than a very few mouthfuls. As the meal proceeded the Emperor grew more and more annoyed, and complained of the insufficiency of the food which had been prepared for him. Such a thing as this had never occurred before in the palace. The Head Cook and all the Under Cooks, the Head Chamberlain and all the Under Chamberlains, the Head Usher and all the Under Ushers, and all the officials of lower degree, were thrown into a dreadful state of confusion and alarm at the event. They rushed hither and thither, between the kitchens and dining-halls, upbraiding the scullions and other domestics for their carelessness, and preparing the most elaborate and copious dishes for the Emperor's table. But after some time the Emperor, wearied by the confusion, and unable, in spite of everything, to make a satisfactory meal, gave orders that the whole of the Cooks and other attendants responsible for his table-service should be imprisoned, and that unless a satisfactory explanation of their negligence could be given before this evening they should be beheaded. I have here, in my wallet, the whole of the viands which yesterday were placed before the Emperor for his consumption, and I propose at the audience to present them to him, and inform him what really happened. He will undoubtedly pardon me when he hears the story, and I shall earn the undying gratitude of all the disgraced officials by procuring their release."

The other two Thieves, on hearing this story, congratulated their comrade warmly upon his daring and success, and the three entered the Emperor's antechamber together, and awaited the time for public audience.

A few minutes later the great doors leading to the audience chamber were thrown open, and a herald appearing upon the threshold proclaimed "Silence." He then gave notice that, on the previous day, the eggs had all been stolen from under the Emperor's favourite pea-hen, and that any person who could find the eggs or give any information concerning their loss should receive a reward; secondly, that for a breach of etiquette the Prime Minister had been imprisoned, and that unless he could explain his offence before six o'clock that evening he was to be beheaded, and that any person who could offer assistance in the matter would be well paid and otherwise rewarded by the Emperor; thirdly, that owing to bad attendance during the Emperor's repast the previous day, all the domestic officials of the palace had been imprisoned, and would be beheaded at six o'clock that evening unless they could give a satisfactory explanation ; and that any person who could assist in the matter would be well rewarded for his pains.

So saying the Herald retired, and the public audience began. When the three Thieves were admitted to the Emperor's presence, they went in together and made a simultaneous obeisance before the Emperor's throne.

" Who are you three men ? " asked the Emperor, " and what do you want from me ? "

" May it please Your Majesty," replied the first Thief, " I have ventured to bring a small gift for you."

And so saying he took from his wallet the pea-hen's eggs, and laid them on the throne.

When the Emperor heard that these were his pea-hen's eggs he was very much pleased, and gave orders that they should at once be taken back to the nest, and the hatching continued; and telling the first Thief to stand back, he enquired of the second what he wished to say.

" May it please Your Majesty," replied the second Thief, " I also have a small gift to make to you."

And so saying he took the soles of the Prime Minister's boots out of his wallet and laid them on the steps of the throne.

When the Emperor found that these were the soles of his Prime Minister's boots, and how they had been removed, he was very much amused, and laughed heartily. He at once sent orders for his Prime Minister to be released, and handed over to him the soles of his boots, and told him to watch them more carefully for the future. The Prime Minister was delighted at being reinstated in the royal favour, and expressed his gratitude to the Thief for his services in the matter.

When the third Thief was asked what he had to say he replied:

"I, too, have a small gift for Your Majesty."

And so saying he produced a plate from his wallet, and laid upon it the various viands which had been cooked for the Emperor's dinner the previous day.

When the Emperor understood that this was the dinner which had been prepared for him, and which he ought to have eaten, he was greatly astonished; but seeing that it was no fault of his Cooks, Chamberlains, or other servants, he ordered them all to be released, and to resume their former functions.

Having issued these various commands, the Emperor again summoned the three Thieves before him, and addressed them as follows:

"Although," said he, "I am very pleased at finding such a satisfactory explanation for the disappearance of the eggs, the misdemeanour of my Prime Minister, and the insufficiency of my dinner, I cannot overlook the fact that you three men have behaved in a very unusual manner. So before rewarding you in accordance with my promise, I desire to put your skill to a further test. If you succeed in this trial to my satisfaction you shall all three be well rewarded, and receive rank and lands in my country; but if you fail, you must take the consequences of your rashness, and you shall all three be put to death."

When the three Thieves heard these words they were greatly frightened, and bowing down before the Emperor they awaited his commands.

"The test which I have in store for you," continued the Emperor, "is as follows: you must know that in my Treasury I have a great number of jewels and precious objects of all kinds; and the Treasury is enclosed within a treble wall ten fathoms in height, closed by iron gates, and is guarded night and day by companies of my most faithful soldiers. If you can produce, before six o'clock to-morrow evening, three of the pearls from my Treasury, you shall be pardoned and rewarded; but if you fail to do so, you shall all three be put to death."

On hearing these words the three thieves consulted together for a few moments, and replied as follows:

"We will do our best to carry out Your Majesty's commands and to succeed in this test which you have given us, but we would call your royal attention to one matter; it is this: supposing we produce before to-morrow evening three pearls as you command, how shall we be able to satisfy you that they come from the Royal Treasury? All pearls look very much alike, and it would be impossible for us to prove to you whence they came. We would, therefore, venture to suggest that, before putting us to this test, you should have a complete enumeration made of all the jewels in your Treasury; then, when we produce the three pearls in question, it will be easy to ascertain whether there are in the Treasury three pearls less than there were when the enumeration was made."

The Emperor, seeing that this was a reasonable request, agreed to act as the Thieves had suggested. So summoning his Treasurer before him, he gave orders that a complete enumeration of all the jewels and other precious objects in his Treasury should be made before nightfall that evening; and having issued his commands he dismissed the audience.

The Chief Treasurer was much perturbed on receiving these orders, for owing to the enormous quantity of jewels and other objects in the Treasury, he foresaw that it would be a difficult matter to have the enumeration complete before evening. The only way in which it could be done was to call in the assistance of all the officials of the palace, and having allotted a section of the Treasure Chamber to each, to order them to make a complete inventory each of his own part. Accordingly, he called together all the officials of the palace to the number of many hundreds, and they proceeded in a body to the Royal Treasury. The three Thieves, who had anticipated this action on the part of the Treasurer, meanwhile dressed themselves up in the complete robes which are proper for a palace official, and mingling unnoticed in the crowd, they followed the Treasurer to the gates of the Royal Treasury. By the Treasurer's orders, the gates were at once thrown open, and the officials, entering the treasury, began the enumeration. The three thieves, in common with the rest, were allotted each a section of the Treasury Chamber, of which they were to make a complete inventory, and whilst so employed they had no difficulty in each one secreting a large pearl after first placing it upon their list. By nightfall the enumeration was complete, the lists were all handed over to the Chief Treasurer, and the Treasury was left locked and guarded as before.

Next day, at six o'clock, the Emperor seated himself in his Hall of Audience, and summoned the three Thieves before him.

"Well," said he, "have you been able to fulfil the conditions which I set you? If you can now produce three pearls from my Treasury, you shall be rewarded in accordance with my promise; but if you are unable to do so, you shall all three be put to death."

The Thieves bowed themselves humbly before the Emperor, and without making any reply each one produced a pearl and laid it on the steps of the throne. When the Emperor saw these pearls he was much astonished; but in order to make certain that they came from his own Treasury, he summoned his Chief Treasurer before him, and ordered him to compare the jewels in the Treasury with the inventory which had been made on the previous evening. The Treasurer hurried off to do so, and after a short while he reappeared, and informed the Emperor that, having carefully counted all the jewels, and having compared the numbers in the Treasury with the numbers on the inventory, he found that three pearls were indeed missing.

On hearing this the Emperor no longer hesitated

in fulfilling his promise to the three Thieves. He raised them at once to high rank, and presented them with lands and money sufficient to uphold their new status, and they lived happily ever afterwards, enjoying the confidence of the Emperor and the friendship of the numerous officials whom they had saved from imprisonment and death.

STORY No. XV.

THE STORY OF THE BOY WITH THE DEFORMED HEAD.

ONCE upon a time there lived a poor man and his wife who had only one child, and this Boy, as it happened, was born with a deformed head, which projected in front and behind, and gave him a very ugly appearance. The parents, although much grieved at their son's deformity, were, nevertheless, very fond of him and brought him up very carefully. Every day, when he grew big enough, he used to drive the cows out to pasture, and all day long he sat about on the hillsides watching the cattle graze. And so he passed his life very happily until, when he reached the age of fifteen, he began to think he should like to marry a wife as other young men did, but he feared that owing to his deformity no girl would ever look at him.

One day it chanced that he drove his cows to graze on the rich pasture on the edge of a small lake, and as he was sitting near the shore of the lake all of a sudden he saw a large white Drake descend from the sky, and light upon the surface of the water. As soon as it was seated upon the water it swam round the lake three times to the right and then three times to the left, and having done so it flew away again and disappeared into the sky.

The Boy watched the behaviour of this Drake with some interest. He had never before seen so large and beautiful a bird, nor one that behaved so strangely. So next day he again sat down in the same place, and kept a sharp look-out for the bird. At the same hour as on the previous day the Drake again appeared in the sky, and descending upon the lake, acted in precisely the same manner as before. And it continued to do so for several days, the Boy always watching its behaviour with increased interest.

At last he determined that he would try to catch this Drake for himself, so he wove himself a long rope of yaks' hair, big enough to completely encircle the lake, and he laid this upon the shore in a loop extending right round the lake; and at short intervals along the rope he fastened loops made of the finest horse hair, the loose ends of which he left floating in the water.

Next day the Drake came as usual and began to swim round the lake to the right. It had not gone very far when it put its foot into one of the loops and was caught. The Boy at once ran down to the shore of the lake, and taking the Drake in his hands, he tied its wings and legs together, and set it down on the grass beside him.

"Now," thought he to himself, "what shall I do with this fine white Drake? I will take him home and kill him, and he will make a nice dinner for father and mother and me."

Just as he was thinking this, to his intense surprise, the Drake spoke to him as follows :

" I beg of you not to kill me, my good boy," said he, " for you must know I am not in reality a Drake as I appear to be, but I am a fairy King just come from the region of the gods. It is my habit every day to descend to this lake in the form of a white Drake, and to amuse myself by swimming round and round. If you will now consent to let me go I will reward you liberally. You shall have gold and silver and jewels and coral, as much as you wish, and sumptuous food every day for the rest of your life.

On hearing this the Boy laughed, and replied :

" You should not tell me such stories as these. How am I to know that you are really a fairy ? It seems to me that all you are in a position to give me is your feathers."

" I hope you will not disbelieve my word," replied the Drake very earnestly ; " I assure you I can do all this, and even more, if you will release me."

" Well," said the Boy, " if that is really so I will make a bargain with you. I do not care at all for your gold or your jewels, but what I really want is a wife. If you can promise to supply me with a wife I will let you go."

" Well," said the Drake, " that, too, can be arranged. I have three daughters living in my kingdom in the skies, and I will give you as wife any one of them whom you desire. Would you prefer the eldest, or the youngest, or the middle one ? "

The Boy was greatly pleased on hearing this offer of the Drake's, and he thought to himself:

"I will not take the eldest girl, for fear she should be too old, nor the youngest, for fear she should be too young. I will select the middle one."

So he told the Drake that he would like his middle daughter.

"Very well," said the Drake, "I will arrange the matter accordingly, and I will meet you here to-morrow with my middle daughter. But there is one condition which always attaches to the marriage of a mortal with a fairy, and that is that she can only live with you for nine years. At the conclusion of that time she is bound to return to her home in the heavens."

The Boy agreed to this condition, and when all the details had been satisfactorily arranged he cut the cords which bound the Drake and let him go. The bird spread his wings and flew up into the sky; and after circling for a few minutes he flew straight upwards and disappeared from sight, whilst the Boy went home to his father and mother.

The Drake flew far up into the blue sky until he arrived at the country of the gods, where he changed at once into the form and raiment of the King of the Fairies. Seating himself upon his throne, he summoned his three daughters before him and informed them of what had occurred; and he gave orders to his middle daughter to prepare herself forthwith to go and marry a mortal. The girl wept bitterly on hearing this, but nevertheless she prepared to carry out her father's orders, and got ready a large stock of beautiful clothes and much gold and silver and jewels to take with her.

Next day, at the appointed hour, the Boy went down to the lake as usual, and seated himself in his usual place; and not long afterwards he saw the white Drake and a white Duck flying towards him from the sky. They descended swiftly until they touched the ground, where they were at once transformed into the Fairy King and his beautiful daughter. The boy was overcome with joy when he saw the lovely wife that had been brought to him; but the girl was horrified at his ugly appearance, and begged her father to take her back to her abode in the skies. The Fairy King, however, insisted upon her carrying out her share of the bargain, so leaving his daughter with the Boy, he again turned himself into a Drake and, flying up into the sky, he disappeared from view.

The Boy now led his bride home to his father and mother, and next day the marriage was duly completed. The Fairy wife, by means of her magic, was able to erect a magnificent palace, and to furnish it in the most luxurious manner with everything necessary for comfort; and she supplied, moreover, horses and servants, and everything else that a married couple could desire. So the two took up their abode in this fine house and, together with the old father and mother, they lived there happily for several years; and as time passed away the fairy wife became accustomed to her husband's forbidding appearance, and year by year became more and more attached to him.

So the time slipped by and at last the nine years of the Fairy wife's abode upon earth came to an end. The young Man, however, had become so accustomed to her presence that he could hardly believe that the Fairy King's words would come true and that he should really be deprived of his wife when the appointed time arrived. So on the last night of the ninth year he went to bed as usual in his magnificent chamber, clothed in rich silks, and surrounded by all the evidences of wealth and luxury.

He slept soundly all night, and when he awoke in the morning and sat up and looked about him, what was his astonishment and horror to discover that, instead of lying upon his fine couch in his magnificent palace, with troops of servants ready to wait upon him, he was reposing upon the bare ground under the open sky, on a bleak hillside near to the spot where he had first conversed with the Fairy King. His palace, his servants, his horses, his furniture, and, worst of all, his beautiful wife, had all disappeared utterly and completely, and nothing remained of them but a memory. Half distracted with grief and chagrin, the young Man ran frantically across the country, thinking to find some trace of his lost happiness.

For some days he wandered on and on, scarcely conscious of what he was doing, and at length, having passed beyond the part of the country which he knew, he arrived one day about noon on the shores of a vast expanse of water which stretched before him as far as he could see. By the side of this lake there arose a jagged cliff, and about half-way up the cliff on a broad ledge he noticed an immense nest, in which appeared some young birds of unusual size. At first he was unable to detect what sort of birds these were, but after examining them attentively for some time he saw that they were three young Gryphons, whose parents apparently had gone off in search of food.

As he stood upon the beach watching the young birds they suddenly began to manifest every sign of terror and confusion, chattering and squealing wildly to one another, and flapping their puny wings; and on turning towards the lake in order to ascertain what was the cause of their alarm, he perceived an immense Dragon—whose head, at the end of its long neck, towered high above the water—making its way rapidly across the lake, with the evident intention of devouring the young Gryphons. The young Man, who was of a courageous and kindly disposition, determined to save the young Gryphons from the maw of this monster; so, drawing his sword, he waited till the Dragon had set foot upon dry land, and then, attacking him fiercely, he engaged single-handed in a desperate conflict. For some time the issue was doubtful, but the young man at length succeeded with one well-delivered blow in severing the Dragon's head from its neck, and the monster fell dead upon the beach.

Scarcely had the Dragon breathed its last when the air was darkened by the wings of some great creature passing overhead, and, looking up, he observed, flying just above him, the forms of the two parent Gryphons

THE DRAGON ATTACKING THE GRYPHON'S NEST.

now returning to their nest. As soon as they had arrived the young Gryphons proceeded to relate to them at full length the terrible danger they had just escaped, and the gallant conduct of the young Man in slaying their would-be destroyer. The parent Gryphons were very pleased when they heard this story, and, looking towards the young Man with some curiosity, they began to remark upon his appearance.

"Have you ever, Mother Gryphon," asked the male bird, "seen any creature of that description before?"

"No, Father Gryphon, I never have," she replied; "but it seems to be both brave and well-intentioned. I observe, moreover, that it has neither beak nor claws, so I propose that we invite it into the nest, and receive it hospitably in return for a good service which it has rendered to our children."

Father Gryphon agreed to this proposal, and he at once flew down to the beach, and addressing the young Man he invited him to enter the nest. The youth accepted the invitation, and having explained that he was unable to fly, he mounted upon the Gryphon's back and was speedily carried up the cliff, and deposited with the young Gryphons in the nest. After making a good dinner off the food which the parent Gryphons had just provided for their young ones, the young Man related to the family all his various adventures since the time when he had first made the acquaintance of the Fairy King.

"Yours," said Father Gryphon, "is a very sad story,

and in my opinion you have not been treated at all well; but if you desire it, I may perhaps be of some assistance to you. What I propose is that you should mount upon my back, and I will then carry you through the air to the kingdom of the gods, where you can represent your case to the King of the Fairies in person, and where you will, at any rate, have the opportunity of persuading your wife to accompany you back to earth."

The young Man gladly assented to this proposition, and mounted on the Gryphon's back; and the great bird, spreading his wings, soared upwards straight into the blue sky, carrying the youth with him. Up and up they flew, whilst the earth seemed to recede into the distance and to grow smaller and smaller, until at length it disappeared from view altogether. Still they flew on until, towards nightfall, they arrived at the country of the gods. The Gryphon, with the young Man upon his back, flew straight in through the great golden gates, and deposited the youth in the centre of a vast court-yard round which were sitting numbers of gods, fairies and other denizens of the sky.

When the gods saw that a human being had been deposited in their midst they rose in great wrath, and began bitterly to reproach the Gryphon for what he had done.

"How is it," said they, "that you have dared, unordered, to bring into our presence an inhabitant of the human world? Do you not know that human beings are of a coarser essence than ourselves and are repugnant and abhorrent to us? How dare you so defile the sacred country of the gods?"

But the Gryphon was not at all frightened at their anger, and he answered them boldly and firmly:

"This young man," said he, "is a valiant and kind-hearted youth. He saved my young ones from destruction by attacking, single-handed, and killing a Dragon who was on the point of devouring them. He then related to me his story of how, after nine years of happiness, he was deprived by the King of the Fairies of his wife, his house, his wealth, and everything which he had possessed. I consider, therefore, that he has been treated in a shameful and unjustifiable manner, and so I have brought him here to plead his cause in person and to claim redress."

While this conversation was in progress the young man's Fairy wife had been hiding in a corner, too nervous to show herself before her husband and all the assembly of the gods. But she could now contain herself no longer, and, rushing forward, she threw herself into her husband's arms, crying out that she loved him and would return with him to earth.

When her father heard this he did not know how to act, but it was decided that a conclave should be held, and the matter debated at length. So the celestial powers met together in a great council, and, having discussed the matter in all its bearings, they decided that, as the Fairy Princess desired to return to earth of her own free will, they would not stand in her way; but that if she did so, she must take the consequence of her own action, and that as the result of mating with an unclean creature like a human being she must herself become mortal and lose her Fairy nature.

On hearing this decision the girl joyfully agreed. So she and her husband mounted together upon the broad back of the Gryphon, and the great beast, spreading his wings, sailed through the golden gates of the palace and swept downwards through the blue heavens to the earth below. He soon deposited the youth and his wife on the ground near their old home, where he bade them farewell and returned to his own nest. And henceforward, although the Fairy had lost her magic powers, the two lived happily together, and grew to a good old age in prosperous and comfortable circumstances.

STORY No. XVI.

THE PRINCE AND THE OGRE'S CASTLE.

ONCE upon a time there lived an old King and Queen, who, although they had been married for many years, had no children to brighten their old age or to inherit their kingdom; and in the King's possession, as it happened, were a favourite mare and dog, who also had no offspring. Now both the King and the Queen were very anxious to have children of their own, and also to perpetuate the fine breed represented by the mare and the dog; so the King posted a notice all over his kingdom, offering a very large reward to any Lama or other holy personage who could secure to him and to his horse and dog the birth of children.

In response to this notice many Lamas and recluses presented themselves at the palace, and by means of prayers and religious ceremonies they endeavoured to obtain from the gods what the King and Queen desired; but all their efforts were in vain, and the years passed by without any offspring being born.

Now it chanced that in a neighbouring country there lived a terrible Ogre, who was an expert in magic and all the black arts; and it came to his ears that this King had offered a large reward if anyone could secure to him the birth of children for himself, his horse and his dog. So he disguised himself as a holy Lama; and coming up to the palace one day on foot, he asked for an interview with the King. The King, who had almost lost faith in Lamas of any kind, received him courteously, and asked him what he could do to help in the matter.

"Oh, King!" replied the supposed Lama, "I, you must know, am a great recluse, and as the result of many years of solitary meditation, I have become proficient in all the magic arts. I will undertake to secure for you and your horse and dog the birth of offspring as you desire. But I can only do so on one condition, which is as follows: three children will be born to you, three to the horse and three to the dog. They will all be of a miraculous nature, and will grow to their full powers in the course of three years. At the end of three years I will return here, and will claim from you one of each to follow me and serve me and to obey my orders in all matters."

The King gladly agreed to this condition, and asked the Lama how he should proceed in order to secure the desired result. The Lama replied:

"Here, oh King, are nine pills; three of these must be administered to the Queen, three to the horse and three to the dog. In three months' time a child will be born to each, to be followed by two others at intervals of one month."

So saying, he handed the pills to the King and forthwith took his departure. The King accordingly administered the pills as directed, and after three months the

Queen gave birth to a boy, the mare to a foal, and the dog to a pup, and these were followed by two others at intervals of one month as the Lama had predicted.

All the young ones grew apace, and at the end of the three years they had all attained to their full growth and powers, and punctually at the conclusion of the third year the Ogre, still disguised as a Lama, returned to the palace to demand his due.

The King and Queen, though reluctant to part with any of their children, resolved to abide by their bargain, and they consulted together as to which of the young Princes should be handed over to the Lama. After some consideration they decided that it would not be advisable to part with the eldest son, as he was heir to the throne, nor with the second, who would have to succeed to the kingdom should any accident or mischance befall his elder brother; so they resolved to send the youngest son, and with him the youngest horse and the youngest dog. These three accordingly were handed over to the Lama, who ordered the Prince to follow him, and started off at once to his own country.

After travelling for some considerable distance they arrived at the top of a high pass, whence the Ogre, pointing down to a great castle standing in the valley below, said to the young Prince :

" That is my house below there ; I shall leave you here and you must go on down to the house. When you arrive there you will find a goat tied up near the door of the courtyard, and a bundle of straw lying near by. You must pick up the bundle of straw and place it within reach of the goat. Then you must go into the farmyard, where you will find many fowls, and in one corner you will see an earthenware jar full of soaked grain, and you must sprinkle this grain for the fowls to eat. These two tasks I give you to-day, and you are on no account to enter my castle until I rejoin you in the evening."

So saying the Ogre went off in another direction, whilst the young Prince, riding on his horse and followed by his dog, went down to the Ogre's castle. When he reached the gateway he found, as the Ogre had predicted, a goat tied up and a bundle of straw lying in a corner of the courtyard. So he dismounted from his horse, and, picking up the bundle, he carried it near the goat and placed it on the ground. Scarcely had the bundle touched the ground when it became transformed into three great wolves, who, leaping upon the goat, devoured it in an instant, and then fled away to the hills.

The young Prince was very much astonished at seeing this, but being of a courageous spirit he did not allow the incident to frighten him, and proceeded to finish the remainder of his task. So he entered the yard where the poultry were kept, and proceeding to the corner where stood the jar of soaked barley, he took out a handful and scattered it amongst the fowls. As the grain touched the ground it was transformed instantly into three wild cats, who leapt fiercely upon the cocks and hens, and in a few moments, having destroyed them all, fled away into the hills.

The Prince's curiosity was now thoroughly aroused, and he determined, in spite of the Ogre's warning, to enter the house itself, and to discover what sort of place he had come to, so he pushed open the door of the castle and began wandering about all over the house. For some time he found nothing to interest him. The rooms were all well furnished and in good order, but he could find no trace and hear no sound of any living creature.

At last, after having explored the greater part of the building, he suddenly turned a corner in a passage, and saw in front of him a room whose walls were composed entirely of glass. Entering this room he saw in one corner a beautiful lady lying asleep on a couch with a flower behind her ear. The Prince was pleased at finding a human being in this desolate and mysterious castle, and, approaching the lady, he endeavoured to arouse her from her slumber. But all his efforts were in vain; she appeared to be in a sort of trance, and all he could do did not succeed in waking her.

At last in despair he took away the flower which was placed behind her ear, and as he did so she woke and sat up upon her couch, rubbing her eyes. As soon as she perceived the young Prince she was much astonished, and asked him what he was doing in the Ogre's castle. The Prince told her the whole story of his miraculous birth through the magic of the holy Lama, and how he was condemned to serve the Lama as his servant through the agreement which the King his father had made, and how he had carried out the two tasks which the Lama had given him that day.

On hearing this story the lady was very indignant and spoke to him as follows:

"You must know, oh Prince," said she, "that the person whom you suppose to be a Lama is in reality a fearful and wicked Ogre. The only food of which he partakes is men's hearts, and this house is full of the lifeless bodies of his numerous victims. He, however, is unable to obtain any power over the body of a human being unless that being directly disobeys his orders. Thus it is his practice upon obtaining a fresh servant to set him strange tasks which terrify and repel him. These tasks grow daily more difficult and more odious, until at last one day the servant disobeys his orders, and forthwith his body is at the mercy of the Ogre, who devours the heart and places the lifeless body in a large chamber at the back of this house. The process has evidently begun with you to-day. You have fulfilled all of his tasks without allowing yourself to be terrified by the strange portents which you have observed, but on his return he will no doubt set you further and more disagreeable duties to perform. I, you should know, am a Princess in my own country, and I was handed over to the Ogre by my parents about a year ago in circumstances very similar to your own. But when he had brought me to his castle, instead of destroying me as he does his other victims, he fell in love with me, and I have remained here as his wife ever since. But he is of a very jealous disposition, and never allows me to leave his castle; and for fear I should make my escape during his absence, he invariably, before going out, places an enchanted flower behind my ear which makes me fall into a trance, and I cannot awake until the flower is removed."

The young Prince was very much interested on hearing this story, and he begged the Princess to give him some further information about the Ogre's habits, in order that he might not unawares fall into his power, and might eventually be able to bring about the destruction of the monster.

"It is very difficult," replied the Princess, "for any human being to kill the Ogre, for he is of a supernatural nature, and even if you were to cut off his head he would come to life again at once, unless you could also destroy his 'mascot'*—that is to say, the object upon the preservation of which his life in this world depends. Now the Ogre's mascot is very carefully concealed, and its existence and whereabouts are known to no person except myself. I, however, have discovered where it is, and I will reveal the secret to you later, but first I will tell you the method by which you may destroy the Ogre's body. You must know, then, that it is only possible for a human being to strike a mortal blow at the Ogre when his face is turned away. He knows this very well, and will never in any circumstances turn his back upon a man. Similarly, if he can make you turn your back to him he may be able to do you a mischief. When he comes in this evening and finds that you have fulfilled both the tasks he has set you, the first thing he will order you to do will be to walk three times round a great stove which stands in the centre of the kitchen; and if you

* Known as "La" in the Tibetan tongue. It is difficult to find an equivalent word in the English language, but the Princess describes its meaning. See also the story of "Room Bacha and Baki," where the same superstition occurs.

obey his orders he will follow you from behind and will possibly do you some harm while your back is turned towards him. When he gives you these orders, then, you must not disobey, but you must tell the Ogre that it is so dark in the kitchen that you cannot see your way clearly, and you must ask him to precede you. This he is bound to do, and while he is going round the stove you may perhaps find an opportunity for stabbing him. If, however, you cannot succeed in doing so, and you both pass through this ordeal successfully, he will set you no further task to-night, and I will ascertain from him during the evening what trial he has in store for you to-morrow."

The Prince thanked the young lady for all her good advice, which he promised to follow faithfully in every respect, and she then said to him :

"It is now near the time for the Ogre's return. I will lie down on the couch, and you must place the flower behind my ear just as it was before; and when I fall into a trance you must at once go out into the courtyard and wait the return of the Ogre, and mind you are careful not to let him know that you have been inside the castle."

So saying, the Princess lay down upon her couch, and the young man having placed the flower behind her ear she instantly fell into a deep trance. The Prince then went out into the courtyard and shortly after the Ogre arrived. He had now discarded his lama costume and appeared in his proper form, and riding up to the Prince he asked him in an angry tone whether he had carried out the orders he had received, and on the Prince replying in the affirmative, the Ogre ordered him to come into the kitchen. On entering the kitchen the Ogre pointed to a great stove standing in the centre, and said to the Prince :

"You must now walk three times round that stove."

"It is so dark in here," replied the Prince, "that I cannot see my way at all clearly. Will you please precede me and show me the way ?"

The Ogre was very angry at hearing this, but he was unable to refuse, so he started off and ran round the stove three times, the Prince following closely at his heels. But he went so fast that the Prince, although he had his knife ready in his hand, was unable to catch him; and the Ogre, seeing that the Prince was not to be outwitted by this stratagem, went upstairs to his wife, leaving the young man locked up in the kitchen, where he spent the night alone.

Next morning the Ogre started off soon after daylight on his own business, and as soon as he was gone the Prince ran upstairs to the glass room, where he found the lady lying in a trance as before. He took the flower from behind her ear, and she immediately woke up and looked about her.

"Good-morning, Prince," said she. "How did you succeed last night ? I hope you followed the instructions which I gave you."

The Prince described to her what had occurred, and she said :

"I have ascertained what the Ogre proposes to do

when he returns this evening. He will seat himself in his chair of state in his great hall of audience and will order you to *kow-tow* to him three times, and if you do so he will seize an opportunity whilst you are lying on your face before him to do you some injury. It will not do, however, absolutely to disobey his orders; but you must explain to him that, being a Prince, you have never had to *kow-tow* to anybody and do not exactly know how to do it, and you must ask him to show you the proper way to proceed. He cannot refuse your request, and you must take the opportunity of stabbing him or cutting off his head whilst he is lying on his face before you. If you succeed in this come at once to me, and I will show you what else is necessary in order to bring about his complete destruction."

The Prince promised to obey the lady's orders, and after again sending her into a trance by placing the magic flower behind her ear, he returned to the courtyard and awaited the Ogre's return. Just before dusk the Ogre came back and as the Princess had predicted he proceeded at once to the great audience hall, and seated himself on his chair of state.

"Now," said he to the Prince, "you must *kow-tow* to me three times."

"I am very sorry," answered the Prince, "that I do not know how to do so. Being a Prince myself, I have never had to *kow-tow* to anybody; but if you will show me the proper manner in which to proceed I will do my best."

This reply made the Ogre very angry, but he was

unable to refuse to do as the Prince had asked him. So the Prince took his seat on the Ogre's chair and the Ogre kneeling on the ground before him proceeded to *kow-tow* three times in the orthodox manner. As the Ogre's face touched the ground the first time the Prince drew his sword; as it touched the ground the second time he raised the sword above his head; and as it touched the ground the third and last time the Prince delivered a violent blow, completely severing the Ogre's head from his body. Leaving the body where it lay, the Prince ran up to the glass room as fast as he could, and having awakened the lady from her sleep, he told her what had happened.

"Well done!" said she. "The first part of your task is now accomplished; but as I told you before, it is still necessary to destroy the Ogre's mascot, or he will come to life again in a short time. What you must do now, therefore, is as follows: you must descend into the vaults below the castle, and having traversed nine dark subterranean chambers, you will come to a blank stone wall. You must rap three times on this wall with the hilt of your sword, exclaiming with each rap, 'Open, blank wall'; and as you pronounce these words for the third time the wall will fly asunder, and you will find yourself entering another subterranean chamber. In the centre of this chamber you will see a beautiful boy seated with a goblet of crystal liquid in his hand. This boy is the Ogre's mascot, and upon his existence depends the Ogre's life in this world. You must at once slay the boy, and taking the goblet very carefully in your hand, carry it upstairs to me. But be careful not to spill any of the liquid, as each drop means a man's life."

On receiving these instructions the Prince went down into the vaults at the basement of the castle, and having traversed nine great subterranean chambers, he found his progress stopped by a blank wall. Raising his sword he rapped three times with the hilt on the wall, exclaiming each time as he did so, "Open, blank wall." As he pronounced these words for the third time a grating sound was heard, and with a hollow clang the wall gave way for him.

Advancing a few paces the Prince found himself in a small dungeon, lighted only by the glimmer which issued from a goblet of crystal liquid held in the hand of a beautiful young boy, who was seated in the centre of the chamber. Without a moment's hesitation the Prince thrust his sword through the heart of the boy, and taking the goblet in his hand, he carried it upstairs to the Princess, being very careful on the way not to allow a single drop to be spilt.

When the Princess saw him entering her room with the goblet in his hand she was very much delighted.

"Now," said she, "the Ogre is effectually destroyed, and can never more come to life in this world. All that now remains to be done is to restore to life his previous victims."

So saying she ordered the Prince, still carrying the goblet, to follow her, and she proceeded by many winding passages and staircases to a remote part of the great castle. Presently, opening a huge door, she entered a long, low, gloomy chamber, lighted only by a narrow window which looked out over the back part of the castle. When the Prince entered this chamber he was horrified to see that down both sides of it were stretched the bodies of many scores of men, women and children, who lay there fully dressed, but to all appearance quite lifeless.

"These," said the lady, "are the bodies of the Ogre's victims; he has eaten their hearts, but the bodies, as you see, remain unharmed, while the spirit of each one is compressed into a drop of crystal liquor with which that goblet is filled. You must now sprinkle the bodies with the liquid, giving one drop to each."

Accordingly the Prince passed down the rows of lifeless bodies, dropping as he went one drop of the magic liquid on each body; and as the liquor touched the body the life returned, and each person, as if awakened from a long sleep, moved and yawned, and finally sat up and began to talk and walk. In a few moments the transformation was complete, and the Ogre's victims, after thanking the Prince and Princess heartily for their good offices, returned to their own homes. The Prince himself bade farewell to the lady, and leaving her in possession of the Ogre's castle and all its belongings, he himself mounted upon his horse, and with his dog following at his heels, set out in search of further adventures.

[This is only the first instalment of the Prince's adventures, which continue to an interminable length. I have given this section as a sample of the whole.]

STORY No. XVII.

THE STORY OF THE STONE LION.

ONCE upon a time there were two brothers whose father was dead, and who lived alone with their mother in a big house in a well-cultivated valley.

Now the elder of these brothers was a smart, clever man, but was of a very selfish, cold-hearted disposition; and the younger brother was simple and kind, but rather dull. The consequence was that after the death of their father the elder brother conducted most of the business of the family himself, and entirely supported his brother and his mother; whilst the younger brother, although quite willing to do his best, was not clever enough to be of any assistance in the household.

After a time the elder brother decided in his mind that he could no longer endure this state of affairs, so he one day called his young brother aside, and told him plainly that he would no longer continue to support such a lout, and that it would be better for him to go out into the world and seek his own fortune alone. The poor boy was much grieved on hearing this decision from his brother; but he was quite unable to protest or dispute, so, having packed up his few belongings, he went to say good-bye to his mother, and told her what had occurred. The good woman was very angry when she heard the news, and she said to her son :

" Very well, if your hard-hearted brother insists on turning you out of the house, I will accompany you. I cannot consent to remain any longer with such an unnatural and cruel son."

So next day the mother and her younger son left the house and set off together to seek some means of livelihood on their own account. After travelling for some little distance they reached an empty hut situated at the foot of a large hill, not far from a populous town ; and finding that the place was apparently deserted and that the owner, whoever he was, had left nothing to show that he proposed to return, they took possession of the hut, and slept there during the night.

Next morning early the boy, taking an axe with him, went out on to the hillside and began chopping wood. By evening he had chopped a fine big bundle of wood, and taking it down into the town he sold it in the market for a good sum of money. Greatly elated at the success of his labours he returned to his mother in the hut, and showing her the money he had earned, he told her that she need no longer have any anxiety regarding the future, for he would now be able to support her without any difficulty. Next morning, shouldering his axe, he started off again, and as before, began to chop wood. He had done a good morning's work, and was walking a little further up the hill in order to search for some better timber, when, in a sheltered part of the hillside he suddenly found himself face to face with a large life-sized Lion carved out of the stone.

"Now," thought he to himself, on seeing the Lion, "this, no doubt, is the guardian deity of this mountain, and to him must be due my good fortune in so easily obtaining a means of livelihood. I will certainly make him some offering to-morrow."

So that evening, after selling his wood, he purchased two candles in the town, and on the following day he went straight to where the stone Lion stood, and lighting the candles, he placed one upon each side of the image, and prostrating himself humbly upon the ground before it, he prayed for renewed good fortune. Suddenly, to his surprise and alarm, the Lion opened its mouth, and asked him what he was doing there.

The young man replied that having been driven from his home by his proud and hard-hearted brother, he was now engaged in earning his livelihood by chopping wood upon that hill; and that, thinking that the Lion must be the guardian deity of the mountain, he had considered it right to make him some sort of an offering, and to request his continued patronage and assistance.

"Very good," replied the Lion in a guttural tone of voice, "come again at this time to-morrow, and bring with you a large bucket, and I will furnish you at once with what wealth you require."

The boy thanked the Lion for his kindness, and carrying his load of firewood down to the village he sold it for a good price, and with the proceeds he purchased himself a large wooden bucket.

Next morning he went up onto the hill again, carrying his bucket, and arriving near the stone Lion, he again prostrated himself upon the ground and announced his presence.

"Very good," replied the Lion, "you must now act as follows: hold the bucket under my mouth, and I will vomit gold into it. But as soon as the bucket is nearly full you must tell me, as on no account must a single morsel of gold fall to the ground."

The young man proceeded to do as the Lion had instructed him. He held the bucket below the Lion's mouth, and the Lion forthwith began to vomit into it a stream of gold pieces. When the bucket was nearly full the young man informed the Lion of the fact, and forthwith the stream of gold came to an end; and the youth, having thanked the Lion most heartily for his munificent gift, carried off his bucket of gold in triumph to his mother. The poor woman was at first quite frightened at seeing so much wealth, but her son, having explained to her how he had come by it, she became greatly excited, and pleased.

Next day the widow and her son set about placing themselves in more comfortable circumstances. They purchased a large farm-house in the neighbourhood, and a large stock of cattle and sheep, and settled down in their new abode, and henceforward they began to live in a very comfortable and prosperous manner.

The news of the changed condition of life of his mother and younger brother soon reached the ears of the eldest son, and overcome with curiosity as to how this result had been brought about, he decided to call upon them, and to ascertain the cause of their prosperity. So, accompanied by his wife, and carrying with him a very small piece of cloth as a present, he set out to pay them a visit. When he reached the house his younger brother was away engaged upon his farm business, but the mother received her elder son and his wife very kindly and made them as comfortable as she could. In the evening, when the younger brother returned, he greeted his brother heartily, and being of a most kind-hearted and forgiving disposition, he related to him fully the manner in which he had come by his wealth, and strongly recommended his brother to act in a similar way.

The elder brother and his wife, as they returned home together that evening, talked the matter over between them, and decided that so good an opportunity of making money so easily was not to be lost. So next day the husband proceeded to the town, and after a prolonged search purchased the largest bucket which was to be had in the whole place. Carrying this with him, and bringing also a couple of candles, he proceeded to the hillside, and following the directions he had received from his brother, he soon found himself face to face with the stone Lion. He at once lighted his candles and placed them one on each side of the Lion, while he prostrated himself upon the ground, and prayed to the Lion for good fortune.

"Who are you?" said the Lion in a gruff voice; "and what do you want?"

"I," replied the elder brother, "am the brother of

THE STONE LION VOMITING GOLD.

Page 121.

the young man who was here the other day, and to whom you gave so much gold; and, following his advice, I have now come to ask you for a similar benefit for myself."

"Very well," said the Lion, "place your bucket under my mouth and I will vomit gold into it; but as soon as the bucket is nearly full you must inform me of the fact, as on no account must a single piece of gold fall to the ground. If this should happen, you will meet with misfortune."

So the elder brother, trembling with eagerness, held his bucket as directed, and forthwith a stream of gold pieces began to pour from the Lion's mouth into the bucket. The covetous fellow shook the bucket slightly from time to time in order to make the gold lie well together and so to obtain a larger quantity; and, overcome by greed, he could not bring himself to inform the Lion that the bucket was nearly full until it brimmed over and a piece of gold, slipping off the heap, fell to the ground. As it touched the ground the stream of gold suddenly ceased, and the Lion, in a hoarse voice, said:

"The largest piece of gold of all has stuck in my throat. Put your hand into my mouth and pull it out."

The elder brother, on hearing this, immediately thrust his hand into the Lion's mouth, hoping to secure a large lump of gold; and no sooner had he done so than the Lion, closing his jaws, held him fast. It was in vain that he struggled and wrenched his arm to and fro, endeavouring to release it; the stone jaws of the Lion gripped him so tight that he was totally unable to effect his escape, and the Lion, deaf to all prayers and entreaties, had relapsed apparently into an insensible figure of stone. And worst of all, when he glanced at his bucket of gold he saw, to his horror, that instead of gold it held nothing but stones and earth.

Towards evening the elder brother's wife grew anxious concerning her husband's absence, and knowing the direction in which he had gone, she set forth to the hillside to seek him. After hunting for some time she suddenly came across him, and asked him what he was doing and why he did not come home.

"Oh, wife," said he, "a terrible thing has happened to me. I put my hand into the Lion's mouth in order to extract a lump of gold which was stuck in his throat, when all of a sudden he closed his jaws, and gripped my arm, and now I am unable to effect my escape."

The poor woman, on hearing this, wept and wailed, but all her entreaties to the Lion proved of no avail, and she went off to her home, and soon returned carrying her husband some food. Every day, for many days after, she returned to her husband, bringing him such provisions as he required to keep him alive; but as she had now no one to work for her, and was obliged to support her husband and her child entirely by her own exertions, she became gradually poorer and poorer, and was soon obliged to sell her household goods to procure the necessary food.

Some months passed away and the poor woman,

falling ill, was at length reduced to such complete destitution that she had not even a morsel of bread to bring to her husband, and one morning she came weeping up the hill, and addressed him as follows:

"I have sold everything in the house, and have now no money to buy any food. There is not a scrap left to eat anywhere, and now nothing remains but for us to starve to death."

On hearing this the Lion was so tickled that he could not refrain from laughing.

"Ha, ha!" said he, and opened his great jaws.

As quickly as he could, and before the Lion had time to close his mouth again, the man withdrew his arm, and, finding himself free, he at once hastened down the hill with his wife. Then, taking their child with them, they proceeded straight to the house of the younger brother, and having related to him the whole of their story, begged some relief from their misery. The young man reproached his brother for his greedy conduct in trying to obtain an extra supply of gold from the Lion in spite of his warning; but being of a very forgiving nature, he consented at last to supply his brother with a sum of money sufficient for him to take a small farm in the neighbourhood. Here the proud brother and his wife settled down in very humble circumstances, whilst the younger son lived for many years very happily with his mother and prospered exceedingly in all he undertook.

STORY No: XVIII.

THE STORY OF THE LAMA'S SERVANT.

THERE was once an old Lama who lived in a small house at the very top of a hill in a lonely part of Tibet. He was a very holy man and spent his time entirely in religious contemplation, and the only person whom he allowed about his house was a certain young man of low birth, who acted as his Servant and used to cook his meals and perform other household duties. This man was a great character in his way. He was an amusing fellow and very fond of his joke, but was quite unreliable and incapable of performing any regular work.

Now the old Lama's diet, in accordance with the tenets of his religion, was a very small one, and he refrained entirely from taking the life of any living creature. So his food consisted chiefly of barley-flour, butter, and so on, and he abstained from meat of any kind. This mode of life, however, was not at all pleasing to the Servant, Rin-dzin, who had a healthy appetite and greatly missed his daily dish of meat, and he was constantly trying to persuade the Lama to allow him to kill a sheep or a goat in order that he might have a satisfactory meal. This, however, the Lama always sternly refused to do, and forbade his Servant on any account to destroy the life of a living being.

One day the Servant noticed a fine fat sheep, which, having become separated from the rest of the flock, was wandering about near the Lama's house. So he pursued it and caught it, and carrying it into the ground floor of the house, he went up into the room above, and letting down a rope through a hole in the floor he hitched a slip-knot at the other end of the rope round the sheep's neck. Having made these arrangements he went into the next room, where the Lama, as usual, was sitting alone wrapt in religious contemplation, deaf to all mundane affairs.

"Oh! Lama," said the Servant, addressing the old man, "I have come to tell you that I have just found a sheep belonging to our neighbours, who live in the valley below, wandering about near the house; so, for fear he should be eaten by wolves, I have caught him and tied him up in a room below. But he is a very violent sheep and is struggling desperately to escape. Will you be so kind as to hold the rope for a short time while I go and inform the owner where his sheep is?"

The old Lama, who never refused a reasonable request, at once proceeded to do as he was asked, and, rising from his seat, he followed the Servant into the next room.

"Pray hold this rope," said the Servant, handing the Lama the loose end of the rope to which the sheep was secured, "and if the sheep begins to struggle, pull it as hard as you can to prevent him from escaping."

The Lama accordingly took hold of the rope, and the Servant went down into the lower storey as if he intended to leave the house. Instead of doing so, however, he went into the room where the sheep was tied and began to poke the animal with a sharp stick, and the sheep began to struggle violently, trying to escape from its tormentor. The more the sheep struggled below the more the Lama pulled above, and at last, when the tug-of-war had lasted for some minutes, the sheep was strangled by the slip-knot round its neck.

After the lapse of an hour or two the Servant returned to the Lama in the upper room and informed him that the sheep had died a natural death while he had been away seeking for its owner, and, in the circumstances, he supposed that they might as well cut it up and cook it for food. The unsuspecting old Lama agreed to this, and for several days the Servant was able to eat his fill of excellent mutton.

It chanced, however, that the shepherd boy who was in charge of the sheep had come to the Lama's house looking for the one which was lost, and peeping in through the window had seen all that had happened. He told the story to his parents, who were very angry, and came to complain to the Lama of the conduct of his Servant. The old Lama was very much incensed at the treachery and wickedness of his attendant, and dismissed him on the spot, telling him to go away and never come back again. So Master Rin-dzin, with his few belongings on his back, marched off into the world to try and make his fortune.

He was a good deal cast down at first, but being naturally a volatile, light-hearted fellow he soon recovered his spirits and marched along the road singing blithely, and keeping a sharp look-out for anything that might turn up. He had not proceeded very far when he fell in with another young man going in the same direction as himself, and the two, joining company, fell into conversation. Rin-dzin soon related to his young friend all his recent adventures, and informed him that he was anxious to make a little money.

"Very good, brother," replied the Stranger, "I am the very man to help you, for you must know I am a thief by profession, and I am always on the look-out for what fortune may bring me. So we will join company, and it will indeed be bad luck if we cannot succeed in hitting upon something profitable before many days have passed."

So they went along together and towards evening they came upon a large house standing in a fertile valley. The Thief went forward alone to make enquiries, and he soon returned to Rin-dzin with the information he had gathered. The servants of the house had told him that the owner had died the day before, and was now awaiting burial in his own room. His only relation was his daughter, who was heiress to the whole of the property, and she was now mourning for her father all alone in the big house. Further, the Thief had learned that the old man had once had a son, who had run away from home many years before and had never been heard of again.

"Now," said he to Rin-dzin, "I have a plan to propose to you. Do you climb in through the window into the room where the old man's body lies awaiting burial, and conceal yourself somewhere. As soon as you are ready I will go to the young lady of the house and inform her that I am her brother, who has returned home after many years' wandering. She will probably disbelieve my story, and I will propose that we should consult the corpse of her father on the matter. When we come into the room where the corpse lies I will address it, and ask whether I am not the long-lost son, whereupon you must reply that I am. On this evidence I shall secure at least one-half of the property, which, of course, I shall share with you. But be careful on no account to leave the room before morning, otherwise you are sure to be detected by the dogs which roam about the house by night."

Rin-dzin agreed to this proposition, and climbed in by the window into the dead man's room, and, concealing himself near the corpse, he awaited the arrival of his friend. Meanwhile the Thief went boldly up to the front door and gave a loud knock; and being admitted by the servants, he went straight to the chamber of the young lady of the house.

"Who are you?" said she; "and what do you want?"

"Oh! sister," he replied, "I am your long-lost brother; do you not recognise me?"

"No," said she, "it would be impossible for me to recognise you, as I was only a little child when you ran away. No one but my father could know you and he, alas! died yesterday."

"That is very sad," replied the Thief, "for indeed it will be difficult for me to prove the truth of my story. Let us, however, go into the room where my father's corpse is lying, and ask it whether or no I am his long-lost son."

The girl agreed to this, and the two went together into the chamber where the old man's corpse was sitting trussed-up for burial, in accordance with the Tibetan custom.

"Are you there, father," said the Thief, as he entered the darkened room; and Rin-dzin, in a sepulchral voice replied, "Ah."

"I have come to ask you," went on the Thief, "whether or no I am your long-lost son."

"You are," replied Rin-dzin.

And on hearing this the Thief at once retired, followed by the young girl, who was now completely convinced of his identity.

"Now, sister," said the Thief, addressing her when they were alone together, "you see that my story is true, but, unfortunately, I am unable to stay here as I am called away this very night on urgent business. I will therefore make over to you the house and the whole of the landed property, and all I ask from you as my share of the estate is a bag of gold, as big as I can carry with me."

The girl accepted these conditions, and handed over to the Thief a heavy bag of gold. He then bade her farewell and started off with his booty as fast as he could, leaving Rin-dzin behind him in the same room as the corpse.

Early next morning Rin-dzin climbed down from the window, and coming round to the front of the house he asked the lady where her brother was.

"Oh!" said she, "I gave him a big bag of gold last night, and he at once started off with it as fast as he could."

When Rin-dzin heard this he was very angry indeed at the Thief's treachery, and was determined to follow and punish him. So, borrowing a horse from the lady of the house, he galloped off down the road as fast as he could. About mid-day, as he was galloping along, he saw the Thief some distance ahead, sitting under the shade of a tree resting; for not knowing that Rin-dzin had a horse, he did not consider it necessary to go very fast.

When Rin-dzin caught sight of the Thief, he first thought that he would at once go up to him and demand his share of the gold, but on second thoughts he remembered that while he himself was unarmed, the thief possessed both a sword and a musket, so that if it came to a quarrel between them he would probably get the worst of it. So, leaning down over his horse's neck, he pretended not to see the Thief, and galloped past him down the road, as if in mad pursuit. As soon as he was out of sight of the place where the Thief was sitting he pulled his horse up to a wall, and taking a new boot out of the bundle on his back, he dropped it in the middle of the road, and then pursued his way for some little distance further, when he took the fellow boot out of his bundle and dropped it also in the middle of the road. Having done this he turned aside from the roadway and concealed himself and his horse in a thicket near by.

As soon as Rin-dzin had galloped out of sight, the Thief congratulated himself at not having been seen, took up his bag of gold and continued his journey. After walking some little way, he came upon a new boot lying in the centre of the road.

"Ah!" thought he, "that foolish fellow has dropped one of his boots in his haste. But one boot isn't worth picking up; it is of no use at all. What a pity it is he did not drop them both."

So leaving the boot where it lay, he resumed his journey. The sun was now very hot, and the Thief, carrying his heavy bag of gold, was getting pretty tired, and by the time he reached the place where the other boot was lying he was nearly worn out.

"Hallo," said he to himself, when he caught sight of the second boot, "here is the other boot. This is really too good a chance to be lost; I must certainly go back at once and pick up the first boot, and then I shall have a pair of new boots for nothing. But I can't carry this heavy bag of gold all the way back with me."

So thinking, he concealed the bag of gold under a

tuft of grass by the roadside, and started off to retrace his steps to pick up the first boot. No sooner was he out of sight than Rin-dzin emerged from his hiding-place, and picking up the bag of gold, strapped it to his saddle and rode on his way.

STORY No. XIX.

THE COUNTRY OF THE MICE.

ONCE upon a time there was a King who ruled over a large tract of country in which there lived a great number of Mice. Generally the Mice were very prosperous and had plenty to eat, but it happened one year that the crops of the country were very poor, and the Mice, who subsisted chiefly on the spare grains left after the harvest, found that their stores were running short before the end of the winter. So the King of the Mice decided that he would make a petition to the King of the country, to lend the Mice what grain they required on condition that they repaid the whole amount the following year.

So he dressed himself up in his best clothes and set off one morning to the King's palace. When he got to the door of the palace the door-keeper asked him where he was going.

"Oh!" replied the Mouse, "I wish to see the King of the country, as I have a petition to make to him."

When the King heard that a Mouse wanted to see him he was very much amused, and he ordered that the little animal should be admitted.

When the Mouse entered the King's presence he

walked slowly up the Hall of Audience, carrying in his hand a little silk thread, which he presented to the King, instead of the usual ceremonial scarf.*

"Good-morning, Brother Mouse," said the King, "what can I do for you?"

"Oh! King," replied the Mouse, "you must know that this year our crops have fallen short, and we are threatened with a famine unless we can borrow sufficient grain to carry us through the winter; so I, who am King of the Mice, have come here to ask you if you can help us in this matter. If you can lend us the grain we require, we will repay you faithfully with interest at the next harvest."

"Well," said the King, "how much grain do you want?"

"I think that we shall require," said the Mouse, "one of your big barns full."

"But," said the King, "if I were to give you a barn full of grain how would you carry it away?"

"Leave it to me," said the Mouse; "if you will give us the grain we will undertake to carry it off."

So the King agreed to present the Mice with one of his great granaries full of barley, and he ordered his officers to throw open the doors, and to let the Mice carry away as much as they wanted.

That night the King of the Mice summoned all his subjects together, and to the number of many hundreds of thousands they invaded the barn, and each one picked

* This is in accordance with Tibetan custom, whereby a scarf is invariably presented upon all occasions of ceremony.

THE CROW AND THE FROG IN THE GUTTER

up as much grain as he could carry in his mouth, on his back, and curled up in his tail, and when they had all finished the barn was empty, and not a single grain of barley was left.

Next morning, when the King went out to look at his barn, he was very much astonished to find that the Mice had been able to empty it so effectually, and he conceived a very high opinion of their powers; and when, in the following spring, the King of the Mice redeemed his promise by repaying with interest the loan he had taken from the King of the country, the latter saw that they were trustworthy as well as clever.

Now it happened shortly after this that the King of the country went to war with a neighbouring kingdom, which lay on the opposite side of the river forming the frontier between the two countries. This other country was far more wealthy and powerful than the country where the Mice lived, and its King soon assembled a huge army on the opposite bank of the river and began making preparations for invasion.

When the Mice heard what was happening, they were much distressed, for they feared that if the enemy entered their country and destroyed their friend the King, they themselves would suffer considerable hardships under a strange ruler; so the King of the Mice set out again to visit the King of the country, and when he reached the palace he demanded an interview with His Majesty. This was at once accorded to him, and finding the King looking very depressed, he addressed him as follows:

"I have come to you a second time, Oh King, in order to see whether I can be of any use to you. The last time I was here you did me and my people a great favour, for which we shall ever be grateful, and if it is now in our power to assist you in any way, we shall be very glad to do our best."

The King, in spite of his grief, was much amused on hearing these words from the Mouse.

"Why," said he, "what could the Mice do to help me in my present predicament? We are threatened with invasion by a foreign army, outnumbering mine by many thousands, and all the men I can muster will not be sufficient to enable me to repel the enemy. I don't see how the Mice can help me."

"Do you remember, Oh King!" replied the Mouse, "that on the last occasion I was here you doubted our ability to carry away the grain you had given us, or to repay you the loan? And yet we proved ourselves able to do both. All we ask you now is to trust us again, and if you will undertake to do one or two things which we ask of you, we on our part will undertake to rid you of the invading army."

The King was a good deal struck by this remark of the Mouse, and he replied:

"Very well, what you say is quite true; and if you will inform me what you wish me to do, I will undertake to carry out my share of the bargain."

"Well, then," answered the Mouse, "all we wish you to do is to provide us by to-morrow evening with one

THE MICE CROSSING THE STREAM.

hundred thousand sticks, each about a foot long,* and to have them laid in rows on the bank of the river. If you will undertake to do this, we on our side will undertake to stave off the threatened invasion and to put the opposing army into a state of confusion and panic. And if we succeed in carrying out all we promise, we will ask you for the future to safeguard us against the two principal dangers which threaten the existence of the Mice who live in your country."

"I will gladly do what I can," replied the King, "to safeguard you against these dangers if you will tell me how to proceed."

"The two dangers to which I refer," continued the Mouse, "are flood and Cats. You see the majority of our burrows are in the low-lying land near the river, and whenever the river rises a little it overflows this level country and floods our nests. What we would suggest to you is that you should build a strong dam all down the river bank so as to ensure that the water cannot overflow into our nests. And as to the Cats they are always the persecutors of Mice, and we ask you to banish them altogether from your kingdom."

"Very well," replied the King, "if you can succeed in averting the danger which now threatens us, I will undertake to do all that you ask of me in this respect."

On hearing this, the King of the Mice salaamed profoundly to the King, and returned as fast as he could to his own subjects.

On the following evening he marshalled all the full-grown Mice of his kingdom, and about dusk, he led down a large army numbering several hundreds of thousands to the edge of the river, where he found the sticks all laid out as had been arranged with the King. In accordance with instructions they had received, the Mice at once proceeded to launch these sticks on the river, and they themselves embarked upon them two or three at a time; and so, pushing off from the bank, they sailed across the river and soon landed on the opposite side.

It was now quite dark, and the enemy's soldiers were all asleep in their camp, some lying in tents and some in the open air, with their arms beside them ready for any alarm. The Mice on a word of command from their King, scattered themselves without delay through the sleeping camp, and each one began to do as much destruction as he possibly could in the shortest possible space of time. Some nibbled at the bowstrings and the slings of the soldiers' muskets; others gnawed the slow-match and fuses; whilst others bit off the clothes and pigtails of the sleeping men. In fact, they attacked fiercely anything upon which their teeth could make an impression, and tents, stores, grain, and provisions of all kinds were soon reduced to shreds or scattered in confusion in every direction; and after a couple of hours' work they all collected upon the river bank, and, embarking again on their sticks, they sailed quietly over to their own shore without having been detected by the enemy, or even having caused any alarm.

Next morning at daybreak, a great outcry arose from the enemy's camp. Each man as he rose from his sleep found himself in a woeful plight—his clothes in rags, his pigtail cut off, his bow without a string, his rifle without a sling, and with no fuse or slow-match to fire it, and no provisions for breakfast. Each one began to accuse the other of theft and treachery, and before many minutes had passed the whole camp was in a state of wild confusion, comrade quarrelling with comrade, or accusing their officers of dishonesty and ill-faith.

In the midst of this uproar the sound of bugles was heard on the opposite bank, and a few shots were fired; and terrified at the thought of being taken unawares, the whole army took to flight, and in a few minutes not a man was to be seen.

When the King of the country of the Mice saw what had happened he was greatly elated, and, sending for the King of the Mice, he thanked him very sincerely for his good offices. And, in accordance with the bargain they had made, he at once had a strong embankment constructed all down his own side of the river to guard against floods, and he issued an edict forbidding all persons, on pain of death, to keep a cat of any kind henceforth within the frontiers of his country, and so the Mice lived securely and happily ever afterwards.

And in order to insure against any more attempts at invasion from the side of the neighbouring kingdom, the King sent a herald across the river to the ruler of that country, to say that, on this occasion, he had only considered it worth while to employ his Mice to defeat his enemies; but that if he was again threatened, he was ready to employ first all the domestic animals of the country; and if they did not succeed, he would have to have recourse to the wild beasts; and in the event of their failing, he was prepared to come himself with his warriors in order to produce the desired results.

When the ruler of the other country heard this message he considered it wiser at once to make a treaty of peace, as he could not hope to defeat the warriors and wild beasts of a country whose Mice had shown such skill and courage. So the two countries remained on friendly terms for many years after; and the Mice, secured against flood and Cats, lived happily and safely, and received every year from the King of the country a barnful of grain as a free gift in thankful recognition of the services which they had rendered in time of need.

STORY No. XX.

THE STORY OF THE TORTOISE AND THE MONKEY.

THERE was once an old Tortoise who lived with his wife and family in a large lake, on the borders of which grew an extensive jungle; and in the forest there were many wild beasts, more especially Monkeys, who swarmed in great numbers all along the shores of the lake.

It happened one day that the Tortoise came out of the lake and went for a stroll amongst the trees which grew near the water. After walking for some distance he became hungry, and looking up into a cocoanut-tree, near which he found himself, he thought how much he should like to get one of the cocoanuts which were growing near the top. He made several awkward attempts to climb the tree, but the stem was so straight and so smooth that he was quite unable to succeed; and he was just about to give up the attempt in despair when he espied a large Monkey sitting among the branches. The Monkey, who had been watching the Tortoise's attempts to climb the tree with some curiosity, felt rather sorry at his failure, and noticing that the Tortoise was a fine, well-grown fellow with a very handsome shell, he thought he would do him a kindness, so breaking off one or two of the cocoanuts, he threw them down to the Tortoise, who gratefully ate the fruit.

The two animals now entered into conversation with one another, and soon striking up quite a friendship, the Monkey led away the Tortoise into the jungle, and showed him a comfortable cave where he could spend the night. The Tortoise was so interested with all he saw and so pleased with his friend the Monkey, that he remained for several days in the forest, moving about during the day and sleeping with the Monkey in the cave every night.

Meanwhile Mrs. Tortoise was becoming rather anxious concerning her husband's prolonged absence. He had never been away from home for so long before, so finally she despatched one of the young Tortoises to find out where his father was and how he was getting on. The young Tortoise accordingly swam to land, and after hunting about for some time in the forest he came across his father near the cave.

"Good-morning, Father," said he, "Mother has sent me to find out where you are and how you are getting on."

"Oh, I am all right, my boy," replied Father Tortoise; "tell Mother she need not trouble about me. My friend, Brother Monkey, and I are just having a good time in the forest, and I will be home in a few days. Now run off to your Mother."

So the young Tortoise went back to his mother and told her what had happened. Mrs. Tortoise was not at all pleased at her husband's conduct.

"It is quite time," thought she, "that he should return to his wife and family, instead of amusing himself with a vulgar Monkey in the forest."

So she sent the boy back again to his father, with a message to say that Mrs. Tortoise was very ill, and that her physician had told her that the only thing to cure her was a Monkey's heart. So he must return at once to his home and bring a Monkey along with him.

The young Tortoise accordingly proceeded to hunt out his father again, and as soon as he met him he gave him Mrs. Tortoise's message. On hearing the news of his wife's illness, Mr. Tortoise became much alarmed, and reproached himself for having stayed away for so long; and in order to secure the necessary medicine for his wife he informed his friend the Monkey that he was obliged to return home at once on urgent business, and he invited the Monkey to come and spend a few days at his house. The Monkey accepted his friend's invitation, and the two set off together to the shores of the lake.

When the Monkey understood that it would be necessary for him to enter the lake, he became rather alarmed, and remarked to the Tortoise that never having been in the water, he was afraid it would be difficult for him to reach the Tortoise's home.

"Never fear about that, Brother Monkey," said the Tortoise; "I can arrange that quite simply. If you will mount upon my back, I will swim with you wherever we want to go."

So the Monkey mounted upon the Tortoise's back, and the Tortoise set out to swim to his house.

As they went across the lake the Tortoise began telling the Monkey about his wife's illness, and in doing so he foolishly let out that the only medicine to cure her was a Monkey's heart. On hearing this the Monkey became very much alarmed, and saw that he was being led into a trap.

"Dear me, Brother Tortoise," said he, "I am very much grieved to hear of your wife's illness, but if she is as bad as all that I do not think that one Monkey's heart will be enough. I should think that three or four at least would be required in order to effect a cure. If you like, I can easily get several other Monkeys from amongst my friends to accompany us to your home."

The Tortoise thought that this was a good idea, and agreed to carry the Monkey back to the shore and await him there while he went off to fetch some other Monkeys. So he turned round and swam back through the lake till he reached the edge, where he waddled out on to the beach.

As soon as he found himself on dry land the Monkey skipped off the Tortoise's back as fast as he could, and climbed to the top of the tallest tree he could find in a twinkling. On reaching the top of the tree he began reviling the Tortoise, and calling out every bad name he could think of.

"You are a nice sort of friend," said he, "to ask me to pay a visit to your home in order to kill me and use my heart as medicine for your ugly wife. Do you call that a proper return for all my attention to you, and for showing you all over the jungle? However, I have

THE MONKEY CALLING INTO THE TORTOISE'S CAVE.

been too clever for you this time, and you will have to do without my heart for many a long day to come. And as to the hearts of those other Monkeys that I promised to you—well, you can just wait till you find them for yourself."*

The Tortoise, on hearing these words, fell into a violent passion, and made several efforts to climb the tree in order to punish the Monkey, but being quite unable to climb at all, he soon gave up his attempt and determined to get even with the Monkey in some other way. So he hid himself in the water until evening, and as soon as it was dusk he came out on the land and proceeded very quietly to the cave where he and the Monkey had lived together, and concealed himself in the darkest corner of it waiting till the Monkey should come in.

The Monkey, however, was a good deal too clever to be caught in a simple trap like this. When his usual bedtime arrived, he came to the mouth of the cave and, looking in, he called out in a loud voice:

"Oh, great cave! great cave!"

The Tortoise lay low in his dark corner and gave no sign of life.

After a few moments' silence the Monkey again called out:

"Oh, great cave! great cave!"

Still the Tortoise lay low and gave no sign.

"Curious thing," said the Monkey to himself in an audible tone of voice, "very curious! There used always to be an echo in this cave, but I can't hear the slightest echo to-night. There must be something wrong," and saying this he again called out :

"Oh, great cave ! great cave ! "

The foolish Tortoise, thinking that if he simulated an echo the Monkey would enter the cave as usual, hereupon gave answer from his dark corner :

"Oh, great cave ! great cave ! "

On hearing this the Monkey chuckled to himself at the simplicity of the Tortoise, and went off to sleep in some other part of the forest.

THE GLASS PILLARS DANCING FOR THE OGRE.

STORY No. XXI.

THE STORY OF ROOM BACHA AND BAKI.

ONCE upon a time, in the country of Room, there lived a King called Bacha, who, having married a young Princess from a neighbouring kingdom, lived with her for a short time very happily. But it happened that both the King and Queen were of a very argumentative turn of mind, and were constantly disputing with one another about all sorts of trifles, and as neither would ever give way to the other, it generally ended in their quarrelling. The King, who was a proud and head-strong man, was not at all pleased that his wife should venture to maintain her opinion against his, and gradually became very much incensed against her.

One night, as the two were sitting together after dinner, a fox began to bark in the palace grounds outside.

"Ah!" said the King, "do you hear that tiger roaring?"

"My dear," replied the Queen, "that is not a tiger, it is a fox."

"Certainly not!" said the King. "Do you think I don't know a tiger when I hear him? There can be no question but that it is a tiger."

The Queen again contradicted him, and a heated argument ensued, in which neither convinced the other. At length, the King said that he could not stand this argument any longer, but would submit the question for decision to his council on the following day. If the council agreed that he was in the wrong, he should be sent adrift on a log of wood on the great river that flowed past the palace; but if the Queen should be found to be in the wrong, she should suffer this fate.

So next day the King summoned a council, composed of all his wisest ministers and men of science. When they were all seated in the council chamber, he addressed them as follows:

"Last night," said he, "some beast began to bark outside the palace. I maintained that it was a tiger; the Queen affirmed that it was a fox. I desire to submit the question to you for decision. If you decide that it was a fox, I agree to be sent adrift upon a log of wood on the great river which flows past my palace; but if you think that the animal was a tiger, then the Queen is to suffer this penalty."

So saying, the King withdrew, leaving his ministers to decide the question. The counsellors, after weighing the matter for some time, summoned to their presence several peasants living in the neighbourhood, and these being all agreed that no tiger ever came within many miles of the palace, whereas foxes prowled there nightly, it was clear to the council that the King was in the wrong. Before any decision was given, however, the oldest counsellor rose and addressed the meeting as follows:

"It appears to me," said he, "that the King is undoubtedly in the wrong in this matter; but I wish to point out to you that if we announce our decision to that effect, the consequence will be that we shall be left without our King, and with only a Queen to reign over us. This, as you know, is a most undesirable state of affairs. I propose, therefore, that in spite of our real opinion in the matter we should make a public announcement to the effect that the King was right in his argument."

The others agreed to these words of wisdom, and the counsellors proceeded in a body to the King's throne-room and informed him publicly that after due deliberation they had come to the conclusion that he was undoubtedly in the right. The King was greatly pleased at hearing his opinion confirmed, and at once gave orders that the Queen should be sent adrift on the river astride a log of wood. So the poor Queen was taken down to the river bank, and placing herself astride of a log of wood, she floated off down the great river.

After floating along for several hours the current at length carried her to the opposite bank, many miles away from her own country, and as soon as she arrived in shallow water she waded ashore and looked about her. As far as she could see, the whole country appeared to be one great plain, covered with high grass, through which it was almost impossible for anyone to force their way; but after hunting about for a time, she discerned a small opening in the grass, which led her to a narrow winding path, along which she walked for some considerable distance. After going some way she came suddenly upon an open clearing in the grass, in the middle of which a very old man, with a white beard reaching almost to his waist, was seated before a small fire cooking himself some food.

"Good-morning, sir," said the Queen, when she saw him; "can you give me a morsel of food, for I am very hungry."

"Certainly, Madam," replied the old man; "you are welcome to all I have," and so saying, he handed over to her the whole of his provisions.

When the Queen had made a good meal, the old man addressed her as follows:

"You must know," said he, "that I am a magician, living in this prairie, and you must carefully follow the directions which I shall now give you. You must first follow the path, which will lead you to the top of a small hill, and when you arrive there a son will be born to you. This boy is not an ordinary human child, but is the incarnation of a very holy Lama, with miraculous qualities, and he will from his birth be able to walk and talk. His name is Baki, and you must follow him wherever he leads."

The Queen thanked the old man for his advice, and following the narrow path, it soon led her to the top of a small hill; and here she was delivered of a child, who, as the magician had predicted, was of a miraculous nature, and was at once able to walk and talk. The boy without any hesitation went forward along the path, followed by his mother, and after travelling for some distance they emerged from the great grass jungle into an open cultivated country.

Now it happened that on that day the three sons of the King of that country were out hunting together, and as they rode along looking out for game they suddenly came upon the Queen and her son. Having heard her story, they mounted her and the boy upon a horse and carried them off to the King's palace. The King at once took them under his protection, and gave orders that the boy should be brought up with his own sons, and he and his mother lodged in apartments in the palace.

Baki grew rapidly in beauty and stature, and soon became an expert in all sports and games. One day he and the King's three sons were out hunting together, when by chance they suddenly came upon a beautiful snow-white doe, who jumped up before them and galloped off towards the mountains. The four young men at once started off in pursuit; but the horses upon which the King's sons were riding gradually tired, and one after another they dropped out of the hunt, leaving Baki to continue alone. As the chase continued the poor doe began to show signs of exhaustion, and Baki, who was close upon her heels, was feeling confident that he would soon catch her. All at once the deer galloped straight up to what appeared to be a precipitous rock, and touching the rock with her muzzle, it flew asunder, revealing the entrance to a great cave within; and as she crossed the threshold of the cave her skin fell from her, and she appeared in the form of a beautiful young woman. Baki, who was of a very courageous disposition, did not hesitate for a moment, but, leaping from his horse, he followed the lady into the cave, and scarcely had he entered when the rock doors closed behind him with a loud crash. Following the form of the lady along a narrow passage, he emerged presently into a great lofty apartment, hollowed out in the centre of the rock, luxuriously furnished and brilliantly lighted, and with a row of great glass pillars running down the centre.

The girl meanwhile had seated herself upon a couch in one corner of the room, and addressing the young man, she asked him who he was, and what he meant by thus thrusting himself upon the privacy of a lady. The young Prince apologised, and explained the circumstances of the case as best he could, whereupon the girl addressed him as follows:

"You must know," said she, "that the place where you now find yourself is the abode of a terrible and bloodthirsty Ogre, and that I, who am human like yourself, was captured by him some time ago, and he proposes shortly to make me his wife. Meanwhile he has taught me certain magic spells, which enable me to transform myself into any animal I please, and to come and go at my pleasure; but without the assistance of some human being it is impossible for me to escape from his clutches. But we will talk further regarding these matters to-morrow. It is now near the time for the Ogre's return, and if he finds you here he will certainly kill you without the least hesitation, so you must hide now before he returns."

So saying she went over to the central glass pillar

and, unscrewing a portion of it, she showed him a cavity inside, within which he concealed himself.

Scarcely was he securely hidden within the pillar when the door of the cave flew open, and a huge Ogre entered the central chamber. Calling the young lady to him, he commanded her to bring his dinner, and after making a sumptuous repast he sat down on some cushions and began playing the guitar. At the first sound of the music all the pillars in the room, with the exception of the one in which Baki was concealed, began a slow and stately dance, his pillar alone remaining firm and unshaken. When the Ogre saw that one of the pillars was not dancing as usual he grew very angry, and seizing a huge hammer in his hand, he advanced upon it, threatening to shatter it into a thousand fragments; but the young lady, seizing him by the arm, begged him to spare it.

"Look," said she "at the position of the pillar. It is the most central and the largest of them all. No doubt it feels some sense of dignity and wishes to be distinguished from the remainder. Spare it at any rate to-night, and it will probably dance as usual to-morrow."

The Ogre agreed to this, and shortly after retired to rest.

Next morning at daybreak he set off about his business, and as soon as he was gone the girl opened the pillar and released Baki, and after giving him a good breakfast, she spoke to him as follows:

"It is a very difficult thing," said she, "for a human being to kill an Ogre, for whatever damage you may do to his body is of no avail unless you can also destroy the object with which his spirit is bound up. Now this particular Ogre's existence depends upon the life of a green Parrot, which is carefully hidden from human view, but I have ascertained where it is kept, and will explain to you how you may find it. Behind the rock in which we are now living you will find another great rock standing by itself. You must go up to this, and, kicking it three times with your right foot, you must exclaim at each kick, 'Great Raven, open the door.' As you pronounce these words for the third time the door will open, disclosing a large cave, in the centre of which, seated upon a red stone, you will see a green Parrot. If you can kill this Parrot you will also destroy the Ogre without any danger to yourself."

On hearing this Baki at once promised to follow the lady's directions, and she released him from the cavern. Going round to the back of the rock, he found himself face to face with another great rock standing by itself. Kicking this rock three times with his right foot, he pronounced the magic words, and as he said them for the third time two rocky doors flew open, disclosing a cave inside. Entering the cave he saw a green Parrot seated on a red stone in the centre, and he at once seized the bird and wrung its neck. As soon as he had accomplished this he ran hastily back to the main cavern, and as he approached the entrance he saw the Ogre, who had just been returning to his home, lying across the threshold stone dead, with his neck all twisted. The young lady was greatly rejoiced at the successful issue of their adventure, and the two, leaving the Ogre's body behind them, proceeded forthwith to the capital of the country, where the King's palace was situated.

On arriving at the capital Baki decided to hire a small house, where he could lodge the young lady and change his own dress before proceeding to pay his respects to the King; so having taken a house in the suburbs, he left the lady there while he went out himself into the streets to hear the news. He soon found out that during his absence the King had announced his intention of marrying Baki's mother, and the poor lady, now that she had no son to protect her, had protested in vain, saying that she was already the wife of another. Baki was very indignant when he heard of this treacherous conduct on the part of the King, and determined to foil his plans. So returning to the young lady, he related to her all that he had heard.

"Do not be anxious," said she. "If you will follow my advice I will show you how you may yet get the better of the King,"

And she forthwith instructed him in certain magic spells, which she had learned from the Ogre.

Armed with these, Baki proceeded at once to the palace. When he arrived in the courtyard he sat himself down upon the King's mounting-block, and muttering the necessary spell, he was at once transformed into a large cowrie-shell. After lying on the mounting-block for some time it chanced that one of the grooms of the palace passed by, and, seeing the shell, he paused to look at it, and remarked to himself:

"What a beautiful cowrie-shell!"

"Yes, I am a very handsome shell," replied the cowrie, to the terror and astonishment of the groom.

"Why," said he, "what sort of a shell are you? What can you know about cowries, or anything else?"

"I know a great deal," said the shell. "For instance, I could tell the King something about Prince Baki, which perhaps he would not like to hear."

When the groom heard this he ran straight into the palace and informed the Prime Minister all that the shell had said. The Minister, having told the King of the matter, the King gave orders that the shell should at once be brought into his presence and placed upon a table before him. When this had been done the King addressed the shell, saying:

"What are you, and what do you know about Prince Baki?"

"I can tell you this," replied the shell, "that if you attempt to marry Prince Baki's mother you will find yourself in a very unpleasant position."

On hearing this the King was very much incensed, and he ordered one of his servants to bring in a big hammer to smash the shell to fragments, saying that he would not be browbeaten by a wretched little object like a shell. So one of the servants, bringing up a hammer, struck the shell a violent blow and broke it to pieces. In an instant each piece of the shell turned into an armed man, and Prince Baki himself appeared amongst them in his proper form.

Great confusion now arose amongst the courtiers;

some fled in one direction and some in another, whilst others, drawing their swords, prepared to fight with the strangers. Meanwhile the armed men, who were in reality demons, placed temporarily under the command of Prince Baki, looked fiercely around them, and waving their swords, shouted to the Prince, "Whom shall we kill? Whom shall we kill?"

Baki now pointed to the King, and in a moment the band of armed men fell upon him, cut him to pieces, and disappeared with shouts of triumph through the roof of the palace. When the courtiers saw what had happened, they hastened to prostrate themselves before the feet of so powerful a magician, and installed Baki as their new king.

As soon as he was seated upon his throne he sent for the young lady whom he had rescued from the Ogre's cave, and, having married her, they lived happily for many years. And the Queen, his mother, soon after returned to King Bacha, and having agreed with him never more to argue on trivial matters, they had no more disputes or quarrels, and long reigned together over a contented and prosperous kingdom.

STORY No. XXII.

THE STORY OF THE HOME-BRED BOY.

HOW HE FOUND THE LOST TURQUOISE.

THERE was once an old woman living in Tibet whose husband had died and left her alone with her only son.

As the Boy grew up, his Mother grew more and more fond of him, and disliked parting from him even for a moment. She was afraid that if he left her house and began wandering about by himself some accident might happen to him, and she would be left desolate in her old age. So the older he grew the more careful she became, until at last she saw that it was impossible to restrain the Boy any longer, and it would be necessary for him to go out into the world to seek his fortune, just as other young men of his age had to do. So when he had reached the age of fifteen she waited till the fifteenth day of the sixth month, which is a very auspicious date, and calling the Boy to her, she presented him with a new suit of clothes, a horse, a dog, a gun and a sword; and she told him that he was now at liberty to leave his home and to go out into the world to seek his fortune.

The Boy was greatly delighted at receiving these gifts and with the prospect of meeting with some adventures, so after saying farewell to his Mother, he mounted his horse, and with the dog trotting at his heels he started away down the road. All day he rode quietly along by himself without meeting with any adventures, and towards evening he reached a high plateau near the top of a range of mountains. As he was crossing the plateau a fox jumped up in front of him and ran off towards the mountains. The dog, on seeing the fox, started to chase it; while the young Man, thinking he was to have some fun at last, galloped after the dog as fast as he could.

After running for some distance the fox suddenly disappeared into his earth, and the Boy, riding up, dismounted at the mouth of the hole, and began to scheme how he was to catch the fox when he came out. So he took off his cloak* and fastened it to the saddle with his sword and his gun, and then placed his horse a little to one side of the fox's earth, whilst his dog stood ready at the other side; and he himself took off his hat and put it over the mouth of the hole, and taking a large stone in his hand, he crouched down ready to slay the fox when it came out.

After sitting waiting for some time the fox all of a sudden darted out of its earth, and ran off towards the hills, with the Boy's hat sticking over its head. It came so suddenly that he had no time to hit

* In Tibetan "chu-ba," the outer garment, like a dressing-gown, worn by all Tibetans.

it with his stone, or to interrupt its flight. The dog, on seeing the fox go off, at once started in full pursuit; and the horse, excited by the dog's cries, galloped off after the pair, and in a few moments all three were lost to sight in the gathering darkness. The poor Boy found himself in a moment bereft of all his possessions—his horse, his dog, his gun, his sword, his hat, and even his outer robe, which he had strapped on his saddle, had all disappeared. After running after his horse for some distance he gave it up in despair, and lay down to pass the night as best he could under a big poplar tree.

He woke towards dawn, and, looking up into the branches of the tree, he saw a large Raven's nest, on which an old Raven was sitting hatching her eggs, whilst Father Raven perched on a branch near by. When day broke the two Ravens began talking to one another.

"Good-morning, Father Raven," said the old bird on the nest, "who is this sleeping under our tree?"

"That," replied Father Raven, "is a foolish home-bred Boy who has no experience of the world. In trying to catch a fox last night he lost his horse, his gun, his sword, his dog, and even his clothes, and now he has not the least idea where to find them."

"Yes, so I see," replied Mother Raven, "but it is clear, nevertheless, that all he has to do is to go towards the villages which lie towards the east from here—there he will meet with good fortune."

On hearing this the Boy at once started off towards the east, and proceeding for some little distance, he met an old Beggar Man, to whom he related the whole of his story, and asked him if by any chance he had seen the missing property. The old Man, seeing before him only a poor Boy, without even a hat or a cloak, did not believe a word of this story, so he only laughed at him and mocked him; and finally, when the Boy grew angry, gave him a sound beating, and left him to go on his way disconsolate.

Wandering on a little further, he came to a big house where a wedding feast was being celebrated. Coming timidly up to the door of the house, he peeped in at the guests, and presently one of the servants happening to pass by, he related his sad story. But just then the Bridegroom caught sight of him, and called out in a rough voice:

"Who are you who come crying here at my wedding feast? We want no woebegone faces here to-day to bring us bad luck. Go away, you ill omened creature."

So the poor Boy slank away sadly, and after wandering about till nightfall he reached another large house further towards the east. After the reception he had received from the wedding party he was afraid to go in or to knock at the door, so creeping into the backyard he dug himself a nest in the manure heap, and crouched down in this for warmth, all hidden except his head. Thus he spent the night comfortably enough.

Early next morning the pigs belonging to the place began to poke about the yard and the manure heap, and several of them, as they passed, rooted at his head with their snouts to see if he was anything good to eat.

He could not stand this very long, so finally, screwing up his courage, he went to the back door of the house, and asked one of the servants to lend him a knife, saying that he wanted it to cut up the dry meat which formed his breakfast. The servant lent him a knife, and as soon as he had got it he enticed one of the pigs away to a quiet corner, where he killed it and cut off its head; and taking with him some strips of its flesh, he returned to his nest in the manure, and hid himself there again, together with the pig's head, waiting to see what would turn up.

Towards noon the Lady of the house came out into the yard, and as she was moving about superintending the various farming operations, it happened that a large and valuable turquoise fell out of her headdress without her noticing it. When, after a few minutes, she went back into the house, leaving the turquoise lying in the middle of the yard, the Boy thought that this would be a good opportunity of getting the turquoise for himself, but he was afraid to leave his nest for fear of being noticed; so picking up a piece of rag from amongst the manure he threw it over the turquoise, concealing it from sight.

Shortly after, one of the maid-servants came out of the house, and seeing a piece of rag lying in the middle of the yard, she picked it up, and the turquoise with it, and thrust them both into a crevice in the wall.

Just then a great uproar arose from the house, where the Lady had discovered the loss of her turquoise. The whole household was summoned, and set to work to search for the missing jewel. For some time great bustle prevailed, everyone searching hither and thither, and ransacking every hole and corner; but no one thought of examining the piece of dirty rag thrust carelessly into a crevice of the farmyard wall.

Finding that all their efforts were of no avail, the Lady of the house sent off in hot haste to summon all the most famous diviners, magicians, and lamas of the neighbourhood, and these, when they arrived, began practising all kinds of spells and casting auguries in the hope of discovering what had become of the turquoise; but all in vain, and when nightfall arrived, they were no better off than they were before.

Towards evening they packed up their various magical instruments and spells, and went away very downhearted; and as soon as they were gone the Boy emerged from his hiding-place, and going boldly to the house, he said that he was a famous magician and could find the turquoise for them; and he asked that on the following morning all the diviners and lamas should again be summoned, as well as the inhabitants of all the neighbouring houses. The Lady of the house was at first inclined to ridicule the idea of this disreputable-looking beggar being able to accomplish what none of these famous sorcerers could do; but thinking it worth while to give the Boy a chance, she decided to do what he suggested, and meanwhile ordered her servants to let him have a good supper, of which he stood badly in need.

Next morning, about ten o'clock, a large crowd of people assembled in the courtyard of the house. In addition to the magicians and lamas of the day before, a great many of the neighbours had obeyed the summons, and amongst them were the people who had treated the poor Boy so badly during their wedding feast, and the Beggar who had reviled and beaten him. As soon as they were all seated in rows ready to see what was going to happen, the Boy, holding the pig's head under his arm, presented himself before them all, and addressed them as follows:

"Now," said he, "I hope in a few minutes to be able to discover the missing turquoise, for I am possessed of magic qualities of unusual power. In my search I shall be assisted by this enchanted pig's head which I hold under my arm. Owing to the spell I have cast upon it, it is able at once to detect a thief or a dishonest person, and also to discover stolen property."

So saying he took the pig's head in both hands, and holding its snout towards the company, he went round from person to person, halting for a moment in front of each. Presently he arrived in front of the Bridegroom, who had been so rude to him some days before, and the pig's head at once became violently agitated, and kept poking itself towards this man.

"Ah!" said the Boy, "here is evidently a dishonest man; it is no good our proceeding any further in our search until he has been beaten and turned out of here."

The other people at once seized upon the wretched man,

One of the Story-tellers, with his Family and Servants.

and after giving him a severe thrashing, they turned him out of the place. Next to him was sitting the Beggar who had so insulted the Boy, and who had disbelieved his story. Here, again, the pig's head became violently agitated, and the Beggar, too, was well beaten and turned out. Having got rid of these two persons, the Boy now began to walk round the yard, the pig's snout apparently sniffing carefully at every part of the wall in the farm buildings. Presently, coming to the crevice into which the rag had been thrust by the servant-maid, he moved the pig's head violently to and fro.

"Ah!" cried he, "the missing turquoise must be somewhere near here."

On hearing this everyone began to search about in that neighbourhood, and in a few minutes the turquoise was found inside the rag thrust into the crevice of the wall.

The Mistress of the house on recovering her turquoise was greatly elated. She took the Boy into the house, and having presented him with a new suit of clothes, and given him all he wanted to eat and drink, she handed him a large sum of money, and he went on his way in a far better plight than when he had first arrived there.

THE HOME-BRED BOY.

HOW HE DISLODGED THE SPIDER.

AFTER leaving the house where he had found the turquoise, the home-bred Boy wandered along until, towards nightfall, he arrived at the same poplar-tree where he had previously stayed the night, and, lying down under its branches, he fell fast asleep, and did not wake up until towards morning.

As day was dawning the two Ravens overhead began talking to one another as before, and the boy overheard their conversation.

"Good-morning, Father Raven," said the hen bird on the nest. "What kept you so late last night?"

"Well," replied Father Raven, "the fact is, I was visiting a farmhouse down yonder, where the mistress of the house, as it happens, is very ill. She is suffering from a severe pain in her left ear, which drives her almost distracted, and no one about the place knows what it is nor how to cure it. They have consulted all of the most famous doctors and lamas in the neighbourhood without, however, affording her any relief at all. Indeed, no one knows what is the cause of the disease except myself. I have ascertained that the pain in her ear is due to the fact that some days ago a large Spider effected an entrance during her sleep, and that the Spider and her young ones have now taken up their abode inside the Lady's head. It is impossible to dislodge them except by a stratagem. As you are aware, Spiders are in the habit of sleeping all through the winter months, and only wake up and emerge from their retreat in the spring. If it were possible to make the Spiders believe that spring had arrived, they would come out of the ear at once; otherwise they will remain there all through the winter."

"Indeed," replied Mother Raven, "that is very interesting; but how would it be possible to make the Spider believe that spring had come?"

"There is a very simple stratagem, which I have often seen employed," replied Father Raven, "which is as follows: a piece of green cloth must first be spread upon a table and well sprinkled with water, and the Lady must bend her ear over this so that the Spiders can see it. It will appear to them to be a green field, wet with the spring rains, and they will imagine it is time to come out; and then, if they still display any reluctance to emerge, it is only necessary to beat a drum to simulate thunder. Thunderstorms, as you know, only occur in the spring, and the Spiders on hearing this noise will feel convinced that spring has really come, and will emerge without any further hesitation. The moment they come out on the table they must be wrapped up in the cloth with the greatest expedition and carried away and killed, for if this is not done, they will always be ready at the slightest alarm to climb back into the ear by the threads which they have left suspended behind them."

Mother Raven thanked Father Raven for his information, and she then said:

"But you yourself are not looking at all well this morning, what is the matter with you?"

"Well," said he, "I am sorry to say I over-ate myself yesterday. The people of the house kept praying to the gods, and were all day long occupied in making offerings of rice and flour. Most of these offerings were thrown out into the garden, and I was able to eat as much as I wanted. In fact, I ate a great deal too much, and I fear that I am going to die. If I do, you must faithfully promise to remain in mourning for me, in accordance with Tibetan custom, for three years, three months and three days."

Mother Raven, on hearing this, was greatly affected, and solemnly vowed to carry out the wishes of her husband, and poor old Father Raven, getting into the nest, shortly after breathed his last.

As soon as he was dead Mother Raven remarked to herself that she had a great deal too much to do in looking after her family and household duties to think for a moment of following so absurd a custom as mourning for a dead bird for any period at all. So she pushed old Father Raven's body out of the nest with her bill and let it fall to the ground below, while she herself flew off to find food for the young ravens, which had just been hatched out.

Meanwhile the Boy, who had listened attentively to the colloquy of the Ravens overhead, went straight off to hunt for the house where the Lady was suffering from pains in her ear, and he decided in his own mind to make this another opportunity for displaying his magical powers. He soon arrived at the house in question, and found the whole family in great grief, and the poor mistress of the house suffering torments with the pain in her ear. Going to the house he asked what was the matter, and on hearing the cause of their sorrow he at once announced that he was possessed of very wonderful magic powers, and was prepared to effect a cure. The people of the house who had seen him on the previous day, when he had found the turquoise, were inclined to believe him, and asked him what they should do to procure relief for their mistress.

"All that is necessary," replied he, "is a square piece of green cloth, some clean water in a jug and a couple of drums."

When these things had been made ready he spread the piece of green cloth on the table and sprinkled some water over it, and he then told the Lady of the house to lean across the table so that her painful ear should come above the patch of green cloth. No sooner had she done so than the Spiders inside, seeing the green expanse with water still lying upon it, thought that the spring had come and began moving about, and the old Mother Spider at once let herself down by a thread to see if it was really spring.

The people of the house were greatly astonished at

seeing the Spider emerge, but the Boy ordered them not to touch her; and having satisfied herself that there was really water on the cloth, she climbed again up her thread, and went back into the Lady's ear to impart the good news to her family. The Boy now ordered the drums to be beaten, and on hearing this sound the whole of the spider family, thinking that the noise was thunder, and that spring had undoubtedly arrived, hastily emerged from the Lady's ear and let themselves down, one after another, on to the green cloth. As soon as they were all, to the number of seven, arrived upon the table, the Boy snatched up the piece of cloth, and wrapping up the spiders inside it, he carried them all outside and destroyed them.

The Lady of the house was now completely cured and overwhelmed the Boy with gifts and compliments, and he left the house carrying with him a large sum of gold, in addition to that which he had received the day before. He now bent his steps towards his Mother's house, and as he was going along the road to his home he suddenly came face to face with the old Beggar who had previously insulted him, and whom he had had beaten and turned out when he was looking for the turquoise. The old man, who was of a very jealous and vindictive temper, was very much incensed against the Boy, and had determined to avenge himself upon him. As the Boy came down the road the old Beggar suddenly emerged from behind a clump of bushes, holding a sword in his right hand and a fly in the hollow of his left fist.

"Now," said he, "I believe you to be an impostor. You have twice made pretence to magical powers, which in reality you do not possess, and I am about to put you to a final test. If you can tell me what I hold in my left hand I shall let you go free; but if you fail to do so, I shall immediately kill you with this sword."

The poor Boy was greatly alarmed at hearing these words, and having no weapon himself he was completely at the old man's mercy. So at a loss to know what to say, he replied:

"Well, then, you can kill me if you like, for I am as much in your power as though I were a fly which you hold in your left hand and which you can crush at your pleasure."

The old man was so much astonished at hearing this reply, which he looked upon as a proof of the Boy's supernatural powers, that he forthwith became one of his most ardent admirers; and as he had seen where the Boy's horse, dog, and other belongings had disappeared to on the occasion when they had all followed the fox, he was able to lead the boy to a distant valley, where he found his horse and dog together. Here having recovered his sword and his gun, his clothing and other possessions, he mounted upon his horse and followed by his dog he returned to his Mother's house a very much richer Boy than when he had left it.

THE HOME-BRED BOY.

HOW HE DEFEATED THE ENEMY.

On his return to his home the home-bred Boy found that he was now famous far and wide for his supposed magical powers, and he was constantly consulted by people of all classes, who wanted his assistance in their various affairs.

It happened not long afterwards that a war broke out with a neighbouring country, and the King sent for the Boy, and asked him whether he would be able to give any assistance in the campaign against the enemy. The Boy was rather alarmed at this request of the King's, for he did not in the least know how he should set about defeating the foe, but he allowed no sign of hesitation to appear in his manner, and he answered boldly that he was prepared to undertake the job; whereupon the King presented him with a magnificent charger and begged him to do his best.

Now as it happened, the Boy was in reality a very bad rider, and did not at all fancy the idea of riding about on a spirited horse, but for very shame he could not refuse the King's gift. So early next morning, when he mounted his horse with the intention of riding out and reconnoitring the enemy's camp, in order to see what could be done, he made his servant tie his feet together with a rope under the horse's belly, so that he should not fall off if it ran away or played any pranks with him. Having ridden for some distance he reached the top of a hill, whence he could obtain a clear view of the enemy's camp, and as he was sitting on his horse watching the scene below a trumpet suddenly sounded. The noise of the trumpet frightened the horse, which, after giving one or two preliminary plunges, dashed off down the hill at full gallop straight towards the enemy's camp.

The poor Boy was much terrified at this untoward event, and did all he could to stop his horse by pulling the bridle and speaking to it, but with no avail. Just before reaching the camp the horse carried him under a dead tree, and the Boy, raising his arms, seized one of the branches with both hands in the hope of checking the horse's mad career; but the rotten bough broke in his grasp, and the horse continued its gallop right into the camp, with the Boy holding in his hands a huge branch of the tree.

Hither and thither rushed the horse amongst the tents of the enemy, trampling the frightened soldiers underfoot, whilst the Boy in his struggles to maintain his balance, swept his great branch to and fro with equally disastrous effect. During his gallop his hair had become loosened, and was now flying wildly in the air, and his shouts and adjurations to his horse increased the terror of his appearance. The enemy's soldiers had never seen such a terrific-looking object before, and one and all came to the conclusion that he must undoubtedly be a demon that was attacking them, and that he would soon compass their entire destruction. So instead of opposing him they tried to soothe and conciliate him, offering him silken scarfs and other presents as he galloped to and fro. But he made no reply to them, and continued to shout fiercely at his horse.

These shouts were taken by the soldiers to be threats of vengeance against themselves,* and, finally, the General and all the principal officers, coming out in a body with scarfs, begged him to make peace and to allow them to go away quietly. The Boy, who heard what they said, was quite willing to agree, but was totally unable to control his horse, so he shouted to them that he accepted their submission on condition that they were able to stop his horse. So running on either side of him, they seized the bridle and soon brought the animal to a standstill, when the Boy formally accepted their surrender, and dictated to them terms of peace; and they on their part were only too thankful to have escaped from such a danger, and gladly consented to withdraw at once to their own country.

When the King heard what had happened, he sent for the Boy and thanked him very heartily for his services; and as a reward for what he had done, he raised him to the highest rank, and presented him with lands and gold, and the young Man and his Mother lived happily ever afterwards.

* There is a play on the words of the Tibetan original here which explains this point, but which is incapable of adequate translation into English.

SOME VERSES FROM TIBETAN LOVE-SONGS.

A woman sings to a man whose affection for her is waning :

" As a great mountain, with its cooling streams,
Nourishes the little fields far down below,
Do you, my lover, with a stream of love,
Nourish the heart of her who loves you so."

The man replies to the woman :

" When autumn chills destroy the honeyed flowers,
The bees must do without their favourite food ;
So when my passion cools, and dies my love,
You should submit to this my changéd mood."

A man sings to a woman :

" Up every rocky cliff some path exists,
If one can find a guide to show the way ;
So to your heart some avenue must lead,
Teach me, forthwith, that path of love, I pray."

The woman replies :

" Were I inclined to grant this fruit* to you,
The gift were thine at once—to-day, to-morrow.
But oh ! I fear that lurking at your back,
Are demons red† to bring me endless sorrow."

* *I.e.*, her heart. She compares her heart ripe with love to a ripe fruit.

† Presumably she means the man's passions. She compares them to the terrific demons (red is the angry colour) of Tibetan Lamaist mythology.

LOVE SONG.

Could I but win the maiden
  For whom my heart doth pine,
I'd prize her as a jewel
  From depths of ocean brine.

I'd guard her fragrant body,
  Like white turquoise so rare.
My wanderings all behind me,
  I'd know no earthly care.

As luscious fruit well ripened,
  Hangs tempting on the tree;
So is thy beauty, maiden,
  Temptation sore to me.

From longing for thy beauty,
  How can I sleep at night?
By day I seek thee vainly,
  My heart is tired quite.

INDIA AND BRITAIN
A MORAL CHALLENGE

INDIA AND BRITAIN

A MORAL CHALLENGE

C. F. ANDREWS

GYAN

Published by

GYAN

Gyan Publishing House
5, Ansari Road
Daryaganj, New Delhi-110002
Phone: 011-47034999, 9811692060
E-mail: books@gyanbooks.com

Distribution Network
gyanbooks.com
India, USA, Canada, UK, Australia

ISBN: 978-93-7014-012-7 (PB)

First Published, 1935

2nd Impression 2025

Printed at: Gyan Press, Delhi.

INDIA AND BRITAIN: A MORAL CHALLENGE
Author: C. F. ANDREWS

INDIA AND BRITAIN

A MORAL CHALLENGE

BY

C. F. ANDREWS

Author of

What I Owe to Christ, Sadhu Sundar Singh

etc.

TO

THE NEW GENERATION OF

MEN AND WOMEN IN

INDIA AND BRITAIN

PREFACE

At last, after many wanderings by sea and land, I have reached an Indian home where I can finish this book in peace, amidst the beauty of the Simla Hills. It is ideal for such a purpose, because my host and hostess are Indian Christians, who love their own country and love England also, where they spent their early days. They have thus been able to criticise and appreciate what I have written, not only from the Indian standpoint, but also from that of Great Britain. Other friends in Simla have done me a similar service.

We have failed—we of the older generation, who led Europe into the abyss in 1914, and have been laboriously building a house on the sands of suspicion ever since. Though we have not yet realised the fact, our greatest failure since the War has been in India. For in spite of long continued effort, worthy of sincere regard, we have neither given nor found peace. Our minds have remained nerve-racked by what has been happening in Europe, and we have not been able to give our undivided attention to Asia.

Let no one, therefore, carry away the thought that the Constitution now offered to India will suffice, and that our debts are paid. The cyclic struggle is not yet over: it has only just begun. A deadlock has been reached, and we have to seek its moral causes together with the will-power needed to remove it.

In crucial times like these the appeal must be made to a new generation—to those men and women who have witnessed the effects of the world-cataclysm of 1914-18, but have not been shell-shocked by it. For this reason I have dedicated my book to them.

C. F. ANDREWS

MANORVILLE,
SIMLA, W.

CONTENTS

CHAPTER I

THE ARGUMENT OF FORCE

I

I HAD gone up to Oxford in order to speak on India at the Union Club in some College rooms at Balliol. The Society had been formed by undergraduates with the object of uniting East and West in friendship by frank mutual intercourse. Generous freedom of speech had been the keynote of the whole evening's discussion. My host took me back to his own rooms, and after a further talk round the fireside, I went to rest.

But not to sleep. The evening had been far too exciting for me to forget it easily, and the discussion went on repeating itself in my brain during the long hours of the night. In the end, it suggested to me the form which this book might take, and I determined to pursue it. We should all talk freely, in its pages, and put our own case forward in the way that appealed to us most. None should be offended, even if bitter words were uttered. For we should honestly set out to face the truth, wherever it might lead us. Only in such an atmosphere could anything worth saying be uttered with good humour, where the subject was so controversial.[1]

II

Anil Bose had recently been "listening in" to Mr Winston Churchill's broadcast from the B.B.C. He had heard the speaker referring to India as Great Britain's chief "possession," which had been won by the sword and must be kept by the sword.

When we met together some days later Anil brought with him the full report of this broadcast from the *Listener*. There were only a few of us present at the outset and it formed the basis of our conversation. We named our discussion on it "The Argument of Force." Neil Munro, a Highlander from Inverness, was with us.

Anil, who was a history student, could hardly restrain his impatience, as he tried to show us how outrageously Mr Churchill had misinterpreted Indian history.

"Listen to this," he said to Neil, with excitement, and he began to read the opening passage thus:

> "If our forbears had been cowed by heavy odds, the British Empire would have stopped at Brighton Beach. It would never have

[1] Of course, the students into whose mouths the arguments have been put are fictitious personalities, and no reference to any real individual is intended.

existed if Clive had not won the Battle of Plassey—not at the odds of five to one, nor at ten to one, but at more than twenty to one. This Indian Home Rule plan strikes at the destiny of the British Empire, and the destiny of the British Empire will not be settled by mere numbers. . . . It will be settled by the march of world events and by the faithful discharge of their duty by men and women spread throughout the land, whose constant thought is for the future of our country and whose will-power is unconquerable."

I had heard this speech, over the wireless, late one evening at Malvern, where I had been speaking at an Oxford Group gathering. We had "listened in" after the meeting was over, and had felt a burning shame that such a public utterance could be made by a responsible statesman more than twenty years after the tragedy of August 1914. It seemed impossible to hold such a theory of brute force, and at the same time be true to the teaching of Christ. This was what we had all felt on that evening at Malvern.

Anil listened with deep interest as I told him all about this. It softened him for the moment, and he recovered his good humour.

"Do look," he said with a laugh, "what an absurd picture he draws of Clive and the Battle of Plassey! Has he never studied Indian history at all? Only the other day I was reading an account of the whole scene described by your two latest historians."

"What history do you mean?" I asked.

"It's called *The Rise and Fulfilment of British Rule in India*, by Thompson and Garratt. Let me read their account, and then compare it with Winston Churchill's picture. Here is the passage:

> "A plot was formed to make Mir Jafar the Nawab. When the plot was nearly ripe Aminchand threatened to divulge it unless he were promised 5 per cent of the Nawab's treasure. Clive drew up double agreements: one on white paper, genuine; one on red paper, fictitious. Both were to be signed by Clive, Watson, and the Select Committee; the sham paper was shown to Aminchand. Watson's signature to this, however, had been forged by Clive. . . . The battle next day consisted of two parts: a morning cannonade, followed by a drenching monsoon downpour, which damaged the Nawab's ammunition: then an attack, precipitated by Major Kirkpatrick's keenness, and ending in a complete victory at a cost of 65 casualties. Even the defeated lost only about 500 men. *As a battle Plassey was ridiculous*. Mir Jafar, who vacillated during the engagement, came timidly round with congratulations and was told he was now the Nawab."[1]

[1] *Op. cit.*, by Thompson and Garratt (Macmillan).

Anil emphasised the sentence which I have italicised and repeated it: "As a battle, Plassey was ridiculous." Neil was about to say something in reply, but Anil continued with emphasis, as if he were giving a lecture:

"Every Indian schoolboy knows how Clive cheated Aminchand and left him an imbecile—a doddering imbecile! Clive took £230,000's worth of loot and was astonished at his own moderation. We have learnt that story by heart in India: and yet here is an English statesman holding up Clive and the Battle of Plassey as the foundation pillars of the British Empire! And you, in London, have put Clive's statue outside the India Office as your model! If you had put Edmund Burke in that place there would have been some decency in it."

Anil threw out this challenge but no one took it up. He was the most brilliant scholar in his year, and this British period in Indian History was his special subject; so he spoke with authority.

"How would *you* like a Clive," he asked, "let loose in *your* country with all his gang of freebooters? Thank God! we have got an honest history of British India at last, which tells the truth. It calls these marauders by their proper name, 'Conquistadores,' and compares them with Cortes and Pizarro. Here is the sentence: 'A gold lust, unequalled since the hysteria that took hold of the Spaniards of Cortes' and Pizarro's age, filled the English mind. Bengal, in particular, was not to know peace again until it had been bled white.' "[1]

III

Anil's excitement had died down when John Murray and Alan Menzies entered the room. I explained the point we had reached. John said, "Oh, we all know Winston. Don't take him too seriously."

"But I do take him very seriously indeed," I answered with emphasis, "for he is that strange mixture of the aristocrat turned demagogue, who can do such infinite mischief. Look what he says here:

> "My friends, to whom I now speak—the working men—let me tell you that India has quite a lot to do with the wage-earners of Great Britain. If we lost India it would not be a hundred thousand unemployed; it would be more like two million bread-winners, who would be tramping the streets. We have, in this island, forty-five millions living at a higher level than the people of any other European country. One-third of these would have to go down, out, or under, if we ceased to be a great Empire with world-wide connections and trade. That would be the fate of the larger population of Little England."

[1] See Note B.

IV

"Don't you see," I added, "how mischievous all that is; how there is not a single word up to this point concerning the wishes and interests of the people of India? Nor is there anything about their national hopes and aims, which a century of British rule and the study of British history have raised. It is all purely selfish. There is no hint given that it might be better for the Indian villagers to grow their own cotton, and spin and weave their own cloth during the 'idle' months of the year, rather than spend their hard-earned pice in buying Lancashire cotton goods. The one thought is, that British goods must continue to be supplied—by force if necessary—to these poverty-stricken villagers, so that the number of the unemployed in Great Britain may not increase, and our own extravagant standard of living may be kept up. The vast unemployment in India, where it is chronic among millions of people, never comes into his picture."

Anil by this time had got hold of the *Listener* again, and read to us, in a Churchillian voice, the following passage:

> "You will say that we must not exploit India. We must not suck the life out of these poor Indians for our benefit. We would scorn to do that: we would rather starve (or 'clem,' as they say in Lancashire) than have them oppressed for our advantage.

"But, my friends, the benefits that Britain derives from India are only a fraction of the benefits we have given to India in return: I do not speak only of the fruitful exchanges of trade. If a visitor came from another planet and looked over this worried, perplexed and tumultuous human scene, he would say, 'Why is this continent of India so different from Europe; so different from the rest of Asia, indeed from the rest of the world? Why is it that one law and one allegiance laps them in a common tranquillity? Whence comes this strange immunity from the perils and disasters which have darkened the life of every other continent? How is it that India has not fallen into the anarchy which has engulfed China, or under the tyranny by which Russia is frozen and enslaved?'

"The answer would be that far away is a small island, shrouded by the mists of the Atlantic Ocean, which by its sea-power, by its heart's blood and its civic virtues, has created and organised in two hundred years a serene and splendid harmony of peace and order, of tolerance, of justice and of law; that a few thousand officials and barely fifty thousand soldiers, renewed from generation to generation, controlled by the Mother of Parliaments, and inspired by the venerable symbols of the British Monarchy, have been able to confer these inestimable blessings and privileges upon India with its three hundred and fifty million

> people, constituting one-sixth of the human race. The answer would be that Britain has done for India, quite surely and firmly, what we all hope the League of Nations will be able some day to do for Europe. . . . That is a proud answer."

"What utter tosh!" said Anil with disgust. "Why, every word is exaggerated. Look at this phrase, 'lapped in a common tranquillity.' Doesn't he realise that India is seething with discontent? We are sick and tired of these 'inestimable blessings' of the patronising type we know so well. Haven't the hundreds and thousands of young men and women offering passive resistance taught him anything? Oh, do look at this gem, 'a serene and splendid harmony of peace and order, of tolerance, of justice and of law.' Why, in India there have always been two standards: one treatment for the European and another for the Indian, one treatment for the white and another for the coloured. And has he never realised that thousands have been kept in prison, and hundreds are still there, without an open trial? Is that a 'splendid harmony of peace and order'?

"Oh, just look here again!" he cried, turning over the page. "Ah! the cat's out of the bag at last!" He read as follows:

> "The other day I urged the Conservative Party to ask themselves one or two blunt questions. Would any other country in the

modern world behave as we are doing about our great possessions and markets overseas? Would France? Would Holland? Would Italy? Those friendly countries stand amazed at British folly! Would Germany? Why, she is preparing to reclaim by force of arms those colonies and possessions of which she had been deprived. Then there is Japan, which is building up an empire while we seem ready to let ours drift away at the ebb of the tide.

"There is one more question we must ask ourselves. The storm-clouds are gathering over the European scene. Our defences have been neglected. Danger is in the air—yes, I say, in the air! The mighty, discontented nations are reaching out with strong hands to regain what they have lost, nay, to gain a predominance which they never had. Is this, then, the time to plunge our vast Dependency of India into the melting-pot? Is this the time fatally to dishearten, by such a policy, all those strong, clean forces at home upon which the strength and future of Britain depends?

"There, you see," Anil exclaimed, "we are back at the old level of conquest and possession and empire. These 'strong, clean forces' he tells about are the bayonet, the rifle and the bomb, to strike down the 'mighty, discontented nations' who are all round like a pack of wolves eager to tear India out of Britain's clutches. The argument amounts to this, that Great Britain must arm herself up to the teeth, because otherwise Japan, or somebody else, is bound to seize India and snatch her away from Britain's grasp."

At this point I broke in with a recollection of my own: "When I heard Mr Churchill repeat these words, he almost hissed them. 'Danger is in the *air*!' he cried, 'Yes, I say, in the air!' It was just as if he was on the stage acting in the play of *Macbeth*, in the 'dagger' scene. It gave one the creepy feeling of aeroplanes just over one's head."

V

John had been silent all this while. My earlier interruption had been too emphatic, and I had regretted it afterwards, for I had noticed, at the Union Club, how very fair-minded he had been during the discussion, and how he had always taken the side that others had dropped in order to give it a fair hearing. He now came into the discussion.

"I must confess," he said, "I was impressed by the argument of Churchill's conclusion, when I heard him on the wireless." John asked for the copy of the *Listener* and read it over:

> "I do not take so poor a view of our moral rights in India as is fashionable nowadays. We are no alien power in India. We are the latest of many conquerors and we are the only conquerors who have ever made the well-

being of the Indian masses their supreme satisfaction. What is the chief shame of this Home Rule Bill? It is that we finally withdraw our guardianship from this teeming myriad population of Indian toilers. We withdraw our protection from their daily lives. We withdraw it, not merely as an experiment which can be brought to an end at any moment but as a solemn abdication and repudiation of duty. We are henceforth to shrug our shoulders about their education and their hospitals, the canals which water their fields, the courts of justice on which they rely; and we cut them from the House of Commons which has so long been their shield."

"Of course," said John, "a lot of that is rubbish." He looked down the page. "Take this, for instance: 'We are no alien power'—that's humbug. And then he brings in the boast about our being 'conquerors.'"

"That's absolutely untrue," Anil said, with vehemence. "Your own historians, like Seeley and others, have proved again and again that India was never conquered by British troops. I remember a phrase of Seeley in his *Expansion of England* where he says, 'We are not really conquerors of India, and we cannot rule India as conquerors.' Every intelligent historian has recognised that fact."

"Yes," said John with a laugh, "and I was going to acknowledge it also, Anil, when you butted in. But all the same this latter part hits me, where he says, ' We finally withdraw our guardianship from this teeming myriad population of Indian toilers.' Just there is my great anxiety. Ought we to make that ' solemn abdication ' ?

" Sometimes I feel like Sinbad the Sailor with the burden of those three hundred and fifty million people on my back. There's *my* Old Man of the Sea, which I can't get rid of ! As Churchill says, we've built canals, and hospitals, and God knows what ! to help these poor people. Can we really tell them now to go and fend for themselves ? What will happen when we go away ? That is a question which I find very difficult to answer. Ought we to transfer the whole burden at once to you and lay it on your shoulders ? I wish we could ! "

VI

It was decided between us that we should continue the discussion which we had thus started. Others might enter in and help us where expert knowledge would be needed ; for we should have to consider carefully the economic effect of British rule on the common people. Furthermore, we should have to find out what was the Christian view of " Empire." From time to time it might be necessary for me to deal separately with some branch of the whole subject of which I had made a special study, such as the "race" question and the treatment of Indians abroad. At these points the form of discussion and dialogue might be dropped.

We all felt certain that we had done the right thing in taking first Mr Churchill's "Argument of Force." For although it had been discredited in Great Britain since the World War, there had been a strong wave of reaction passing over Europe bringing back among the multitudes the old fatal appeal to violence in new forms.

CHAPTER II

TAGORE'S APPEAL

I

WHEN we met again other students had joined us. One of these was Safdar Ali from St Jude's, a Muhammadan, who was loud in his indignant protest against Mr Churchill's broadcast. He, like Anil, was a brilliant student, who was likely to be a leader in India in the near future. Mulchand, a Hindu from the Punjab, and Abdul Majid, another Moslem, were also present, and their eyes flashed with fire as they declared to me how keenly they had felt the insult and how deeply it had pained them to go on listening to Mr Churchill. His constant use of the word "Empire" and his mention of India —their own Motherland—as Britain's "possession," had made them furious. His speech had the underlying assumption running through it that their own country belonged to people like him, and they could not bear the thought. His very tone was insulting, as he threw out his racial challenge on the air, little caring that Indians themselves were listening to every word he said.

Abdul Majid told us how, on that night, he had been the guest of an English friend, who had specially invited him to hear this broadcast on India.

"When it was all over," he said, "my friend apologised to me; for he saw what pain I had suffered. But all that night I couldn't get a wink of sleep for thinking about it. It made me wonder if Mr· Churchill realised what Young India is thinking to-day. How would *he* like it if we talked about *his* country in the same manner? When we hear him, we are inclined to give up all that Mahatma Gandhi has taught us about non-violence and civil resistance. We say to one another, 'Brute force is the only thing that an Englishman like him can understand.'"

II

My own sympathies were naturally with these students, apart from any plea for violence. It had seemed to me incredible that Mr Churchill, who had passed through the agony of the World War, and as a Cabinet Minister had given solemn pledges to India at its close, could now put forward again the exploded theory of ruling India by force as a conquered country.

For the mischief of such an utterance would not stop with the small number of Indians resident in Great Britain. The occasion was one of critical importance, and the full report of his speech would be circulated through the Indian press in all the great cities.

The British students who were present at our

discussion thoroughly disliked Churchill's Indian policy and were inclined to discount it. This seemed to me to be shortsighted, and I tried to explain that his attitude, however much we might deplore it and protest against it, could not be dismissed with impatience, because we were living in one of the most difficult periods of modern history and were still suffering from the after-effects of the World War. Ever since the economic collapse of recent years a much more selfish view of world politics had spread from one country to another.

" Churchill," I suggested, " claims to be able to interpret this new expression of public feeling in England. His mind's quite saturated with the idea of power. This gives him his strength of conviction. For he means exactly what he says and he believes the country is with him. All this is quite different from the England I can remember when I was a boy. For though my father was an ardent Conservative in politics, he brought me up as a lover of English freedom. Since then I've learnt to distrust profoundly any such words as 'conquest' and 'possession' applied to India. Yet to-day we all find ourselves confronted by these strangely disturbing forces. We seem to have gone back, not forward."

John Murray had been silently listening. " Most of us," he said, " have been astounded at the swing over on the Continent. Even here, in England, when we speak of giving a free

Constitution to India we don't get the same response as before."

Safdar Ali raised an objection. "Aren't those all mere excuses?" he asked.

"No," I answered, "I am afraid not. We can't count upon Great Britain remaining uninfluenced by this reactionary spirit. For, with Europe in such an unsettled state, we are within the danger zone. The ultimate resort to violence may at any time be made once more. Then impatience may gain the upper hand, and make any reasoned consideration of the Indian question impossible."

III

Alan Menzies now took up the subject. He had many close Indian friends and stood on their side in most discussions. After taking his degree he intended to go out to the Far East. In all probability he would finally settle down in China as a medical missionary. But he had not yet made up his mind.

"Isn't there," he asked me, "a violent spirit rising in the East, just as destructive as this 'clean, strong force' to which Churchill appeals in the West? Aren't we playing with fire, while the whole world has become like a powder magazine?"

Anil, who was Alan's closest friend, answered for me. He assured us all that nothing could keep violence in check in India if the present repressive policy continued much longer. Revolt was certain to spread far and wide. He then went on to tell us his own story.

His father was a Government servant, and therefore he had been brought up in an atmosphere where everything English was praised. He had intended to follow in his father's steps, and had received the highest education possible at the Presidency College, Calcutta. But many times over his heart misgave him; and more than once he had almost determined to give up everything for the sake of his country, as his sister Asha had done; but he had not the strength of will to do so, for it would have been contrary to all that his father had planned out for him. He had won a Government scholarship, which had enabled him to get to Oxford, and he had finished his first year at College. His sister, after suffering imprisonment as a passive resister, had already passed three years at Oxford. They were devoted to one another.

"Frankly," said he, "I often feel that I have been a coward for not joining in the National Movement. While young men and women also, like my sister, have gone to jail without any resistance, I've felt thoroughly ashamed of myself for making no sacrifice at all."

"I remember someone telling me," said John, "how those who stayed at home, at the beginning of the War, felt desperately ashamed of themselves. It must have been something like that with you."

"Yes," said Anil eagerly, "that was just what

happened; and again and again the thought came back to me that I had failed to help my country in her hour of need. This made that broadcast all the more galling. I've seen Mahatma Gandhi and asked him about my future, and also Rabindranath Tagore: for they are the two greatest and noblest men in India to-day."

"What did they tell you?" asked Neil Munro.

"They both told me," said Anil, "to go on with my studies; and whenever the despondency comes over me their advice gives me courage and I don't feel such a moral coward as before."

Tagore's name carried me forward to the point I had intended to reach if possible. For I had brought down with me some passages from his writings. They seemed to me to offer, better than anything else, the answer to the broadcast, which had given such great offence to the Indian students. For Tagore could take the moral issue for us into a far higher region of thought, above the murky atmosphere in which politicians usually dwell.

The poet is now approaching his fourscore years, which is a great age in a climate such as India. He spends most of his time in retirement at Santiniketan, watching the course of human events without taking active part in them. His mind is as detached and free from bitterness as it is possible to keep it in an age of violence and strife.

For three generations past the Tagore family—

the most famous in all India for artistic and literary achievement—has followed closely in the steps of Raja Ram Mohan Roy. It has attempted to build up a true moral harmony between East and West on honourable terms. All through the nineteenth century this larger hope of a union of hearts and minds had been retained, and further steps have been taken by the poet himself towards its accomplishment. For he has founded an institution called *Visvabharati* (World Culture), where East and West meet together for the common pursuit of art and learning.

In the moral debacle which followed the World War Tagore, in despair, surrendered his title. He could not bear to be silent after the humiliation of Amritsar. Yet even this shock has not altered his belief in the true meeting of East and West. His whole heart is still bent upon its fulfilment.

I asked Anil to read the passages I had chosen from Tagore. He did so with such feeling that it seemed almost as if Tagore himself was entering into our discussion.

IV

" When I was very young," the poet writes, " we were all full of admiration for Europe, with its high civilisation and its vast scientific progress, and especially for England, through her glorious literature, which had brought a new inspiration into our young lives. The English authors whose books and poems we studied were full of love for humanity, freedom and justice.

"This great literary tradition had come down to us from the Revolution period. We felt its power in Wordsworth's sonnets about human liberty. We gloried in it, even in the immature productions of Shelley, written in the enthusiasm of his own youth, when he declared against the tyranny of priestcrafts and preached the overthrow of all despotisms through the power of suffering bravely endured."

V

At that point I broke in for a moment, saying, "It was just the same with the poet's elder brother, whom we used to call 'Borodada.' He was an aged recluse, but none the less an ardent lover of India. When his country's wrongs in any part of the world came up before his notice his eyes would kindle with indignation. But whenever he spoke of Shakespeare, or Dickens, or Sir Walter Scott, who were his three favourite British authors, his whole countenance would soften with deep affection, and his patriotism would take a different tone. For these British authors were kindred spirits. They were his very own. They stood out clearly on his side in all his highest ideals. He could appeal to them direct against the acts of repression which were being committed in Bengal."

"We can sympathise with Tagore there,"

said Alan Menzies. "We British can never lose our own love of freedom as long as we have Shakespeare and Milton, and the poets of the Revolution period. Scott, again, was an ardent Tory, but he loved liberty—and what a gentleman he was!"

"Listen to this," said Anil, reading from his manuscript of Tagore as follows:

"'We believed with all our simple faith that, even if we rebelled against foreign rule, we should have the sympathy of the West. We felt that England was on our side in wishing us to gain our freedom. But there came a rude awakening as to our actual relations. We found them at last to be those of force rather than freedom.

"'This not only disturbed in a great measure our youthful dream: it also began to shatter our high ideas concerning our English rulers themselves. We came to know at close quarters the Western mentality in its unscrupulous aspect of exploitation, and it revolted us more and more. During the twentieth century, and especially since the European War, this evil seems to have grown still worse and our bitterness of heart has increased.

"'*Those who live in England, away from the East, have now got to recognise that Europe has completely lost her former moral prestige in Asia.* She is no longer regarded as the champion, throughout the world, of fair dealing, and the exponent of high principle, but rather as the upholder of Western race supremacy and the exploiter of those outside her own borders.

"'For Europe this is, in actual fact, a great moral defeat that has happened. Even though Asia is still physically weak, she can now afford to look down on Europe where before she looked up. This carries with it tragic possibilities of long-continued conflict.

"'I cannot truly point to any short-cut to win relief. What is most needed is a radical change of mind and will and heart. What I really believe in is a meeting between the best minds of the East and the West in order to come to a frank and honourable understanding.

"'Meanwhile, let it be clearly understood in the West that we, who are born in the East, still acknowledge in our heart of hearts the greatness of European civilisation. For we acknowledge, in the very act of striving for liberty, the noble character of the Western education which has roused us from our slumber.'"

VI

Neil Munro had become impatient as Anil read on. "Surely," he cried out, "Tagore contradicts himself. He says in one place that Europe has completely lost her moral prestige in Asia; and then he goes on to say that those who are born in the East still acknowledge, in their heart of hearts, Europe's greatness."

"Don't you see," I explained, "how desperately he tries to win back our affection? In spite of heart-breaking disappointments in recent years, he still goes on hoping against hope. There he is truly noble."

"Just look," said Anil, "how he continues, 'I myself,' he writes, 'have a firm faith in what is human in your nation, and the credit is yours for the very struggle for freedom that has been made possible to-day in India. The courage to suffer that has been aroused in our country carries with it an unconscious admiration for your own people in its very challenge. At heart it is a moral challenge, being sure of moral response in your mind when our claim to freedom is made real to you by our suffering.

"'Such sufferings have won your admiration. You secretly feel shame at the enormities that you allow to be perpetrated in a state of panic upon a people who are no match for you in power. Let, then, the best minds of the East and West join hands and establish a truly human bond of friendship between England and India.'"

Just as Anil finished, his sister Asha came in from St Ursula's. She was always a welcome member of the Union Club, and had been its president in her second year. Now she was preparing for her examination and her attendance was less frequent. Among the Indian students at Oxford she was well known for her patriotism.

John Murray continued the conversation.

"How is it," he asked, "that this repeated challenge of Tagore—to get the best minds to meet—is never taken up?"

"England is far too busy with her own concerns," said Safdar Ali impulsively. "If you put forward a business proposition, at once every one is on the alert. But talk about Persian or Arabic culture, and you won't get a single listener."

Asha was anxious that another passage should be read from Tagore. "I remember well," she said, "how we had to go an hour before the time in order to get a seat, when he gave the Hibbert Lectures in Oxford. The hall was crowded out. Couldn't you let me hear what you have chosen?"

I had left to the last the finest passage of all, which I had heard Tagore deliver at the Friends' House, in London. His speech had made a profound impression. I had watched the whole audience swayed by his appeal. For he spoke with prophetic earnestness, as though he were giving his parting message. He had taken the privilege of old age to utter the last words of a lover of the West, who had been deeply wounded in his love.

"In its relation," he had said, "to the people of the East, the aspect of Western character which has now come uppermost is not only insulting to us, but also to the West itself. Nothing could have been more unfortunate in the history of Man than this. At the moment when Europe came to our door the whole of Asia was asleep; the darkness of night had fallen over her life. Her lights were dim, her voice mute. She had her wisdom shut up in her books. Thus the East was not ready to receive the West in all her majesty of soul. We have not seen that which was great in the West because we have failed to bring out the great that was in ourselves.

"In the lives of the best individuals in Western countries there is a love of humanity; their keen intellect and indomitable will are both leagued together for human welfare. This reveals itself in loyalty to the cause of Truth, for which so many of them are ready to suffer martyrdom—often standing heroically alone against some fury of national insanity. When this wide human interest takes a moral direction, it grows into an intelligent service of mankind that can ignore all geographical limits and racial traditions.

"But what is most unfortunate for us is the fact that the advent of Europe into Asia has been accompanied not only by Science, which is Truth (and therefore welcome), but by the impious misuse of Truth for the violent purpose of self-seeking; and this converts it into a disruptive force. . . . It is difficult for us to acknowledge what is best in European civilisation and accept it when we are humiliated. This has been the reason why the West has not yet come home to our heart, why we struggle to repudiate her culture. It is because we ourselves are under the dark shadow of her dominance. We need freedom; we need that generous vigour of receptivity which the sense of self-respect alone can give to us.

"Let us, the dreamers of the East and the West, keep our faith firm in the life that creates; in the power that hides its force and blossoms in beauty! Let us know that Science is great when it destroys Evil; but *not* great when the two enter into an unholy alliance.

"I believe in the individuals of the West; for on no account can I afford to lose my faith in Man. They also dream; they love; they intensely feel pain at the unholy rites of demon worship. Their lamps of sacrifice will burn bright along the great pilgrim track of the future, when the triumphal tower of skulls, heaped up in memory of war lords, has crumbled into dust."

VII

As Anil finished a silence fell on us all. We seemed to have listened to the cry of a soul in pain; a sensitive mind, which had come

> between the fell incensed points
> Of mighty opposites,

and was crushed and bruised and torn. No one can fail to recognise the magnanimity of Tagore's spirit while he thus speaks out with all his heart. There is also a noble restraint, as he tries to control the sense of humiliation within. He does not weakly lay all the blame at the door of the West, but acknowledges the fact that when Europe came with its new message to Asia, the "East was not ready to receive the West in all her majesty of soul."

CHAPTER III

THE BRITISH POINT OF VIEW

I

AFTER the silence was broken, John Murray asked if he might put the case from the British point of view.

"We're entirely one with Tagore," he said, "in his plea for goodwill between the races. That is what we're aiming at, and we repudiate the doctrine of force. We don't look upon India any longer as a 'possession' of Great Britain, and we can now see much more clearly how insulting that word has been. The last thing we should desire would be to hold India in subjection to ourselves, if she can manage her own affairs."

"When did you learn those lessons?" asked Mulchand.

"The World War," John replied, "taught us many things. We're not so proud of our old 'imperialism' to-day. On that subject, for most of us, the Churchill School is out of date. We've learnt at last to consider the feelings of other people; and since the war-spirit is very closely connected with race supremacy, we're eager to repudiate that as well."

"Why then," inquired Safdar, "do you insist on keeping everything still in your own hands by means of safeguards and reservations?"

"The main difficulty," John answered, "arises from quite another quarter. We have on our consciences the destiny of these countless millions of very poor people in India whom we've tried to protect from oppression. We sincerely feel that we've a duty towards them, which we can't relinquish until we're certain that it will be fulfilled by you after we've gone away."

"Aren't you there," Safdar questioned, "concealing from yourselves your real motive?"

"No," said John with emphasis. "The question raised in our minds is a vital one. It is this: What would happen to the Indian villagers, and especially the depressed classes, if we left to-morrow? Would oppression begin over again?"

"Isn't your own rule," asked Abdul Majid, "the worst form of oppression?"

"Not intentionally," said John. "But I'm thinking of something far different from what is happening in India to-day. Take a comparison, ready to hand, in China. The Chinese are a virile and capable people. Yet a single flood, four years ago, swept away and drowned more than two million cultivators, whose lives were lost owing to culpable negligence in failing to keep up the embankments. On another recent occasion a single famine destroyed millions of poor people, and many millions besides were driven by starvation to emigrate to Manchuria, with women and children dying all along the road. Such things used to happen in India; but owing to scientific methods of rendering help the villagers have been saved in some measure from such disasters. Can we be quite certain, if we leave everything in Indian hands, that the standard of efficiency won't be lowered?"

"We can only learn by experience," Safdar answered. "We *have* to take over responsibility —why not at once?"

"At any other time," said John, "that answer would have satisfied me; but now I'm not so certain. We're taking tremendous risks, and the welfare of millions is at stake."

"Yet all life's made up of taking risks," came the quick reply from Anil. "Sooner or later the responsibility must be ours; for they're our people after all, not yours."

"Yes, I know that very well, but somehow that answer doesn't ease my mind in the least. The world's so upset in these days that we're all learning to put politics in the second place, and economics in the first. We simply can't afford to let things go to pieces, and then clean up the mess afterwards. In former times we used to believe in the old slogan of political freedom as the cure for every social ill; but now we think more of food supply and unemployment. We're not so sure as we were that mere political changes will work wonders."

"But won't you let us learn those lessons for

ourselves?" asked Anil; "why should you dictate?"

"Anil," said Alan, very seriously, "may we be absolutely open with each other? Can you assure us that there would not be open war between Hindus and Moslems if the British left, and that the 'untouchables' would not be left in the lurch? Please don't think these are lame excuses for hanging on."

"Well," said Anil, "as to Hindus and Moslems you have both in this room now, and you will find in all Indian student circles they work together quite happily. Then in the Labour Movement or the Women's Movement there is little or no communal friction. We know the older generation are often bigoted, and we admit they were all at sixes and sevens in the Round Table Conference. But I must remind you that we didn't elect those men to represent us. They were chosen by your Government. Anyway, we of the younger generation are working together. In India to-day the chief divisions are social rather than religious. That brings us to the 'untouchables.' You say you mustn't leave them in the lurch. But do you really look after their interests to-day? When big financial interests in London required a balanced Indian Budget, some years ago, you insisted on doubling the salt tax, which only hits our poorest people. We all told you not to do this, but the Viceroy insisted on it—and you've gone and certified it again this year!

Does *that* show any love for our 'untouchables'? Once more, you were as anxious as possible to satisfy every objection of the Princes in order to get them into the new Constitution. But when the downtrodden subjects of the Princes appealed to you for justice, you refused to hear them, and so all the old evils of a feudal system remain as before.

"The truth is this," Anil continued, "we distrust your motives. You want to realise the full interest on all your money invested in India. You want to keep in your own hands every form of exploitation. You've safeguarded these things in your new India Bill. All this money goes back to England; it's not spent among our poor people in India—not a penny of it. Where, then, comes in your consideration for the 'untouchables'? Believe me, we are not the degraded inhuman beings Miss Mayo makes us out to be! We are human, just as you are, and we are humane also. Do let us avoid hypocrisy."

II

Alan saw in a moment, from Anil's growing excitement, that something had hurt him in the discussion. "I'm so sorry," he said. "I've hurt badly, Anil. I can see it. And you must forgive me. But I assure you that our own sympathy with your poor people is quite genuine. Please don't make a mistake there."

"Even then," Anil replied with more composure, "there's one thing we feel so much, that we can't ask for your help any longer. You always want to occupy the chief place. You can't work with us, or under us. You insist on being over us. That's why the present state of things has become intolerable."

"I grant that," Alan acceded. "But even there things are not as bad as they were. Indians now are taking the highest positions in the Civil Service, with English officers under them. And there's another point I should like to make. Can we be sure that the peace of India, on which the security of the civilised world depends, will continue after the British authority is withdrawn? The whole world seems going to pieces. Won't India fall into ruin if we depart? This isn't a mere smoke-screen, set up selfishly in order to keep things in our own hands."

"There we differ," said Anil.

"I'll tell you the truth, Anil," said Alan. "However much we may dislike Churchill's attitude, we have an uneasy feeling that he's right when he declares that we oughtn't hastily to make, what he calls, 'a solemn abdication and refusal of responsibility.' For opposite reasons from his, we're afraid to take risks. We cling on, as you say, to power; but it's not for power's sake. We'd only too gladly hand over everything, bag and baggage, if we could. Indeed, we've done this already in Canada and South Africa. But just as some of us regret now that we didn't make better provision in

South Africa for the coloured races, so we feel now that we ought to make provision in India for the depressed classes."

III

It would be shortsighted on the part of those who feel intensely the need of immediate Swaraj, if they made light of these conscientious objections which some of the best Englishmen are putting forward. Furthermore, it would merely confuse the issue to indulge in wholesale condemnation of British rule, as if it had been an evil thing from beginning to end. Abdul Majid appeared anxious to take up that position, when John Murray forestalled him.

"You tell us," he said, "that because our rule in India is 'foreign' it has been altogether bad: but is this in accordance with the facts? First of all, there are abundant records left by Indians themselves stating in unequivocal terms the benefits derived from British rule in days gone by. Even if we deduct a large percentage for the conventional manner of speech common to that age, there is still first-hand testimony contrasting British rule with the hopeless anarchy which went before it. We've no right to doubt either the sincerity of these men, or their knowledge of the facts."

"But the debit on the other side," Abdul argued, "has far outbalanced those assets which we admit."

"Then let's take a test case. Whenever the choice has been offered for a local area to be transferred from British India and placed in the territory of an Indian State, the people concerned have always preferred to remain in British territory. Doesn't this imply that British India is more advanced than the Indian States?"

"That couldn't be said of Mysore," Anil replied quickly. "No one would want to leave that State."

"There may be exceptions, I grant, which prove the rule; and Mysore is a big one. But don't you see how even to-day the Princes who wish to federate with British India are determined not to have their States represented by elected candidates. Only their own nominees will be appointed. How would you like that in British India?"

"The truth is," said Anil, "that the backwardness of the States, politically, is itself due to their being buttressed up by the British rulers. That is one of the greatest evils of your rule."

"Very well," said John, "let's leave that question, as I see it's controversial; but there's still one further mode of reckoning which I have kept to the last. It's purely historical, and seems therefore almost beyond the pale of controversy."

Anil listened with attention, while John set forward at length the following argument:

"Consider," he said, "the advance made in the nineteenth century under British rule through movements which sprang from the heart of the people. This period has been rightly called the Indian Renaissance. We see, from historical records, how art, literature, language, culture, and above all, religion, gained a new life. We can see, also, how this modern intellectual and spiritual impulse, acting from within, has broken down social and religious barriers. It has also produced outstanding personalities, who became world-famous and made Indian culture widely known in the West. Let any one consider India's place in the world of thought to-day, as compared with a century ago, and he will almost certainly come to the conclusion that this Renaissance couldn't have happened if it hadn't been for the impact of foreign rule, which broke down all barriers and opened the doors of India wide to the science and thought of the West."

IV

The argument may pause here for a moment, and certain conclusions be drawn from the discussion.

Any attempts, from the material side, to prove the benefits of foreign rule—such as the extension of irrigation, canals, railways—do not appear to carry final conviction. For evils may have been introduced along with them; and, in any case, such artificial works may be utilised for a time and then as rapidly disappear. Mesopotamia, long ago, made provision for myriads of the human race by means of its irrigation system. But nothing except a malarial swamp remains to-day. New Delhi, with its costly buildings set over against the hovels of the poor, is another of those ephemeral things that will either pass away, or else be used for a different purpose when foreign rule itself disappears. We have striking examples in Soviet Russia and Germany, where the palaces of Emperors have been turned into museums for the common people.

But the intangible things of the human spirit, which gave rise to the Indian Renaissance, are of a different order. They abide; they become the common property of mankind. Therefore, at that point, the argument quoted above did not go astray.

The presentment of the case which appears to be most nearly in accord with the facts of history is this:

The foreign British rule, which came by sea to India more than three centuries ago, had its primary importance in the annals of mankind owing to a concurrence of events. It differed from everything that had entered India before, and by its complete divergence gave the shock and stimulus needed to rouse, first of all, Bengal, and then the rest of India, out of a state of anarchy which might have ended in death.

At first, indeed, it only made the anarchy more

rampant and the confusion worse confounded. For, during the early freebooting days of the Company's merchant-adventurers, the ruthless plunder of Bengal and Madras went on unchecked. This impoverished India and corrupted Great Britain through and through. Never, perhaps, did a great change in human affairs take place under worse auspices. The political life of England had sunk to its lowest ebb. The misery of India had also reached its lowest depths.[1]

But, in spite of all this, which was so bad that it can hardly be overstated, there were very great men on either side who won through, and in this way changed the course of history and introduced a new epoch, which we call the Modern Age.

Bengal produced, during that period of decay, one of the most tenderly pathetic of her own poets, Ram Prasad. Beyond this, she gave birth to a world genius in Raja Ram Mohan Roy.

Great Britain was also able to bring forth, out of the corruption of those days, a vital religious movement under John Wesley, which led up to the abolition of slavery and other great humanitarian reforms. There were statesmen such as Burke in Parliament, and scholars like Sir William Jones in Bengal, who raised the standard both of political morality and intellectual culture. The biography of Warren Hastings, by Mervyn Davies, shows what a deep interest the first Governor-General took in the philosophy of

[1] See Note B.

the East, and how he sought to mould his life upon it.[1]

Starting from Bengal, where great personalities on either side gave the new impulse its creative power, the Indian Renaissance spread in wider and wider circles. The period also witnessed an advance in scientific thought in the West, which led on to all the vast discoveries of the nineteenth and twentieth centuries. It was of the utmost importance to the human race as a whole that Asia should share in that advance as quickly as possible, so that there should be no time-lag between East and West, which would cruelly divide mankind. Bengal had the innate intellectual capacity and alertness of imagination which enabled her to make that effort.

At other epochs of human history, such as the beginning of the Christian era, Asia had taken the lead. When the soul of the brooding East made its own inner message known to the world through the Christian Church,

> She heard it—the victorious West,
> In crown and sword arrayed.
> She felt the void which mined her breast,
> She shivered and obeyed.

A new life began, which we have inherited as our birthright to-day.

In the same way, when Europe took the lead, not by a conquest of the spirit, but through

[1] See Note C.

scientific discovery, Bengal was the one country in the East which had still smouldering embers to be fanned into flame.

One other factor, mentioned by Tagore, helped to rekindle the intellectual fervour of Bengal. The literature of the Revolution Period in English Poetry was opened out before the eyes of the East just at the right moment of awakening. The passionate love of freedom, which runs through English poetry, was like new wine in its intoxicating power.

Long before China and Japan had become aware of these fresh springs of human thought, Bengal was wide awake; and the other parts of India were roused to action in their turn. Each language began to develop its own literature, following the footsteps of Bengal. When future historians look back at this Renaissance, they will make special reference to the revival of vernacular literature in every part of the country. For it shows how the fresh impulse of creative thought reached down to the masses of the common people and did not merely influence the tiny circle of the intellectuals.

VI

But just because the shock thus given to India by the impact of foreign rule, at a time when vitality was at a low ebb, had such a penetrating power, the danger was all the greater of its becoming destructive, if the shock itself was too prolonged. For as soon as ever the intellectual life-stream in the body-politic ran in full flow once more and circulation had been restored, the employment of any further stimulus from without would check the natural processes of recovery, and in this way do more harm than good.

No doctor would wish to use artificial respiration, or employ a violent stimulus, after the patient has begun to recover. He would rather, if he were a good physician, leave Nature herself to do her own healing work.

VII

Thus far the argument has had its double aspect. It acknowledges the value of the stimulus that India had received, yet it shows with equal clearness how grave the disaster may be if this subjection is further prolonged.

The crying need now is for the transfer, as rapidly as possible, of responsibility into Indian hands. Not less, but more responsibility is what India needs, because the form of rule by the foreigner has gone on too long. It has served its turn. To carry it on further would merely undo whatever good may have been done before.

> The old order changeth, yielding place to new,
> And God fulfils Himself in many ways,
> Lest one good custom should corrupt the world.

VIII

" Have you ever thought," I asked, before we parted, " of the analogy to India in British history, when Saxon England for a time came under the Normans ? "

" Do you mean to say," asked Safdar incredulously, " that England herself was ever in subjection to a foreign rule ? "

" Yes," I replied ; " the Norman was in every way a foreigner, and he did any amount of harm. But the Saxon character, which had to submit to this alien rule for a time, had its own serious defects. It had become isolated from the intellectual life of the continent of Europe. Nothing broke down this isolation and overcame Saxon sluggishness more effectively than subjection to the Norman."

" Surely," said Safdar, " that was because the Norman and Saxon were so near akin. There was no colour bar."

" I grant you," I replied, " that the analogy is imperfect. But the Norman shook the Saxon out of his mental lethargy and awakened a new intellectual life. We English to-day owe an immense debt of 'awakening' to the Norman Conquest, just as I believe you in India to-day owe a debt of 'awakening' to the British occupation.

" At the same time, history tells me plainly that if the foreign rule of the Norman had been prolonged, and England had become merely an integral part of a Norman empire, the good effect of the earlier impact would have been destroyed.

" In exactly the same way, I can see clearly that if the foreign rule of the British in India is prolonged, the good effect of the earlier impact will be destroyed. For this reason, I can never wish that India shall remain for all time, without her own consent, an ' integral part of the British Empire.' When she is strong enough, she must choose her own course."

Alan ended the discussion. " As Christians," he said, " we have one clear duty. We have to follow the Golden Rule which Christ has set before us. We have to do to others what we should wish done to ourselves. That's the only final solution of the moral tangle between India and Britain."

We decided, before we parted, to consider next the chief moral evils of subjection. We should discuss, also, some of the counter-balancing factors which had been present right through the British period and had led on to the Indian Renaissance.

CHAPTER IV

THE MORAL EVIL OF SUBJECTION

I

"WHAT would you regard," I asked, "as the greatest of all the moral evils which arise out of foreign rule?"

"The fact," Anil answered, "that it *is* foreign! It's not our own. So it tends to destroy personality. It degrades us by forcing upon us a second-rate imitation of another people. We hate ourselves for this imitation, and yet we go on with it. Thus it humiliates us all the while. When, further, the foreign rule is made to depend on brute force and abject fear, it becomes altogether vicious. The poison eats right into the soul."

"Mr Churchill," said Safdar, "never suffered from loss of national freedom. He has never felt the misery of belonging to a 'Dependency.' He has never experienced the bondage of racial subjection. Therefore it costs him nothing to paint a glowing picture about a serene and splendid harmony of peace and justice. Why, he has never lived in India, except as a young subaltern! So the phrases he uses are quite empty. For there's no real peace and order based on equal laws between the white and coloured people. The white man remains privileged throughout. If he kills or injures one of us in India, or an African in Africa, he gets an entirely different punishment from that meted out to a coloured person who kills or injures a white man. There's no equal justice."

"If only Mr Churchill," said Anil, "could look below the surface, he'd soon realise the canker that is eating out the heart of self-respect among us. That's why every young man and woman in India is determined to stand it no longer."

"How did the fact come home to you?" asked Alan.

"Once, long ago," said Anil, "a sentence of Sir John Seeley suddenly struck me like an electric shock:

"'*Subjection for a long time to a foreign yoke is one of the most potent causes of national deterioration.*'

"When I read that sentence it roused me as nothing had ever done before; because I could see in a flash how true it was. The harm that's done doesn't begin at once. Only after a long time can the evil be clearly traced. What's more, it's injurious to both sides. It's the opposite of what Shakespeare says about mercy. Instead of being twice blest, it's twice cursed. It curses him who rules, and him who is ruled."

"The worst of it is," said Safdar, "it's quite impossible to make people understand in England what British rule means in India. They won't believe what we say."

"How would *you* explain it?" I asked.

"You come from a country with a cold climate thousands of miles away and live out there in isolation. You're completely out of touch with our daily life. By the way, that's our fault as much as yours, for we're a clannish lot ourselves. The gulf grows wider, and you make no effort to cross it. You're not interested in our art, or literature, or music, or religion."

"That's rather a bad character you give us," said John Murray.

"Then look what it means for *us*!" said Mohanlal, who was a new Hindu member of the group. "We've always got to be under restraint when any official is about. We've got to put up with all sorts of humiliations and bow constantly to your over-ruling, though we know the country much better than you do. Indeed, we have often to watch one mistake after another being made through sheer ignorance on your part, without saying one word to put things right."

"Do you have to live a double life like that?" asked Neil Munro.

"There's no help for it," said Mulchand. "If you want to get on you have to do it, however much you may dislike it. Every day we have to think of these things and weakly submit to them, for the most part. Don't think we don't know our own weakness. We're only too conscious of it. But what are we to do?"

"May I tell you," I asked, "without giving offence, a story about what happened to me one day in India some time ago?"

"Please do," said Mulchand, "and we'll let you know afterwards whether it's typical or not."

"Once," I said, "while talking with an Indian friend, I suddenly noticed the change which came over his face as he stood beside me. He had become aware, by a glance of the eye, of the approach of the Deputy Commissioner. Up to that time he'd been perfectly natural with me, and we had carried on a frank conversation together. Then in the twinkling of an eye, as the British official approached who'd got full power in his hands to promote or degrade at will, his whole manner changed and he became all smiles and effusiveness towards the official. As far as I could judge there wasn't a single sincere word in all that he said while he spoke to the Deputy Commissioner in my presence.

"As soon as we were quite alone," I continued, "I challenged him about it as a friend. He told me that he hated himself for such double conduct, but what was he to do? As long as the rule of the foreigner continued, this 'kow-towing' to the ruler who had all power in his own hands had to continue. Sooner or later, every one who wished to stand well with the Government was obliged to act thus."

"How long ago," asked Mulchand, "did that happen?"

"More than twenty years ago," I answered, "when the National Movement was still in its infancy."

"I thought so," he said, and remained silent.

"It was chiefly due," said Safdar, "to Mahatma Gandhi that this has now been stopped. He first gave us the power of saying 'No,' and abiding by our decision."

"Yes," Mulchand agreed, "the National Movement has swept away a lot of hypocrisy. But it hasn't made the British rulers themselves any more friendly. For that old submissiveness appealed to their weaker side, while the modern spirit of independence makes them always suspect that we're up to mischief."

"When our Professor of English," said Anil, "at the Presidency College used to teach us Wordsworth, we tried to ask him awkward questions. There were some lines in the *Golden Treasury* which we all knew by heart. 'Sir,' we'd ask him, 'can you please tell us what Wordsworth meant when he wrote,

> We must be free or die.

Is that meant only for Englishmen, or does it apply to Indians as well?' He used to get awfully confused when we put to him questions like that."

Alan laughed rather uneasily. "I can see where the fault lay," he answered. "If we'd only made an attempt to settle down and assimilate ourselves to the life of your people, and thus make ourselves one with you, things might have been very different."

"That's true," said Abdul Majid. "The Moghuls did that, and for a long time everything went very well indeed."

Alan remained thoughtful and we all paused in the discussion. "The one thing," he said at last, "that's drawn me to go out to do mission work in China, rather than India, is bound up with this very point. Out there, in China, it is easier for us to adopt Chinese dress and to live, not as strangers, but in the heart of the country among the common people. There's no British rule there which brings 'awkward questions' with it every moment."

"Mere dress by itself is of very little importance," said Anil, "but it means a great deal when it implies the desire to be one in spirit and not racially aloof. I do wish you'd change your mind, Alan, and come out to India. We shouldn't put those 'awkward questions' to you: for we know you're on our side."

II

Asha now joined in the discussion. "You can't tell," she said, "how weakening it is for any of us to indulge in self-pity and then go on to make excuses for our own failings. You've only got to read modern psychology to see what happens. If I'd my own way I'd try to get every Indian worker to promise never to throw the blame on others. It makes us moral invalids."

"But don't we really owe our weakness to the British domination?" asked Safdar.

"Let me put it round the other way," said Asha. "Don't we really owe the British domination to our weakness?"

"I never thought of that," said Safdar. "How stupid of me! Asha, you've taught me a lesson."

"I wish I had," said Asha laughing. "I've repeated that lesson a hundred times, but it hasn't gone home yet. This self-pity is our great national fault. That's why we women mustn't let you indulge in it."

"What would you say was *our* national fault?" I asked.

"Oh, you," she replied. "Here at Oxford you're quite decent; but in India you're—I don't know what to call you!"

Everybody laughed at Asha's lame conclusion.

"Do tell us what you really think," said Alan.

"Shall I tell you?" asked Asha. "I think I've got it now exactly. You're never yourselves! That's your great fault! Oh, what *could* be more artificial than your life out in India, where you hold yourselves aloof from us, in most places, and live in a tiny club circle of your own? I wonder how you can endure it!"

III

An incident had once brought home to me very forcibly indeed this factor of aloofness, and I ventured to relate it; for at the time it had made me think out many things afresh from the Christian standpoint.

An important post had been vacant and I had strongly advised a brilliant young Cambridge scholar, who was a prominent member of the Student Christian Movement, to go out to India as a Government servant in the Education Department rather than as a missionary. Circumstances made the latter vocation almost impossible. While putting the opportunity before him, I had explained how affectionate Indian students were when they met with real goodness in their teacher. He was quite eager to go out, but a few days later was thrown back by the words of a retired civilian, who had spent his whole life in India. This older man, whom he deeply respected, had told him that if he *did* go out it would be wise to hold himself aloof and not come closely into touch with the students. His casual remark was perhaps quite kindly meant, but the foreign attitude of a ruling race, which it implied, so disgusted the younger man that he changed his plans and went elsewhere.

This story seemed almost incredible to Alan. "Do you really mean to say," he asked, "that this senior officer actually told him that he would have to hold himself aloof if he went out as a teacher of young students ? "

" Yes," I said, " that's a perfectly true story. But, just as Mulchand said about his own countrymen, things have moved a lot since then. We look back on the years since the World War and they seem to us hateful, miserable years, full of bitter quarrel and dispute ; but much good has come out of them after all. *You* are not by any means so weak and feeble as you were. And we—well, we've moved a great deal too."

" *Some* of you," said Anil, " but by no means all. The trouble is we have Diehard Englishmen in India. There are still people who are ready to turn us out of railway compartments in order to keep up British prestige, and others who glare at us if we don't show the old slavish respect. We never know when we're going to meet them, and this puts our minds in a perpetual ferment."

" Not here, I hope ? " asked John Murray.

" Oh, no," said Anil. " Here we're as free as the air we breathe. You can hardly realise what a difference that makes ! Only think, if we talked like this in India——"

" Why, what would happen ? " asked Alan quickly.

" Oh, it couldn't be done over there. The atmosphere's entirely different. Here we're perfectly free. That's one of the great glories of Oxford, which makes us love her so much. Oxford gives us perpetual beauty and a perfect sense of freedom."

IV

A sudden thought had once on a sea voyage come home to me like a flash, and I determined at this point to bring it forward as a part of the discussion.

"There's no one in the world," I said, "who'd be happier to see India free than I should; for I can trace every day more clearly how this prolonged subjection to a foreign rule is injuring something vital in her soul. That's the tragedy of it all, and Mr Churchill never in the least realises what it implies when he uses that hateful word 'possession.' Isn't it really the same issue over again as that of the slave traffic a century ago? No man, it was said then, has the right to 'possess' the person of another man. In the same way, we've got to understand with burning conviction to-day, a century later, that no *nation* has the right to 'possess' another people who are of a different character and race. Human personality is involved. To put it in moral terms, the person of a nation is sacred."

"How ever did you come to put these two things together?" asked Safdar, with enthusiasm. "That's quite a new thought to me. I'd never seen things in that light before. But it's perfectly true."

"It was off West Africa, just as we approached Sierra Leone. Slavery had been carried on there in days gone by. My own country had gained the very lucrative monopoly of the slave traffic.

The slave ships, which plied to and fro, on what was called the 'middle passage,' were British. Yet when once the wrong done to the person of human beings was clearly understood, Great Britain performed one of the most wholly unselfish acts in her long history. She abolished slavery at a very great cost."

"I see the analogy," said Anil. "But do you really think that she will perform an even more unselfish act to-day and set India free?"

"If once," I replied, "it was made absolutely clear that India was unjustly treated, owing to this retention of power by Great Britain, I am sure our people would do what they did before. They would release India from bondage. But the issue has become so involved, that even the most earnest Christian men and women somehow feel doubtful. They still feel that British rule is protecting the poorest of the poor. There is the real difficulty. They want to do the right thing by India, but they are confused. They wish to be truly Christian, but they don't know how to act. If they saw clearly that there was a united moral demand for further freedom, from rich and poor alike in India, then they would abolish this bondage just as they abolished slavery itself a century ago."

"Obviously," said Neil Munro, "we have to go much deeper still into this whole question of subjection. We haven't got to the bottom of it yet. If what you and Seeley and others say is perfectly true, and foreign rule leads on at last to national deterioration, then your analogy with the abolition of slavery holds good. Just as we mustn't retain the 'person' of an individual by force, so we mustn't hold by force the 'person' of another people."

"The argument would be greatly strengthened, said John Murray, "if you could prove that the injury done to the foreign ruler is no less grave than that which is done to the alien subject who is ruled. This would then imply that Great Britain herself might become demoralised if the present subjection continues."

"That's what's really happening to-day," I said. "Moral deterioration on both sides is going on. The life lived by Englishmen and English-women is artificial, and so is the Indian life also."

"Could you give us," asked Alan, "another example from your own experience, like that one about the senior officer? It seemed to me quite incredible that an Englishman could have acted like that."

"Here's the first that occurs to me. It happened in the War, when all letters were censored. A kindly old retired general, at one of the ports, who was doing war service, invited me to see him and told me he had been looking through all my private letters. 'I hope you found them interesting,' said I. 'Oh, yes,' said he, 'they're very interesting indeed. But I find you write to your Indian friends exactly as you do to your own family. Now, as one who knows the East much better than you do, I want to tell you one thing. You shouldn't write to your Indian friends like that. There are certain things we can discuss among ourselves; but it's not safe to discuss them with "natives"—especially in war time.'"

"Good heavens!" Neil blurted out. "Did he say that?"

Alan turned to his friend Anil, "Just imagine my treating *you* like that, Anil! What would you think of me?"

Anil laughed. "You couldn't do it, Alan," he said, "even if you tried."

"Time's up," said Neil, "just as things were getting to the point. Couldn't we continue the same subject next time?"

"I've got a paper already written," said I, "on 'Anglo-India.' It was put together about twelve years ago, when the Non-Co-operation Movement was active."

"Oh, do read it!" said Asha eagerly. "We'd love to hear it. But I hope you don't merely speak of your own British failings. You must speak of ours too, for we need plain speaking very badly."

"You must remember," I said, "how long ago it was written. Much of it is now out of date. But it does show what happened, and what might happen again, if the old spirit in any way revived."

CHAPTER V

" ANGLO-INDIA " [1]

I

THE discussion was thus held over, and at the next meeting I read the following paper:

" India is a country which can never be suitable for the average Englishman to settle down in. Owing to difficulties of climate, it involves for him, in most cases, enforced separation from his wife and children during a great part of the year. For this and other reasons, his character becomes subtly modified in unperceived directions; and the change which has taken place is at once noticed when he retires and lives at home.

" There has thus been evolved a type of character which in English literature has been called 'Anglo-Indian.' It has met with good-natured chaff from such novelists as Thackeray on account of its eccentricities. Among these have been a short temper, imperious voice, and an autocratic manner of addressing servants.

" If these peculiarities were analysed they

[1] The word is here used, in its old literary sense, to denote the environment of one who has spent his life in India and developed a certain type of character.

would be found mainly to be due to the submissiveness with which the 'Sahib' had been treated by his Indian servants and subordinates, over whom he had exercised unlimited sway during the time he was in office abroad.

"Such perpetual domination over another race, accepted with submission, is in itself a demoralising process, for it leads insensibly to an exaggerated humility on the one hand and an equally exaggerated self-importance on the other. India is the worst place in the world for such distinctions to be emphasised, because these very things have all along been its curse in the past, and they need to be got rid of rather than encouraged in modern times.

"History shows how the Brahmin ascendency led to one type of racial subservience, which left as its evil legacy millions of so-called 'untouchables.' The Moghul supremacy led on to servility of another kind, carrying with it fatal results. All sorts of princes, great and small, added a third form of debasement, owing to a feudal despotism unrelieved by modern ideas of liberty and justice. With the British came, last of all, a new ascendency, along with its inevitable train of hangers-on and time-servers, eager to please the official in order to get rich and earn a title. Those Englishmen who came out, unspoilt by race and colour prejudice, soon began to think of their own prestige. They learnt in this manner to accept the position of a new ruling caste.

" Yet in spite of all this evil growth, notable friendships between Indian and British have been common. For there have always been those who have successfully resisted the noxious atmosphere around them and have chosen their Indian friends and associates wisely and well, treating them with a generous courtesy which surmounted altogether any barrier of race or caste. Some of the truest friendships in the world have been those between individuals who have broken down every distinction of race through mutual love and respect.

II

" Modern Indians, who have imbibed to the full the new national spirit, are in open revolt against any kind of outward expression of servility towards the ruling race. Indeed, they call it by the harsh name of ' slave mentality ' which Mahatma Gandhi has made current coin. They are justly indignant at the gross flattery which went on in earlier days, and they encourage in all with whom they come in contact a manly independence which is clean and wholesome when compared with the impure atmosphere of false submissiveness which went before.

" Above all, they realise that political freedom must be inward as well as outward, if they would become a truthful, sincere, and self-respecting people.

III

"When I came out for the first time to India, my associates at once sought to drill me into the mentality of the 'Sahib.'

"'Never,' they said, 'for a moment forget that in this country, as an Englishman, you depend entirely upon your prestige. You must never let that down; for if that goes, everything goes with it. Therefore, though you have come out as a missionary, you are an Englishman first. You will do an incalculable injury to your fellow-countrymen if you let your sympathies carry you away and allow any "native" to become familiar with you. Never give way to them. They don't understand it; and they will take it as a clear token of your own weakness. None of them are to be trusted in the same way that you would trust an Englishman. Above all, never forget that we have English ladies out here, and the least familiarity, if you allow it, is going to do harm to their position in this country, which entirely depends on every Englishman keeping up his white prestige.'

"It was racial poison of this kind that was distilled into my ear, night and day. Fortunately, an antidote was always ready to hand in the words of Christ, my Master, and I was able to survive those first few months, spent in language study at Simla, without any serious infection. But the strain of it is a very severe ordeal for a young Englishman to pass through. Repeated small doses of this toxin have a terribly depressing effect even on one who has come out with a strong determination fearlessly to fight under Christ's banner.

" A story will make this clear. One of my English friends told me that he had come out on business to a great commercial firm in India. He had formed, while at Oxford, a close friendship with an Indian student who was a member of his own college; so he had written beforehand telling him that he was expecting to see a good deal of him on his arrival in India. His friend met him at the steamer and the old college comradeship was renewed. They dined together and were often seen in each other's company.

" Very soon, however, his conduct was noticed by his fellow-countrymen, who warned him that he was not properly upholding his British character, and that his actions were being severely criticised at the Club. One of the senior partners took him aside and rebuked him.

" ' Look here,' he said, ' you are young; you don't understand this country yet and our position in it. You can't carry on your Oxford friendship with that ' native ' out here. It's not done!'

" ' But,' said my friend, ' he is a member of my own college.'

" ' We can't help that,' said the other. ' These things aren't tolerated out here by decent people.'

" Some of those who come out from England surrender at once in the face of a heavy frontal attack of this kind. Now and again, however, a really brave spirit makes a good fight, just as this young Englishman did. For he gallantly refused to give up his Indian friend and was boycotted in consequence.

"But human nature, after all, has its gregarious instincts, and in these racial conflicts, with their divided loyalties, the struggle is never ended; and there is no place for a non-combatant. That is the deep tragedy of the whole matter, when once hostilities begin.

IV

"It ought, long ago, to have become abundantly evident to the Civil Service, which had the unchallenged conduct of Indian affairs in its own hands, that in any circumstance this unnatural submissiveness would not continue, and also that when the revolt began, its reaction was likely to be overwhelming.

"The reaction has now come. No nationally-minded Indian to-day will submit to the old 'Sahib' attitude. The thoroughly bad habit, that used to be so common, of employing flattery as a subtle weapon of defence against this arrogance, is now only used by those who are paid subordinates. The servants, who still cluster round the 'Sahib,' with little work to do, not seldom continue to exploit him, if his weakness for flattery lays him open to attack. They have learnt to know every foible and to play upon each of these in turn. It is a cruel game—a kind of defence mechanism, that ought to have been abandoned long ago, and would have been left behind in any normal state of society.

" This undermining of character on both sides is the worst nemesis that has arisen out of all the numerous evils that have been introduced with foreign rule. At the same time, it needs to be recorded that, even with racial feeling as strong as it is to-day, if any Englishman or woman is prepared to drop the 'superior' attitude and be perfectly natural and human, there are no retainers in the world more loyal and devoted than Indian servants.

" How utterly inconsiderate this forceful upholding of racial prestige may become can hardly be imagined by those who have never seen it practised. It appears to override all the finer instincts in our own characters.

" 'I hate this country,' has been a passionate word which I have heard many times over, and I have wished to reply with very deep conviction, 'Then you can only do harm by staying here, and you should, if possible, go home at once.'

V

" It seems as if the cumbrous traditions of the past had strangely paralysed any initiative in the reform of these bad manners. Therefore the old abuses of an Englishman's power die very hard. Now and then an altogether wholesome change is ordered from above, such as that which forbade the use of the objectionable word 'native' in any public document. But even such official orders appear to have had but little effect upon the daily conversation that goes on when Englishmen and women are alone.

"Lest I should be thought to be exaggerating, let me relate an incident which happened to me some years ago in Delhi. I had gone daily to call on one of the leading gentlemen of the city, a man of culture and refinement. We used to read English poetry together, and he had become my intimate friend. He was much older than I was, and of high repute in the city. One day I asked him to take me in his carriage to the Deputy Commissioner's bungalow for some purpose. He did so, and his carriage was stopped at the outer gate of the compound, which was some distance from the house. To get out at that spot would have entailed a walk in the blazing sun, without any protection from its rays, and it was approaching midday heat. So I asked my friend to tell his driver to drive on up to the house. He said to me with shame that he could not do this: he would be turned back, for Indians had to approach the Deputy Commissioner's bungalow on foot. The thing was so monstrous that at first I treated it as a joke, but it was nothing of the kind. It was one of the ways of 'keeping the native in his proper place.'

"My old friend was gentleness itself, but his

eyes blazed with fire as he told me how these 'foreigners' insult them in this manner. While speaking to me he had never used that word 'foreigner' before with reference to Englishmen. At heart he was loyal to the ideal of British rule and he had a deep veneration for Queen Victoria, who was to him the embodiment of all that was good. But petty tyrannies like these, exercised by those who strut across life's stage wrapped round in brief authority for a few moments, cancel out a large credit balance of goodwill.

" When I challenged the D.C. about his action he said, in weak self-defence, that it had been the custom in the Punjab for 'native' gentlemen to wait in that manner, and he did not see his way to change it. Let me state at once that such discourtesies are much less frequent now.

" The result of all this action and reaction has been visible in recent years. Nationally-minded Indians have learnt to assert themselves, not seldom in an exaggerated manner, which reveals by its own excess how sadly the balance has been upset. Englishmen, on their side, have begun to understand that they cannot any longer take liberties as they used to do in the past. They are more on their guard and less autocratic than before.

" Outwardly, therefore, there has been an improvement in the general situation, especially among higher official circles. But while certain unwholesome things have thus been finally abandoned, the actions and examples of those in higher authority have not been sufficient in themselves to bring about the desired result of true friendly relations.

"H. W. Nevinson, whose generous spirit had been stirred to righteous indignation by what he saw of 'Anglo-India' many years ago, proclaimed the urgent need for 'what our forefathers called "conversion"—a change of heart.' Mere prohibition cannot effect this; and not seldom there has been left behind no change of heart at all, but an inward contempt of all things Indian, which finds an outlet at the Club.

VI

"There is one new feature which needs to be mentioned in a paragraph by itself, because its all-pervading influence is now manifestly apparent, and it has led not only to racial, but also to moral antipathy.

"The rapid spread of the film industry and the establishment of cinemas which cater especially for the middle classes, have brought about a revulsion of feeling against the West which has added to the general confusion. For the last vestige of respect is destroyed, when films of Western life, illustrating all that is base and brutal in it, are exhibited day after day, and night after night, to a perpetual stream of young people. It would therefore be entirely wrong to underrate the influence that this new factor is exercising over Young India.

VII

" While I have set down, in unqualified terms, the bad customs which have been kept up in India by a false sense of prestige, it needs to be repeated with emphasis that there are officials who detest this anti-Indian racial spirit and have done what they could to stand out against it. These men, and their wives also, have been the soul of courtesy towards Indians with whom they have come in contact. Still further, there are signal examples of those who in times of grave calamity have been ready to put every selfish consideration on one side and sacrifice even life itself in the service of the poor. However bitterly Indians have suffered from the racial arrogance of others, they have never been slow to acknowledge this aspect of British rule embodied in individuals whom they admire."

CHAPTER VI

THE LIBERAL PRINCIPLE

I

THE picture of Anglo-Indian society which I had drawn in my paper would be incomplete if I were to leave it as it stands. For all along there has been a noble tradition which has struggled to represent worthily in India the higher principle of fellowship which Christ's teaching so clearly embodies. Since the disaster of the World War, which shattered for a time the larger mind of Europe, two currents of thought—the liberal and the racial—have constantly come into conflict, but the outcome of the struggle as yet has remained uncertain.

At Allahabad, the two great rivers of Northern India, the Ganges and Jumna, meet. For some space, one stream can be traced by a brown, mud-laden current, while the other remains almost blue. The analogy is, of course, imperfect; but hitherto we have chiefly been tracing what may be called the "racial" current, as it runs strong and carries with it much decaying matter which needs to be thrown aside. But we can at the same time distinguish the

" liberal " current, with its clearer waters, making its way through every obstacle in its onward flow.

II

This " liberal " tradition in British rule had been chosen for our next discussion. Meanwhile my own paper on " Anglo-India " had been circulated and had come in for much criticism. Neil Munro had read it and did not like it.

" You've been far too hard," he complained, " on the average British official. My own ancestors have been connected with India for some generations, and I can even trace a distant relationship with Sir Thomas Munro himself, so that I'm not likely to err on the conservative side. But surely the racial complex hasn't been so widespread as you've made out ; and there have been thousands of officials and others all along determined to help forward the cause of political freedom in India."

" We're just about to discuss this ' liberal ' view," was my reply. " But don't under-estimate the strength of the racial bias ; for it has been the curse of British rule in India from the very first. Why, your own ancestor, Sir Thomas Munro, found this out more than a century ago. (I looked up the passage.) Here is what he says :

" ' Foreign conquerors have treated the natives with violence, and often with great cruelty, but none has treated them with so much scorn as we; none has stigmatised the whole people as unworthy of trust; as incapable of honesty; and as fit to be employed only where we cannot do without them. It seems to be not only ungenerous, but impolitic, to debase the character of a people fallen under our dominion.'

"Such a quotation," said I, "shows that this scornful contempt of the Indian, about which Sir Thomas writes, is of very long standing. The only thing that saved the situation was that liberal statesmen were found who detested whole-heartedly such conduct towards the people of another race, and were convinced that the only way forward was through equality freely acknowledged in every concern."

Anil supported my position. He knew this history period well. "The great Victorians," he said, "always assumed that the day would come when India would decide freely her own destiny. But since the War, with its repressive spirit, even to speak about separation from the British Empire is regarded as 'seditious'! Yet those earlier statesmen definitely faced that possibility without any reservation whatever."

"Can you prove that?" asked Neil. "It's a very important point. I've never heard it made before."

"Yes," answered Anil. "Sir Henry Lawrence uses these very words: '*When the connection between Britain and India ceases.*' Surely that means separation. He adds the prayer that, whenever the time should come, it might happen, 'not with convulsions, but with mutual esteem and affection.' That was a noble aim, and we can still keep the same hope before us to-day."

Neil returned to his original proposition. He urged that the racial discrimination, about which we had been talking, had played very little part in Anglo-Indian history. Safdar Ali strongly dissented. He told how his own father, an old man, had been assaulted on the railway. "I can assure you," he said, "these things are by no means over yet. Instances happen every day that are never reported."

Mohanlal agreed that the evil was still rampant, but qualified this by saying that in higher official circles an entirely different attitude had begun to prevail. He praised, especially, the recent Viceroys, who had taken a strong line about courtesy and good manners. They would not tolerate the least atom of rudeness, and this had set a salutary example at headquarters.

"To me," said Alan, "the whole idea of race prejudice is so vulgar and coarse and brutal that I can hardly believe such snobbery ever occurs. I can't even dream of an Englishman acting in that manner; and yet you all make it perfectly clear that a monstrous scandal exists, and I only wonder how you've been patient so long."

Anil turned to his friend with affection. "Alan," he said warmly, "you haven't got the least touch of it yourself. The moment we met you we knew it, and that's why we trust you. But we feel it at once in others."

"Perhaps we'd better get on to the main subject," I suggested, "and take up what I've called the 'liberal' tradition."

"Won't you fire away, then?" asked John.

"No," said I, "let Anil open the discussion."

"It's quite clear," said Anil, "that Burke's protest pioneered the way to a cleaner rule in India. He was the real hero of the eighteenth century, and we in India have kept our hero-worship for him, and also for Lord Ripon in the nineteenth; and we're not far wrong in both cases. After Burke, we have a succession of other great men, Munro, Metcalfe, Elphinstone, Macaulay, Bentinck, Lawrence. There were outstanding men also in Bengal—Ram Mohan Roy, Dwarkanath Tagore, Maharshi, Keshub, Ramkrishna, Vivekananda.[1] Other parts of India awoke later. Swami Dayananda roused the North. But I mustn't get on too far, because I want to make my earlier point quite clear. It is this. They looked forward to the time when India should be free to make her own choice. They believed in political freedom, not in political bondage."

"How on earth," asked John, "had they got as far as that a century ago? Why, they were miles ahead of where we stand to-day!"

"You forget this disastrous World War and its reactions," said I, breaking in. "That set-

[1] See Note G.

back of the War has to be taken into account all along the line. Then you must remember also the fine liberalism of those early Victorian days. It was the era of the Reform Acts and the abolition of slavery. Freedom was stirring the hearts of men, and there were statesmen ready at hand to promote the spirit of freedom. Ram Mohan Roy felt it when he landed in England. It was a tragedy that he died at that critical time; for great men make human history, and he was very great indeed."

"What brought all this to an end?" asked Alan.

"The Mutiny," I answered.

"But wasn't that for us, in India, a fight for freedom?" asked Abdul Majid.

"There were such gross provocations that a fight almost *had* to come. The racial evil on the British side had increased tenfold and had become wellnigh intolerable in its arrogance. But it was a sordid struggle in its origin, excited by human follies and human lies as thick and gross as those of the last World War, from which we are all suffering to-day. No, if it had been a real struggle for independence, it would have gone much further. Let us hope such a 'war to the finish' will never have to be fought out, with all the inhuman lethal weapons which are being devised by science to-day. Mahatma Gandhi has been like a 'voice crying in the wilderness,' telling us that the only warfare God can bless is a *moral* warfare, and this can never be decided by poison gas and picric acid bombs."

"What do you yourself make of the Mutiny, then?" asked Safdar Ali.

"It was a thunderbolt and an earthquake combined," I replied, "and it has deeply infected the very air with hatred ever since. The brutal deeds, at the outset, committed by the mutineers had already been recorded; but Dr E. J. Thompson's book, called *The Other Side of the Medal*, has now made clear the brutalities which followed from our own side. Those have to be honestly acknowledged and admitted, because the racial poison they engendered has never been eliminated from our blood ever since. It has created Jallianwala Baghs and other horrors."

"May I come in to your discussion?" asked someone at the door, and Hara entered. He was one of the few Japanese members of the Union Club, and we welcomed him warmly.

"We are just being told," said Neil, as Hara took his seat, "that all war in modern times is an unmitigated curse, and that the racial spirit is a vile poison, which maddens men's minds till they brutally kill one another. Is that so?"

Hara smiled, but refused to be drawn into the discussion.

"Britain," said Abdul Majid, "will never let India go unless she is forced to do so?"

"Didn't we abolish slavery?" asked Neil Munro. "Was that forced?"

"No," Majid answered, "that was a purely unselfish act. But will it ever be repeated?"

"There's no reason," said I, "why it shouldn't. But let's see what really happened in India, after the Mutiny. Our histories rightly tell us a good deal about Lord Canning—'Clemency Canning' as the Europeans nicknamed him in anger—but the greatest asset among the Indian village people was the character of Victoria the Good. The story of her long widowhood, her devotion to her husband, her deep religious faith, and her love of the Indian people travelled very far. I've traced it in most unlikely places."

"So have I," said Mohanlal. "There's one story from my own experience. In a village not far away from us there was a very aged priest, with white hair and beard, loved by everybody for his goodness. On one occasion an innocent lad was cruelly imprisoned on a false charge owing to police corruption. At first the old priest wouldn't believe it; but when the boy's mother came to him weeping and told him it was true, he said: 'Now I know that Queen Victoria is dead. Such a thing would not have happened if she had been alive.'"

This incident struck me, and I told a somewhat similar story concerning a deeply-revered old friend, Munshi Zaka Ullah of Delhi.

His own life had nearly been forfeited, in spite of his innocence, in the reprisals which followed the sack of Delhi. An English officer saved him. For a time his heart was broken by the horrors he had been through, but at last he rallied from the shock and spent many years in writing his Urdu History, called *Victoria Nama*. He wished to show that only through Queen Victoria's goodness had the spirit of hatred been restrained and a new order of righteousness established. He felt, in a sense, that he owed his life to the good Queen. Her great Proclamation of 1858, declaring racial and religious equality as the basis of her rule, formed the title-page of his book. The most interesting thing is that the story of the good Queen is as well known in African kraals as it is in Indian villages."

"What destroyed all this goodwill?" asked John.

"First of all there was the Partition of Bengal," said Anil. "But that was partly remedied before the War; and in the War itself we did our utmost to help the Allied Cause, sincerely believing it to be the cause of freedom. We made no sordid bargains with Great Britain; but we were absolutely certain that if we helped to win the War, we should gain our own Swaraj. And when, after the War, we got the Rowlatt Acts and Amritsar instead, we non-co-operated. We couldn't fight you: we didn't even wish to fight you. But we were quite determined that the whole world should know how you had betrayed us."

Those are very hard words," said Neil,

"and very ungrateful words, in return for all that we've done for you! What about the Reforms?"

Safdar Ali answered hotly, "Reforms! Humbug! We of the younger generation, Muslims and Hindus alike, are quite fed up with them. They merely play with us. Your British Parliament has the last word in every single thing. You never treated South Africa like that, or Canada, or even the Irish Free State."

"They belong," Majid almost shouted, "to the white race, but we—we are a coloured race, and that makes all the difference!" (Neil, at this point, tried to demur.) "No! It's no use your denying it! That's the *real* difference! You're white and we are not! You're free and we are not! Oh! it's quite easy for us to talk like this in Oxford, but you good people here don't know what things are going on abroad. In Kenya, in South Africa, in India itself, we're up against the white race every time, and even your Parliament rubs it in—your Churchills and others—till we can bear it no longer!"

Safdar's short-lived excitement died down, but evidently there was a volcano underneath, which this subject of the "white race" had roused into violent action. Anil was equally excited, but he had kept to the argument more closely.

Neil had become excited on his side. He challenged the racial bias of the British Parliament. "You mustn't," he said, "confuse Parliament with the Diehards like Churchill. After all they're a very small minority."

"What about this, then?" asked Anil. "Here is the Preamble which, we are told, is to be put at the head of the new Constitution: 'The time and manner of each advance can be determined *only by the British Parliament*, upon whom responsibility lies for the welfare and advancement of the Indian peoples.' Can't you realise what an insult that is?"

"No," said Neil bluntly.

"What!" cried Safdar. "Would you dare to tell the Irish Free State that each advance towards self-government must be determined *only* by the British Parliament? Would you dare to tell De Valera that *he* was not responsible for the welfare of his own people, because the British Parliament had taken on the job? You tried to do things like that with Ireland once, and also with South Africa, but you had to give it up, and you don't try now any longer. Let's say it quite plainly. The real reason that you make such a sharp distinction in our case is because we don't belong to your own white race! That's the real difference all over the world. If we were your kith and kin, sprung from your own blood, you'd give way quick enough, just as you've done in Canada, in South Africa, and now in Ireland. All that we ask you to do is exactly what you are doing here in this room: treat us as racial equals, not as racial inferiors."

III

This brought us as far as the discussion could adequately reach on that evening, for it clearly had never even dawned on those undergraduates at Oxford that the white race prejudice meant incessant humiliation in the larger world outside Great Britain. Neil Munro, perhaps, had a suppressed instinct in his blood, from his forefathers, as to what it might mean: but to Alan and John and others the question of colour and race distinction hardly existed. They were as innocent of these things as little children are.

It seemed best, therefore, for me to set out in another paper what this issue implied, and after this had gone its round, we should decide what was our Christian attitude towards it all. For there was very strong feeling on the part of those who came from the East that the Christian Church had encouraged this imperialism in some of its worst forms.

CHAPTER VII

IMPERIALISM

I

THE paper which I wrote ran as follows:

"What I tried to set forward with regard to 'Anglo-Indian' character represents the extreme reaction in the past towards a foreign domination on the part of those who submit to it, and, by so doing, experience humiliation.

"I have explained how such an unnatural condition corrupts the finer instincts on both sides; how it creates in the rulers a domineering temper, which is far removed from the Christian spirit, and implants in the ruled a subservience that destroys all decent moral standards. Race feeling, with bitterness on both sides, becomes intensified. For Lord Rosebery's definition is correct.

"'What is Imperialism,' he says, 'but the Predominance of Race?'

"Everything that is happening to-day in Europe proves this to be essentially true.

"This racial evil of imperialism is found in its acutest form not in India itself, but in those parts of the world to which Indians have gone as settlers. For nearly three million Indians are now living in different parts of the world outside India, and if those in Burma are added this number must be doubled. They are to be found scattered abroad in almost every land, and where the white race confronts them, it tends to react against them. It excludes them, if possible, as a menace and a public danger, fearing their virtues of thrift and industry even more than their vices.

"There are laws which prevent any further admission of Indians, even though they are British subjects. In certain cases, where they have already been admitted and have gained the right of domicile, they have been prevented from having a vote. They are also brought up against the social barrier of the colour bar, which confronts them at every turn. Vast areas of the British Dominions are in this way closed against Indians for residence, though these lands are empty while India is crowded. Therefore it is a hollow mockery to ask Indians to take pride in the 'Empire,' when they are excluded by the strictest anti-Asiatic regulations from residing in two-thirds of it.

II

"It is this unjust racial discrimination, inflicted on Indians outside India itself, that has most of all poisoned the springs of human-kindness and tainted the sources of good fellowship. Therefore it is no cause for wonder that extreme resentment has filled the hearts of those who have travelled and settled abroad. For the treatment meted out to them has often been disgraceful. Whether on board ship, or on the railway train, at hotels, restaurants and lodgings, at frontiers and places of embarkation, the Indian traveller is in danger, at a moment's notice, of having to submit to some insult, often in front of those who look on with open scorn and contempt.

"One of my Indian friends, whose special duties compelled him to travel, told me that while he had met with kindly people on his journeys, yet the slights from which he had been made to suffer had caused him to be perpetually on the alert. He could never tell from what quarter the same mischief would return. He assured me that he would not stay a day longer in the place where he lived abroad, if his livelihood and that of his family were not dependent on it.

"When I asked him in what countries he was most badly treated, he first of all put to me the question whether I wished to know the truth; and when I pressed him to tell me the whole truth, and nothing but the truth, he replied that the Anglo-Saxon, in his opinion, was the worst offender. It was no protection to himself, but rather the reverse, to be a British subject. While he gave generous credit to the English people in their own homes, and praised their hospitality, he could not give the same character to the Anglo-Saxon race when they went abroad.

" There, he told me with sadness, they seemed to lose all their kindly feeling and to bow too easily to the convention of the place where they were stationed. Only a few held out bravely against the current of their surroundings when the final test came.

III

" The height and depth of this human tragedy (for it is nothing less) lie in the historical fact that the Indian people have inherited a civilisation that makes them intellectually and spiritually among the leading peoples of mankind. Their Emperor Asoka, more than two centuries before the birth of Christ, had established a genuine love of peace and a profound aversion from the cruel bloodshed of war in the hearts of his own people all over the north of India. This created a repulsion against every form of violence, which has remained strong right up to the present time.

" The influence of the Buddhist Movement, which he championed, spread as far as Ceylon and Burma, and also to the island of Java and the farther East. Thus, the Indian people have still deep within them an old inherited instinct which makes them abhor brute force. They have also carried the same peaceable and reasonable temper with them into their daily lives. Such characteristics place them very high in the scale of human values as an ancient civilised people, who have maintained up to the present time the true inner life of the spirit.

"Since this can be proved historically, the claim made by the white race to-day, to be superior in every respect, bears no relation at all to the spiritual realities underlying human history. The mere possession by Europeans of deadly weapons of precision carries with it no *moral* standing as a ground whereon to base the racial supremacy that is now being claimed.

IV

"As Christians we have been very greatly distressed of late by a strange racialism springing up in a neighbouring country. Germany had become very dear to us on account of its evangelical devotion to Christ whom we worship. We are startled, therefore, by the sudden reversion to a racial cult, even among those who still profess and call themselves Christians. Our hearts go out to those who are fighting the good fight of faith against tremendous odds, in order to bring back the Christian religion from racial narrowness to its first principles of racial fellowship.

"Yet our own Anglo-Saxon intolerance should give us pause and be no less disturbing to us. For as soon as ever we leave England, with its higher Christian ideals, we seem at once to assume a domination over other races, and even to institute a 'white race' creed, with ceremonies and formulas which deny altogether the unity of mankind in Christ. We erect our 'white churches' wherein no coloured person is welcomed. We tell the non-white races to worship in churches of their own. Thus we have brought wilfully these racial distinctions within the fold of Christ.

"On one occasion, while I was staying in Durban, a young Indian with high qualifications as a teacher began to tell me what he had suffered since he had come out to South Africa to take up work there among his own people.

"'If only your skin,' he said to me, 'were the same colour as mine, you would soon understand in South Africa what it means to belong to a subject race. The most harassing thing of all is this, that here in Natal I can never tell from one moment to another when I am likely to be insulted; so, unconsciously, I begin to look out for some expression of ill-feeling towards me, and suspect the insult even when it is never intended. In this way, it becomes almost a second nature to me to be always on my guard.'

"'Tell me," I asked, 'how this extreme sensitiveness first arose.'

"'One day,' he said, 'not long after I had come out to South Africa I had to go into a post office. So I just went up to the counter, when a European came up and assaulted me. That was my first lesson. I could not retaliate nor make a scene. To do so would only have made things worse. There were other Europeans standing there, but they didn't interfere or take my side. When such a thing as this has happened once, if you are very sensitive, you find yourself suspecting that it will happen again at any moment.

" 'There are, of course, good Europeans in South Africa who are ashamed at such incidents, but there are others who are on the watch in order to keep, as they call it, " the coloured man in his place."

" 'In earlier days, when I was at home in India, I was glad that my country was linked with Britain, where freedom was so highly honoured. It is true I had received now and then haughty treatment from Englishmen whom I had met. But I had been brought up in a Mission College and my teachers there treated me as a friend. It is true, also, that my own people had told me what to expect when I went out as a teacher to South Africa. But somehow I didn't understand the full meaning of what they said, till I came out and saw it for myself. On the way, I stayed for a short time in Kenya, and there things are just as bad as in Natal. The very look in the white man's face is one of domineering superiority. He lets you know all the while that Kenya is "a white man's country," and that the Indian is an intruder.

" 'I must confess,' he went on to tell me, 'I never understood before how guilty we were in India for treating our own depressed classes as "untouchables." I don't think I ever seriously offended in that respect, except for the fact that I didn't openly protest against it—taking it all for granted. Here in Natal, however, we ourselves have become "untouchables"! We cannot travel in the same railway compartments with Europeans, and we are plainly told that we must not mix with them. Sometimes when we invite Europeans to our social functions a few come, but they usually sit apart, as if they were doing us a favour, and there is nothing that hurts us more than being "patronised." They hardly ever invite us back in return. We are "pariahs" out here, and we feel it most acutely. I would not stay a day longer in Natal, if I had not signed a contract.'

VI

"An incident from my own experience in South Africa may illustrate what he said; for my thoughts went back, as he spoke, to what once happened in the railway station at Johannesburg. I was travelling alone, and had already reserved a seat on the train. Ramdas, Mahatma Gandhi's son, had come to see me off, and was taking my small bag into the compartment, when a European schoolboy, on his way back to school after the holidays, lifted up his hand to strike Ramdas for entering that part of the train. Only just in time I caught hold of the boy and prevented the blow from being struck. The lad looked back on me with surprise. He could hardly imagine being prevented by a white man from thus dealing with a 'coloured' person.

"But this was by no means the worst thing which I had to encounter on first coming out to South Africa, for I found that even the Churches were tainted through and through with the same colour prejudice, so that there were 'white' and 'black' churches. Indian Christians were not allowed to sit with European Christians in many of these so-called Christian churches.

"Thank God, things have altered for the better since those evil days. The Student Christian and Oxford Group Movements in South Africa have already accomplished wonderful things. But even among earnest Christians, who sincerely profess the name of Christ, many further changes have yet to be made before the House of God is wholly cleansed from impurities and scandals of this kind.

VII

"It would be quite easy for me to fill a book with narratives concerning disgraceful happenings like these which I have witnessed on a hundred journeys in all parts of the world; and I have suffered many untoward incidents for protesting against such treatment. In this way I have learnt by bitter experience to understand the sufferings which Indians themselves have been called upon to endure. While, every now and then, we can register some improvement, and can be deeply thankful to see a change for the better, yet on other sides things appear to be going back instead of forward.

"In London, for instance, the metropolis of the British Commonwealth, where in earlier times there was no serious infection, the epidemic of white race prejudice has begun to spread in wider and wider circles. Both Indians and Africans have been treated in an insulting manner, and instances of such conduct appear to be multiplying. The Christian conscience has been unable hitherto to overtake this growing evil, and Christian public opinion has seemed almost indifferent, even when outrageous things have happened.

"It may be argued that such treatment would still go on, and insults would have to be endured —the world being what it is—even if India were free. But this is not borne out by the facts. The Japanese, who are a free people, very rarely suffer such treatment as Indians have to endure, and the reason is obvious. Once, in Durban, an insult was offered to some Japanese sailors who had gone on shore, but immediately a public apology was made. The incident has never happened again. Yet with Indians, although they are British subjects no such apology would be thought of. Indeed, in their case, the very words 'subject' and 'subjection' appear to run together. Every Indian believes that if his country were free he would be an enfranchised citizen of the world, and receive and give respect in an entirely different manner. Those who have never been held in subjection cannot even imagine how the iron enters into the soul and corrupts the inner life.

" The European who brutally assaults a member of another race, when he cannot retaliate, is a coward and a bully. He takes advantage of the fact that the other person is unable to hit back. As the world goes at present, the forceful retention in subjection of another race which is gentle and refined, and at the same time helpless, sets a premium on bullying in the race that rules. The evil of such subjection does not stop with those who are thus ruled over. As I have already shown the evil that is even more deadly is the deterioration which takes place in the character of the foreigner who rules.

" Every one has noticed the change which takes place in this respect in the character of an Englishman who goes out East. At first he behaves himself like a gentleman. After that, this race imperialism seems to get into his very blood, and so subtle is the poison that he is hardly aware of the demoralisation that has taken place.

" The main thesis, therefore, that Indians would put forward is this, that only when India herself is a free nation will they be able to possess the full inner sense of personal freedom. For then they will be able to meet the British everywhere on equal terms and receive equal treatment from them. All the present 'patronising' on the one hand, and 'bullying' on the other, will cease. Then and then only a healthy friendship between members of the two countries will be made possible.

"Once I was giving a lesson on some of the simpler English poems in a junior class at St Stephen's College, Delhi. We were learning by heart 'The Village Blacksmith.' After the English class was over, one of my students, who was best of all at games and athletics, said to me, 'Sir, there is one line in that poem which I keep repeating to myself ever since you taught it to us.'

"'What is it?' I asked.

"'It is that line, sir,' he said to me, 'where it says about the blacksmith,

> He looks the whole world in the face.

We shall never be able to do that until India is free.'

VIII

" The phrase 'Helots of the Empire' has been ascribed by Indians themselves to their own position within the British dominions. When a faint protest is made against such a title, the Indian answer is that it is far better to face the stark realities of life than to be fooled with specious phrases. For the word 'Helot' represents the glaring fact that Indians have not been welcomed as yet as racial equals, but only as 'hewers of wood and drawers of water.'

"Mahatma Gandhi has often pointed out, in his campaign to remove 'Untouchability,' that Hindus belonging to the higher castes have deserved to suffer in South Africa from the same indignities which they themselves have heaped upon others in their own country. He is quite unsparing in his condemnation of racial segregation whenever he meets with it among his own people, and his efforts have already been rewarded by encouraging results. The whole system of 'Untouchability' in India appears to be tottering to its fall. His stern and salutary teaching concerning the treatment of Indians as 'untouchables' in South Africa has been taken to heart.

"But while this act of noble reparation towards their own fellow-countrymen is being made by Indians themselves, it is surely a sorrow, too deep for words, that the Christian Church should be unable to rise to the height of a great occasion. For it is nothing less than a moral defeat that those who profess to follow the teaching of Christ should be busily occupied in building up a 'white race' religion within the bounds of Christendom itself.

"For those in Great Britain and the Dominions who have imagination and insight, it must surely be plain that things like this cannot go on indefinitely without an explosion far greater than anything that has been witnessed in the past. For India is slowly and painfully realising what these things mean, and her marvellous patience will in the end become exhausted. When she has got rid, from within, of her own evil of 'Untouchability,' she will feel all the more intensely the wrongs that are done to her by others."

IX

When I had finished the paper Alan said with much feeling, "I never thought for a moment that things were as bad as that."

"Nor I," said Neil Munro.

"What I should like to do," said I, "would be to examine the Christian principles which are entirely opposed to this imperialism, and also to consider whether they are put into practice."

This was agreed by every one present.

CHAPTER VIII

THE CHRISTIAN ATTITUDE

I

"PLEASE don't think for a moment," said Mohanlal, "that our real quarrel is with Christ and His teaching. We revere Him with all our hearts. There's not an Indian to-day who would speak a word against Him. But we don't find His teaching carried out in practice."

Mulchand agreed and so did Safdar Ali. Christ, he declared, was a Prophet. The Quran called Him the "Word of God." But though He was born in Asia, many Christians in their hearts despised the East. They would have rejected Christ if He had been born in the East to-day and had come in lowly guise to Europe from Asia.

"The Germans who follow Hitler," said Anil, "and believe in race supremacy and the policy of force are honest in their professions. They despise the Jews who come from the East, and so they have gone back to racialism pure and simple. Ludendorff was only telling the truth when he said he was not a Christian! But the British who go abroad, full of racial prejudice and altogether believing in violence, insist on calling themselves Christians; and yet they never carry out Christ's teaching."

"That may be," said Alan sadly, "but, in India, can you tell me why there is often a bitterness even against the missionaries, who are such self-sacrificing men and women? I am hoping to go out to the East as a medical missionary, and you know how Christ is all in all to me. I want you frankly to explain to me, Anil, what the missionaries have done to give offence."

"We've nothing whatever against *you*, Alan," said Anil, "and medical missionaries, who quietly carry on their Christ-like work, are loved by us for their pure goodness. But there are others, who come out and soon become members of the dominant race; they domineer and interfere and always want to put us right. They think of us as heathen and even speak evil of our religion. Christ would never have done that! Then they go back home and paint everything in the darkest colours. They are thus doing harm to our cause as a people struggling to be free, and are in league with the imperialists who want to keep us in subjection."

"Only think for a minute," said Mohanlal, "what happens when sermons presenting the darker side of Indian life are delivered year after year in England. It's like the dropping of water on a stone. It wears the stone away. These missionaries are, as you say, self-sacrificing people; they are, therefore, trusted far more than Miss Mayo was. For every one took her as a sensation, and most of us just read over what she had to say and then forgot all about it. People knew she hadn't spent her whole life in India. But these missionaries have done so. That's where the trouble comes. Their word carries more weight."

"You wouldn't have them," asked Neil, "hide things from us, would you? We're not babies!"

"Not at all," said Mohanlal, "but we *do* claim that what is good should be appreciated. *You* wouldn't like all the foul things that are happening to-day in the slums of London to be placarded in India, while nothing is said about the beauties of English home life and the purity of English home ideals."

"I see the point," said Neil. "To tell you the truth I couldn't stand Miss Mayo, so I'm altogether with you there."

"Can't you do anything to stop this one-sided propaganda?" asked Anil. "Somewhere I read a passage of Tagore about the missionaries, which seemed to put the whole of our case in a single sentence. 'We honour,' he wrote, 'the beauty of the character of Christ, and we admire His teaching in the Sermon on the Mount, but we feel indignant when His followers go back to the West and openly misrepresent us. That is not Christ-like.' What Tagore says there is true. It's not Christ-like. Don't you see what harm is being done to your own Christian religion? You come to our shores as our guests, and we freely offer you our hospitality. At least, you should show us the same courtesy in return by putting our case forward impartially when you go home. But when you draw a lurid picture of everything evil and call that 'India,' those who listen naturally begin to question whether it is wise and safe to grant full self-governing powers to us, if things are as bad as they have been painted."

II

"Do let me say something on that point," I pleaded. "Most missionaries, I believe, would frankly acknowledge the wrong that was done by such one-sided propaganda in the past. They started, unfortunately, with a conventional mode of speech, due to bad theology, and this has terribly handicapped them ever since. I read the other day some words of the first Lord Minto, written at the very beginning of last century, and I copied them down. Here they are: 'Pray read,' he said, 'this miserable stuff addressed to the Gentoos (pagans), in which the pages are filled with hell-fire, and hell-fire, and still hotter fire, denounced against a whole race of men for believing in the religion which they were taught by their fathers and mothers. Is *this* the doctrine of our Christian Faith?'

"That was written," I continued, "more than a century ago, and this 'miserable stuff,' as he rightly calls it, was repeated for a long while afterwards. I had the painful task of wading through many volumes of old missionary literature, and found the same dark picture being drawn all along. There was no attempt at any Christian appreciation of the village life of India, that was blossoming all around with singular beauty. Christ said, 'Consider the lilies how they grow,' and in village homes of India there was always to be witnessed a gentleness of human goodness unspoilt by that luxury of wealth which He sternly condemned. Just as in Galilee, so all around them there were innocent children in Indian homes, whom Christ would have taken in His arms and blessed. There were also the flowers of the field and the birds of the air, from which He would have drawn His lessons of simple trust in God. But they seem to have ignored all this when drawing their dark picture."

"We in India," said Safdar Ali, "love that part of Christ's teaching about the lilies of the field."

"Yes," I said, "you understand it. I remember on one occasion, when I had been picking some blossoms from a flowering tree, a simple village woman rebuked me saying, 'When the blossom falls to the ground, God gives it to you to take home and use for worship. Why do you tear it from the tree? The flower has as much right to live its own life as you.' That rebuke went home to my heart, and I have grown more tender towards God's flowers ever since. This village life of India, so similar to that in the midst of which Christ was born, was before their eyes in those earlier days when the missionaries first came to India; but many of them seem to have been blinded by a narrow creed, which they called the religion of Jesus. What a mockery! Fancy St Francis of Assisi, who came nearest of all to Christ, talking as they did! It would be unthinkable!"

"Surely," said Neil, "the missionaries weren't all of that character. Dr Duff for instance, who was the friend of Raja Ram Mohan Roy; Dr Pennell of the Frontier; Dr Miller of Madras, and a hundred others."

"Ah!" exclaimed Mohanlal, "Dr Miller was a *rishi* (saint). His pupils are to be found all over India. *He* never went home to Scotland and slandered us behind our backs."

"No indeed," I said, "and I think you'll find that, as the nineteenth century advanced, a much more generous type of missionary came out to India who tried to recognise the beauty in all they saw around them, without minimising the evil. Some of the finest appreciation of Hindu religious poetry has come recently from the missionaries themselves, and I have read noble tributes to Islam also. Times have changed."

"But there's one thing," said Safdar Ali, "that still goes on and we can't stand it. We've read about Christ, how, like our own Prophet, during the days when persecution was abroad, He had not even a place whereon to lay His head. He was humble and simple. But some of those who seek to represent Him in our country live in large bungalows with lots of servants, who are rude to us and make us sit in the verandah till the 'Sahib' invites us to come into his office; and when we go into his presence, he treats us as inferiors. Christ never lived like that or treated people who came to Him in that way!"

"Safdar," I protested, "that's an old story. Surely, it hardly ever happens to-day, does it? I thought such treatment had vanished long ago."

Safdar was by no means as certain as I was. "You don't know," he said to me, "how many of us have been hurt by such treatment, when we never expected it."

III

"Shall I speak very frankly indeed?" asked Anil.

"Do, by all means," said I; "the franker the better."

"The World War," said Anil, "destroyed all our respect for the Christian West. When Christian brothers killed one another and Christian sisters sang hymns of hate, we said to ourselves that the West hadn't even begun to understand what Christ taught. We had in Calcutta a young Bengali poet, Satyendra Nath Datta, who died soon after the War. One of his last poems was called 'Christmas Day.' He wrote in it:

Come, Lord Christ, come to this Asia of ours,
  There is no place for you in Europe.
Bring your message to us in Asia:
  Our heavy-laden hearts will find comfort in you.

He was not a Christian, according to your way of thinking, but he was a much better Christian than those in Europe who were shedding one another's blood. Do please forgive me, if I've gone too far; but you asked me to be frank, and I've taken you at your word."

"Anil," said John Murray, "we respect you all the more when you hit us hard like that! We much prefer that to the way some of you—not you, personally—say nice things about us, just to flatter us."

IV

"I can't tell you how glad I am," said Alan, "that we've had this talk together, and I owe a debt to you, Anil!"

"Yes, I agree with you," said I, "but what we want now to consider is the attitude of Christ Himself towards these racial problems. As I interpret the story of the Gospel, He came into our midst to break down these racial barriers and do away with these hard and fast distinctions between man and man."

"And between man and woman also," said Alan. "He took woman, from the very first, as man's equal."

"Yes, indeed," said I, "and what a place in His heart He gave to little children! He loved the beauties of Nature and called us God's sons and daughters. All this was utterly contrary to the sour religion of the Pharisees, whom He condemned. It came from His absolute sense of union with the Father. 'I and my Father are one,' He said; and again, 'One is your Father, and all ye are brethren.' There cannot be any doubt as to what His standard was. He was universal. Look at this great word, 'He that doeth the will of God, the same is my mother and my sister and my brother.'"

"Why, that surely is the essence of Islam!" said Safdar. "Did Christ say that?"

"The amazing thing is to see how simple these utterances are. They can so easily be understood and yet they are so profound. They are like the deep, fundamental laws of the Universe. The noblest example of His teaching," I went on, "is that of the early Christians themselves, who suffered martyrdom for what they believed and practised. The Apostle Paul spent a whole lifetime in breaking down the worst barrier of all in the ancient world between Jew and Gentile. Even Peter, at first, could not get over that barrier and sit down sensibly to eat and drink with those of another race."

"We're still in that backward state in India," said Anil, "with 'Hindu pāni' (water) and 'Musalmān pāni,' being called out at every railway station."

"That cry makes my blood boil!" said Abdul Majid.

"And mine also," echoed Mulchand.

"Yes," I added, "and I have to confess that in South Africa and other places, Christians are just as bad. In Capetown, for instance, or Durban, you will find teashops, with notices written up, 'For Europeans only,' and I well remember the row we had when I took an Indian friend into one of them by mistake!"

"Why, even in London," said Safdar, "that kind of thing is beginning. The Americans from the southern United States, and Europeans from South Africa, have started it. We go to a lodging house, where there's a notice, 'Apartments to Let'; but when the landlady sees that we're Indian she says that she's so sorry her last room has been taken, and we know all the while it's untrue."

V

"I would like to tell you," said Mulchand, "an incident in my own life, which made all the difference to me."

"Do, please," said Alan eagerly. "It would help the discussion and bring it to the point."

"I know you'll pardon me," said Mulchand, somewhat timidly, "if I speak out from my heart, as Anil did. First of all, I would like to tell you how deeply we feel pained when the missionary calls our sacred religion 'heathen.' We have dropped the insulting word 'mlechcha' on our side; but we still hear this word 'heathen' from yours. We recognise at once any man of religion when he is lowly, as Christ was lowly; and considerate to others, as He was. But we don't recognise as true followers of Christ, those who come out as strangers to our shores and despise us and expect every one to bow down to them. We used to have respect for Englishmen once, but we have very little left after what we have seen and heard."

"What made the difference?" asked Neil Munro.

"First of all, as Anil has told you, the World War; then Amritsar and the 'crawling order,' and then the brutal *lathi* charges which were ordered by European officers in Bombay. These have destroyed the old respect. They made us quite certain that the West believes in violence. That's what Young India thinks to-day."

"But let's have this incident in your own life," said Alan. "Tell us that."

"I was obliged to begin in a round-about way," said Mulchand, with more confidence, "just to show you what made me reject your so-called Christianity, which has come to us from the West. I had been deeply drawn in my heart by the portrait of Christ in the Gospels; and I once saw a picture of His face which also drew my heart strangely towards Him, as the Man of Sorrows, forsaken on the Cross, and yet pleading with His dying lips, 'Father, forgive them.' That prayer so moved me that I kept on repeating it to myself—'Father, forgive them.' Christ's face of love and sorrow, as He said those words, quite haunted me."

"What then?" asked Alan.

"It was just at a time like this that I came more closely into touch with Englishmen than I had ever done before. At first I was very greatly attracted by them, especially by one who often spoke to me about Christ. He was very friendly and kind. Up to that time I had kept to my own Indian dress, because I loved everything that belonged to my own country. I mention this, because it led to the incident I am now going to relate. One night I was travelling by train all alone in Indian dress, when an Englishman came to the door of my compartment and ordered me out. He wanted the carriage to himself. He said, with great rudeness, that he objected to travelling with a 'native.' The stationmaster asked me to give way in order to avoid a disturbance, and I weakly consented to do so. But the insult, right in front of the people who had collected round me, had gone very deep, and my mind was on fire. That fire raged within me all through the night, and I tried to pray, 'Father, forgive him,' but it was too hard for me."

"You should *never* have given way to him like that!" said Abdul Majid, hotly.

"Yes, that rankled most of all: but—do you know?—my heart is still bitter, whenever I think of what happened, and I can't get over it even yet, though it occurred many years ago."

"Mulchand," said Alan, with pain in his eyes as he spoke, "I'd do *anything* to make up for that insult, if I only knew how to do it! But aren't you too hard on us Christians, to judge us by that single incident ? "

" You're right," said Mulchand, " I know I oughtn't to dwell on it ; but these things can't be settled by any logic, or rational way of thinking. The wound somehow remains open, and even your own friendship and the freedom here at Oxford haven't been able to cure it."

Every one had listened in silence, with the exception of Abdul's sharp interruption. Mulchand then went one step further. " May I add just one word ? " he asked, making a great effort. " This is how I look at it. So long as you continue with your Colour Bar and your 'white' churches, where only white men may enter, it seems clear to me that the Christian religion can never heal this running sore of the world. For *we* shall never be able to look you in the face till we have thrown aside our 'Colour Bar' ; and *you* will never be able to look us in the face till you've done the same ! "

VI

" Don't you think, after all, that things are really getting better ? " Neil Munro asked, with an anxious look. He was fervently patriotic in religious matters as well as in political affairs, and could hardly bear to listen while Mulchand was speaking.

Some of those present were quite certain that the younger generation was throwing religion aside altogether and including with it the excessive nationalism of the past—just like garments which had become outworn. Others said that the general feeling was becoming more bitter and that the racial spirit was rising.

"Look at the continent of Europe," said John Murray. "Surely racialism is worse than ever, and we shall soon have to fight once more against it as they did in the early days of Christian martyrdom. The world's gone back since the War, not forward—at least, as far as Europe is concerned."

"Asia's just as bad," said Mohanlal. Safdar agreed, but declared that Islam was attacking these things all along the line, while other religions were only standing still. This appeared to be leading to controversy, when Anil interrupted.

"Oh, what an awful mess we're in," he said in disgust. "When shall we get rid of it all and live like decent, rational human beings? Sometimes I'm almost ready to throw over religion altogether, and call it the dope of the common people."

"What on earth would be the good of that?" said Neil. "That would only make matters worse and drive us back into despair. None of us here could ever go that way. No, what's needed is to purify religion—not to cast away the greatest gift which God has given us."

Anil still looked doubtful. The iron had entered deep. He detested the irrational element in man.

VII

" May I tell you one thing," said Mohanlal. " If only this hateful racial stumbling-block, in all its different forms—religious as well as political—were removed, and we were ready to treat one another as simple human beings requiring sympathy, it would revolutionise the whole world."

At this point the discussion closed. " There's still something about India on the same subject," I urged, " that I haven't yet written down. It will explain the disabilities under which Indians suffer in different parts of the world, owing to this evil. I don't like to let go this central moral issue until the whole case has been made so abundantly clear that it can never be forgotten. So, if it's no burden to you, I'll put this also in writing and get it sent round before our next gathering. Then, when we meet, we shall be able to take up the economic aspect, which in some respects brings to the surface new moral issues still more fundamental."

The following chapter contains the short paper which I wrote, setting out in detail certain facts about the Colour Bar.

CHAPTER IX

THE COLOUR BAR

I

MY third paper read as follows:

"The incessant indignities from which Indians suffer abroad, owing to the Colour Bar, have become familiar as household words in the homes of Indians themselves. Things that are happening in Africa reach Bombay through those who travel to and fro across the Indian Ocean. The Press is full of them. Public meetings are held about them. Thus what Indians suffer in those countries goes directly to reinforce the bitter sense of subjection which is felt in India itself. While the situation which I have described in this paper has shown some signs of improvement in recent years, the Colour Bar still remains.

"'Only when India is free,' the well-known saying runs, 'will Indians in other lands be respected as citizens of a free nation.'

"The racial insults which have been inflicted upon Indians abroad are one of the most potent causes of political unrest. People in Great Britain do not in the least understand what it means for Indians to be treated as unwanted and unwelcome in almost every part of the King's dominions.

"When, in November 1913, a flagrant act of injustice in Natal led on to the shooting of Indians on a sugar estate, the resentment aroused in India brought about a grave crisis. Mr Gokhale, who was careful in his use of words, declared that no outburst of public feeling had ever reached such an explosive pitch since the Mutiny.

"When, again, ten years later, in 1923, the British settlers in East Africa threatened to take up their rifles and 'drive the Indians into the sea,' the excitement all over India became so intense that only the immediate summons of the different parties to London prevented an irreparable disaster.

II

"The history of the first emigration of Indians abroad in large numbers, which happened just a hundred years ago, is full of tragedy. The humiliation of it can never be forgotten by those who love the good name of their country.

"For when slavery was finally abolished, in 1833, a crisis followed in the colonies where slave labour had hitherto been employed. The emancipated slaves refused to go back to work on the sugar plantations, because this labour carried with it still the old stigma of slavery. Therefore, in order to save the sugar industry from extinction, the Governor-General was induced to allow indentured labour to be recruited in Indian villages for the colonial sugar plantations. Mauritius was the first colony to receive this Indian labour, in 1835. After this the system spread to other colonies also. Thousands of Indian villagers were sent out year after year. They were despatched in what were called 'coolie' ships to all parts of the world.

"The immoral conditions under which they lived in their barracks, called 'coolie lines,' were appalling. This was due to the extreme disproportion of women and the lack of married couples. Sexual jealousies arose. Suicides and murders were frequent. All the brutalities of the old slave days reproduced themselves wherever the employer himself was a hard taskmaster; for he had almost unlimited power. Adequate government inspection became practically impossible. Labourers who suffered from bad treatment were terrorised into silence.

"There were good masters as well as bad. Under the former the labourers' lot was often a happy one. Many also settled down in the colony after the indenture was over. But the accumulation of misery and moral evil was immense.

"That such a system—inevitably carrying with it the old stigma of slavery—should have been imposed upon India by Great Britain, so soon after the slave traffic was abolished, and should have gone on for over eighty years, shows very plainly indeed in what low esteem Indians were held. Sir William Hunter, the historian, has called the system 'semi-servile'; and that is what it really was, in its degrading features.

"The struggle to obtain its abolition was a very painful and arduous one. Indians of all classes took an honourable part in it. Above all, the leading women of India, ladies of high rank from every province, indignant at the treatment meted out to their own sisters, actively supported abolition. They went to the Viceroy in person and held meetings all over the country.

"It is also good to note that the women of Australia, who had been shocked at the evil conditions of Indian labour in Fiji, helped nobly in the final stages of the struggle. The Abolition, which came on 1st January 1920, is a red-letter day in Indian history. Thank God, the whole evil thing, which was an offence against humanity, has now been banished from the earth for ever, just as slavery had been banished in 1833.

"But its after-effects cannot be so quickly remedied. For just at a time when it was pre-eminently necessary to raise high the reputation of India among the nations the spectacle of Indian 'coolie' labour, working in the old slave-cultivated colonial plantations, dragged it down.

III

"When Mohandas Karamchand Gandhi, who had been called to the Bar at Lincoln's Inn, London, went out to South Africa, he was commonly spoken of as a 'coolie' barrister. There could hardly have been a more ignorant use of this word 'coolie' from an Indian point of view; yet Indians in South Africa, however educated, were wont to be called by this name of 'coolie,' or else 'Sammy' (a corruption of Swami), which was equally a word of contempt. All were bundled together as 'coloured people,' and any nickname was good enough for them.

"The treatment which Mr Gandhi received from the day he landed in South Africa was often so outrageous that it will hardly bear repeating. Once he was nearly lynched by an excited Durban mob, when their passions were roused by colour prejudice of the worst kind. On one occasion his life was saved by an English lady's heroism. Her name was Mrs Alexander. In his Autobiography Mr Gandhi has paid a grateful tribute to her bravery. Simply on account of his race and colour he was despised and rejected. He was even excluded from a Christian church where I was preaching. Had I known it, I should have refused to preach that sermon. The really amazing thing is this, that, in spite of all he has suffered, he has kept in his heart a very deep affection for the South African Europeans and has remained quite free from any bitterness of spirit.

"In the Transvaal, the racial prejudice against Indians is probably strongest of all. A considerable proportion of domiciled Indians are obliged to live in separate 'locations' apart from the

Europeans. The insanitary condition of these places is deplorable.

" Last year, to mention a slight incident which explains the situation, I did my utmost to obtain sanction from a municipal council in the Transvaal for the purchase of a site for an Indian school. This site was to be paid for by a generous Indian merchant. It would cost the municipality nothing, and would provide for the education of the youngest Indian children. But the elections were near at hand, and the Mayor, who was a candidate for that special ward, was not ready to advise the municipality to accept this gift.

" When I went to him about it he said that the Europeans in the neighbourhood might object to an Indian school being built near their own houses. Though I pointed out the great harm that would be done to the children if they remained uneducated, he was still unmoved. The few Europeans in the neighbourhood who had the vote might object; and he could not risk his seat. Such colossal selfishness is due to race prejudice alone; for what harm could these tiny Indian children do to the Europeans if they had a school of their own?

" In addition to these numerous disabilities a Colour Bar Act has been passed prohibiting African workmen from undertaking certain forms of skilled mechanical labour. No one yet knows how far the provisions of this Act will be extended, under the pressure of the European

Trades' Unions, which have the voting power. Already this Colour Bar Act has been applied to certain skilled work in the mines, and it has tended indirectly to affect Indian interests also. Thousands of Indians have been thrown out of employment in order to make room for what is called 'white labour.' Administrative acts of this kind, penalising on racial grounds African and Indian labour, are sinister and strange. It had been the proud boast of the British Constitution hitherto that it was free from racialism, and stood for equal justice for all races. But the whole conception of a 'Commonwealth' has been undermined by what has happened in South Africa. For it seems that a 'White Race Empire,' in which Indians are to remain in subordination under the white race, has now been substituted for it.

IV

"For many years past British Columbia has shut her own doors fast against any new Indian immigration. This exclusion of Indians was enforced at a time when only a few thousand emigrants from the north of India had made the very difficult journey by sea from Calcutta via China and Japan, to Vancouver.

"The fact that one of the finest races in the world, the Sikhs of the Punjab, had been prohibited by Canadian law from entering British Columbia has left behind a deep resentment.

The bravery and chivalry of the Sikhs is well known, and I can assert from personal knowledge that their nobility of character is equal to their bravery. Whenever I have met them abroad they have received me as their guest and admitted me to their temples. A more affectionate and generous people it would be impossible to find. Yet they were prevented for many years from bringing over their wives and children to British Columbia, even in the case of those who had obtained their domicile before the exclusion laws were passed. Only with great difficulty was this small concession obtained. Even now they are still regarded as aliens without a vote, and the Exclusion Law remains in force.

V

"The harsh treatment of Indians in Kenya has had its repercussions all over India and has led to grave political results. The whole history of British East Africa, from the time it was first annexed, on the pretext of helping Indians who were British subjects, has been one long record of hopes held out to India and then withdrawn.

"'Since South Africa,' Major Grogan declared, 'has closed the back door into Africa, so that no Indian may enter Durban, in the same manner the British in East Africa must close the front door at Mombasa.'

"If the British settlers had been successful in this racial policy, and Kenya had finally been closed against Indians, this would have meant that not only were all the larger Dominions shut out from Indian immigration, but even in tropical Africa, opposite their own shores, Indians would have had no place. Their leaders would naturally ask, 'Are you going to exclude us from the tropics as well as from the temperate zone? Of what use is your "Empire" to us, where you close every door against us and hold us in subjection?'

"At the end of the European War, in which India had provided more than a million combatants, a mischievous *Economic Commission Report* was published in Kenya, signed by Major Grogan and Lord Delamere among others, strongly advocating the full 'exclusion' policy. So libellous were its terms concerning Indian moral character that it had to be disowned by the Colonial Office. The next few years were spent in a very bitter struggle, with the wildest threats on the part of the European settlers of an armed revolt if any major concession was made to Indian interests by the Colonial Office. In the end the Highlands of Kenya were reserved exclusively for Europeans, and a new Colour Bar was thus established.

"Ever since that highly critical period, from 1919 to 1923, the racial demands of the British settlers have continued, and opportunities have been eagerly seized by them for extending their powers. Thus, Indians have found to their cost that so long as the India Office remains a subordinate department at Whitehall there can be little hope of any satisfaction. They may register one protest after another, but no sanction lies behind them. For India is a 'Dependency,' and therefore has no independence.

VI

" Mahatma Gandhi relates how at one time he 'fell in love' with the British Constitution. It held his affection, he told us, because at that time it had no place for racial or religious distinctions. Mr Sastri also was devoted to it for similar reasons; and this accounts for the pain which was in his heart when he found the Colour Bar receiving authorisation from the British Parliament in respect to the Kenya Highlands. In this connection he uttered his famous sentence, which has since become proverbial: 'If Kenya is lost, all is lost.' For should it once be proved that the exclusive racial principle has been finally established within the framework of the British Constitution, divided loyalties of the most disastrous kind are certain to occur."

CHAPTER X

INDIAN POVERTY

I

BOTH John Murray and Neil Munro were anxious to get away from the race and colour question as quickly as possible. It worried them every time it was brought forward, and had evidently got on their nerves. It seemed also to disturb, somewhere within them, a guilty conscience with regard to British imperial affairs. For it was not easy for them to use the familiar word "Commonwealth" instead of "Empire" where the Colour Bar was so pronounced.

"We agree," said Neil, with a quick gesture of his hand, "that this colour prejudice exists; but you only make matters worse by continually harping on it."

Alan at once demurred. "I'm afraid," he said, "that's rather like the ostrich putting his head in the sand. Surely, Neil, it's much better to face the music and own up where we're wrong. We'll never get these things right unless we face up to them fairly and squarely."

"It's easy enough for you," said Anil to Neil, somewhat bitterly, "to keep the skeleton locked up in the cupboard, for *you* enjoy the privileges of the white race! But we're just the opposite. We get all the kicks, while you get all the halfpence."

"At any rate," said Neil, laughing, "we've had the old skeleton out of the cupboard all the while in *this* discussion. Why, we never seem to get away from it." Then he turned to Mohanlal. "Good lord, Mohanlal," he said, "I never knew that Indians had to put up with all those things before! Empire Day can't be exactly popular with you over there, when you've been shut out from all the Dominions, except on a temporary permit."

"Oh, do let's change the subject," said John Murray, "unless Hara's got something to say about it."

"Japan," said Hara quietly, "will never be satisfied until racial equality is fully recognised as the first article in the Covenant of the League of Nations."

"Well, Hara," said Alan, "I can assure you, as far as the Union Club is concerned, we're all agreed there; for that's the basis of our existence. But I must confess to you, all the same, that the chief reason why this clause was not embodied in the Covenant was because all the British Dominions objected to it, and the United States also—in spite of the Declaration of Independence. How could Australia agree to it, with its own White Australia policy? And how could the United States, with its Asiatic Exclusion Act? Kenya also flatly denied it."

"What about Japan herself?" asked Neil.

" What about racial equality in your own Empire, Hara ? Do you mean to say that you're advocating racial equality in North China, Korea and Manchuria ? "

" Yes," said Hara, " our policy has been greatly misunderstood ; just as your policy has in India."

II

It seemed best, in order to avoid a heated argument over this issue, to return at once to the question of India's poverty, which was the subject we had chosen for discussion; and this brought us face to face with the character and programme of Mahatma Gandhi. For while Abdul Majid and Mulchand represented the Congress Socialist party, the majority of those present wished most of all to understand the economic work which Mahatma Gandhi had carried forward with such remarkable success throughout the length and breadth of India.

" What is Gandhi like ? " asked Neil. " Can't you give us, first of all, some idea about his character ? "

" Very gladly," I replied, " because the man and his work are one. He is entirely absorbed in it, and that gives him his amazing driving power. The British working men and women in Lancashire and in the East End of London soon found that out. He was like one of themselves. I was with him during his visit, and they took to him at once."

"Didn't they try to mob him in Lancashire?" asked Neil. "We heard he was under police protection."

"Exactly the opposite," I answered. "The police were quite unnecessary. The Lancashire working men and women cheered him wherever he went."

"You don't know how difficult it is," said Alan, "to get correct news about him. The newspapers always make him out to be an eccentric, and repeat from time to time that his influence is on the wane."

"The wish there is father to the thought," I replied, "and it's quite untrue. He remains, just as much as ever, the one man in India whom the masses in the villages revere and obey."

"Surely," said John Murray, "his economic programme, of substituting hand-spinning in the villages for mill-yarn, is quite absurd. There he seems to us to be an idealist, like Ruskin, looking back to a Golden Age which can never be repeated."

"On the contrary," I replied, "in very many things I've found him to be a pioneer blazing a trail into the future. It's true he's intensely conservative and looks back to the past for his inspiration. But he's also ultra-modern, and adores science when it can show him how to raise the level of the life of the poor."

"But he'd do away with all machinery, wouldn't he?" asked Alan. "At least that's what we're told."

"There again you've been told wrong," I answered. "He'd welcome electricity in every village, if it could raise the power of village production and keep the villager in pure country air, eating wholesome country food. Have you ever thought of the absurdity of our own 'machine' existence in Europe, wherein more than twenty million workers, who have been sucked into the towns, are unemployed, and the country villages are becoming deserted? Gandhi is dealing with that whole problem of unemployment. He regards it as unnatural, and tries to go to the root of things, dealing with moral causes which lead to bad economic conditions. You mentioned Ruskin a moment ago. Gandhi owes one of the greatest of his inspirations to the little book *Unto This Last*. He took Ruskin for a long time as a master on these moral concerns of the economic life, just as he took Tolstoi for a master in the concerns of non-violence, which he calls *Ahimsa*."

III

"Didn't he go, once upon a time, to the Sermon on the Mount for his ideal?"

"Yes," I replied, "both to that and also to the Gita, which is his favourite Hindu Scripture. He found the Sermon on the Mount, in a living form, in Tolstoi and Ruskin. That's how things developed with him. But since those earlier days he has launched out in all kinds of creative ideas on his own account, following an inner voice which seems to warn and direct him in the way of Truth.

"Have you realised," I continued, "that Sir Daniel Hamilton, one of the shrewdest of Scotsmen and finest of Christians, immensely admires Gandhi's practical economic programme, and has constantly corresponded with him?"

"Is Gandhi a holy man, such as we read about in Indian stories?" asked Neil. "Is he one whom the villagers worship as a kind of god? Do they come to him and do *puja*? Is that where he gets his magic power from?"

"No one hates that kind of thing," I answered, "more than he does. It worries him to death, and he tries to get out of it. He is most delightfully human. Let me explain that at some length. No one enjoys being laughed at more than he does: for he has a never-failing fund of laughter always rising to the surface, and he is essentially a man of the people. He dresses in the simplest Indian village loin cloth—as a villager, not as a *sannyasi* (ascetic). He never holds himself aloof, and no one is afraid of him. His greatest friends and companions are little children, who have uproarious fun with him. Thus he is no plaster saint with a halo round his head, set on a pedestal to be admired, but a very gentle and lovable one. Like St Francis of old, he's a 'little brother of the poor,' ready to share everything he has with any one who might seem to need it more than he did himself.

"He has also," I continued, "that unique faculty which St Francis possessed, of feeling the inner suffering of another as if it were his very own. I've been with him when the pain of it has suddenly come upon him, and at such times I've realised how entirely he has identified himself with those who suffer most—especially with the outcastes, whom he calls 'God's children.'

"Because he's got no private interests to serve and no popularity to win or lose, his will remains as hard as steel when he believes that the cause he advocates is right. At such times he is as uncompromising with his own followers as he is with himself; prison and death have no terrors for him. Yet, the moment the fight is over, which he has waged on behalf of what he feels to be the truth, his heart is set upon peace. If the spirit of reconciliation is present, a settlement can be easily won from him. Thus he is a chivalrous opponent and a most loyal friend."

IV

Safdar Ali, in economic matters, was an ardent follower of Mahatma Gandhi. He believed with all his heart in what has been widely called the Khaddar (home-spun) Programme. Since this fact was well known in the Union Club, we turned to him at this point and asked him to explain Gandhi's position.

"To put it briefly," he said, "India must, by its very geography, be always an agricultural country. Its mineral resources are not great, but its supplies of sun and rain are abundant. There are rich alluvial plains, covering hundreds of thousands of square miles, not only in the great Ganges Delta itself, but also in the south and west and north. This alluvial soil, exposed to the sun and watered by the monsoon, seems to recover its fertility with amazing rapidity year after year. It can be made still more fertile by modern scientific methods. Gandhi by no means refuses to utilise these methods, provided they are within the means and competence of village people. This is his one and only test."

"Would he use tractors, as they do in Siberia and Russia?" asked John Murray.

"No," said Safdar, "the Indian village conditions are entirely different. Siberia is a vast wilderness of uncultivated land, India is a closely cultivated area with a dense village population. Any large use of tractors would at once throw out of employment hundreds of thousands of villagers, and drive them into the slums of Calcutta, Bombay and Madras."

"Let's get back to the Khaddar argument," said Alan. "We want very badly to get the picture of that home-spun industry and understand how it helps the poor people."

"Mahatma Gandhi," Safdar continued, "holds that the Indian villagers have all the moral qualities needed for carrying out practical agriculture in a wholesome and worthy fashion.

They are God-fearing, industrious and thrifty; inured to hard country fare and able to bear the hot climate. In the past they have shown themselves capable of maintaining a level of prosperity which is strangely lacking to-day. They are peace-loving, in a world of strife. The different conquerors who have swept over their country were not able, in former times, permanently to reduce their standard of living, though it sank from time to time. For as soon as ever the tyranny was over, they started to thrive again."

"What about the British?" asked Alan. "Were they just the same as the rest?"

"The British penetrated much further and deeper than any who had passed over the villages of India in earlier days. According to Gandhi's estimate, they have ruinously impoverished the village workers, both physically and morally. In former times, he says, the villager had two lungs wherewith to breathe, two hands wherewith to work—Agriculture and Cottage Industries. This twofold occupation was a necessity in the Indian climate. For during the dry heat of the burning, rainless months, home industries, such as the spinning and weaving of cotton goods, alone are possible. The ground is too hard for the plough and there is little to be done in the fields. On the other hand, throughout the damp heat of the monsoon, when the ground is soft and rain is plentiful, agriculture takes up every moment."

"What about the supply of cotton?" asked Neil Munro. "Where does that come from?"

"The cotton plant has always been indigenous to India. It can be grown almost anywhere with little trouble. Therefore, the home spinning and weaving during the dry, hot months of the year used to provide clothing at a minimum expense, while the rice cultivation in the monsoon months provided food. But the Lancashire cloth came into competition everywhere with these old hand industries. Machine-made goods won their way into the Indian market by their cheapness, novelty and smoothness. Yet even then they would not have penetrated so far into the remote villages, where home-spun was still worn, if they had not received all the prestige of the East India Company to carry them forward. The Government acted, as it were, like a great salesman for the benefit of Lancashire."

"But in England also," said John Murray, "the Industrial Revolution swept away the spinning-wheel and the hand-loom."

"Yes, just what had happened earlier in England has been taking place more slowly, but no less relentlessly, in India. The only difference has been that while Britain was able to recover her economic balance owing to her mineral resources, there has hitherto been no such possibility of recovery in India. For when once the village industries had been abandoned, the poor people were bereft, as Gandhi puts it so forcibly, of one of their two lungs, and they have remained in an anæmic condition ever since. Owing to enforced idleness, they have lost many of the moral qualities which they possessed in the past."

"What has been the result of all this?" asked John.

"Since they have now got into the habit of buying their cotton cloth, instead of manufacturing it for themselves, their family income has been diminished. The vicious circle of penury, with its pitiful brood of children born only to die, has been closing in upon them, and there is little chance of escape. That circle of evil becomes still more gruesomely complete when opium and 'country liquor,' sold under Government license, are consumed by the villagers. Idleness for such a long period during the year has proved a fatal temptation, leading them to opium or drink."

"What you've told us," said Neil, "is plain common sense. There's nothing mystical or medieval about that!"

"Certainly not," said Safdar. "Gandhi's programme of hand-spinning and weaving is by no means the fantastic thing which the West has imagined it to be. It has already added millions of rupees to the villagers' yearly income, besides saving the money which they would have spent upon mill-made cloth. No one but Gandhi could have persuaded the villagers to take it up again; but since they have resumed it, there are facts and figures which prove conclusively its working value. It may have a place also in other parts of the world, which are situated as India is, with a long dry season wherein agricultural work is slack."

V

At this point an opportunity occurred to enter into the discussion with a personal experience; for I had just come back from touring with Mahatma Gandhi.

"I've actually witnessed," I said, "this recovery of villages. They were sunk in penury before and seemed almost past help, being given over to idleness and vice. Their restoration has been due solely to a faithful adherence to Mahatma Gandhi's methods. Therefore, even if he has not yet completely proved his case, he has gone a long way towards it. The very simplicity of his proposal is its greatest merit: for it can be universally applied."

"But what attitude has he adopted towards the Government?" asked Hara, who had listened with attention.

"So eager has he been," I replied, "to help the villagers that more than once, even when non-co-operating, he has offered to co-operate with the Government if it would side with him in this vital concern. He has added one further demand, that the spread of the drug and liquor habits, which have been encouraged rather than repressed by the Government licensing system, should be stopped.

VI

"It is interesting to note how rapidly these ideas have gained ground. While in earlier days Mahatma Gandhi was almost alone in his appeal, he has steadily gained support owing to the sound wisdom of his proposals. One example may suffice. Sir George Schuster, the late Finance Member of the Viceroy's Council, speaking at the Royal Society of Arts on the prospects of Indian economic life, said:

"I have always dwelt on the disadvantages of huge urban industrial concentrations, and expressed my doubt as to whether India made any gain for her people in the truest sense by finding employment for a few hundred thousands in this way. I must confess that I have always had great sympathy with some of Mr Gandhi's economic ideas—though it seems to me that his particular proposal of reverting to the hand spinning-wheel involved so great a departure from economic methods of production as to make it impossible on a large scale. But would it not be possible to achieve essentially the same object in a manner that would not be open to this criticism? . . . I should like to see agriculture supplemented by moderate-sized industrial establishments.

"If such a declaration from a Finance Member of the Government of India does not go the whole way with Mahatma Gandhi, it at least generously acknowledges the soundness of the principle for which he is always working, namely the supplementing of agriculture with village industries. Assuming that Sir George Schuster had been able to obtain Mahatma Gandhi's first-hand knowledge of the extreme simplicity of Indian village life, he might have been inclined to consider even such a primitive method of industry as hand-spinning. In the far north of Scotland, in Norway and Iceland, the spinning-wheel is still used to produce a beautiful yarn, which can be woven into hand-made cloth more durable than that which is made in the mills. The hours of the long dark winter evenings are used in this manner, just as in India the long hot days of the dry weather may be employed for the same purpose."

VII

We all felt that we had entered into a new region of thought based upon a living experience. We should need to consider what we had heard before coming to any practical conclusion. In the end, British rule would be morally judged by the two supreme tests—

1. Whether the daily lot of the millions of peasants had been made easier or harder to bear.

2. Whether the inner resources of the mind and will had become strengthened or weakened.

We decided to meet again, and if possible to gain the help of an economist who had made a special study of Indian affairs.

CHAPTER XI

THE PRICE OF FOREIGN RULE

I

JOHN MURRAY was studying "Economics" at Balliol, and he had brought with him to our meeting an economist, with a good book knowledge of India. His name was Bruce Martin. As a new-comer, he had gone carefully through the minutes of the previous argument. He told us that he had been impressed most of all by what had been written about the moral evils caused by foreign rule. Strangely enough, these had not attracted his attention seriously before.

"I like your medical analogy," he said. "That comparison with a person who needs a stimulus in order to bring back vital circulation is a good one. From the general study I've made of the earlier period, before the British occupation, it appears to me that things had got very low indeed. You're right there, even from the economic side."

"Yet we're apt," I said, "to exaggerate, and to forget that the Indian villager was going on with his own field cultivation all the while. Many of us were astonished at the way the

French peasant continued his farm work in the rear of the trenches during the World War. I've read also, in the records of the Intelligence Department at the time of the Mutiny, how just outside the military area round Delhi there were fields ripening with a golden harvest."

"That's true," said Bruce Martin, "and I've taken it into account. But the records of the eighteenth century seem to show that in the north of India very large areas had gone out of cultivation altogether. It was something like certain districts in China to-day, with bandits let loose in all directions. One of the facts which I have noticed has been the increase in the area of cultivated land during the nineteenth century. This can't go on for ever, of course; but it has certainly staved off the evil day of over-population so far."

"But the villagers," said Anil, "have become half-starved in the process."

"Would you call the Punjabi villager half-starved?" asked Neil, turning to Anil quickly.

"No, he's an exception, though even he is getting poorer," said Anil. "But look at Orissa, Bengal, Bihar, and a great part of the United Provinces. Even to-day, as in Sir William Hunter's time, there are millions of human beings merely half-existing, who have hardly as much as a single meal of rice a day with a pinch of salt, and never know what it is to be free from hunger; who wake in the night with the pangs of hunger unrelieved. Nothing can describe the misery in those provinces, and they are lands where British rule has been long established."

"I've actually seen this tragedy," said I, "both in Orissa and Bengal. But there's one thing further that I've noticed. The worst poverty in India is mixed up with 'Untouchability.' In the United Provinces, for instance, it's the 'untouchable' who lives at such an indescribably low level. I've seen it. It is the same in South India also."

"Mahatma Gandhi," said Safdar Ali, "has fully recognised that, and for this reason he has linked all his village movements together."

"We've got somehow to find the answer," said Bruce Martin, "to the vexed question whether there has been any improvement in the lot of the poorest, who are outcaste, and therefore untouchable."

"I'm afraid there's been very little *economic* improvement hitherto," said I. "Recently I've had abundant opportunities of seeing things and forming a personal judgment. For instance, it's impossible for me ever to forget an experience I had in Orissa, where a succession of disasters had weakened the whole morale of the people. Year after year there had been either drought or flood. We had come down there to undertake relief work after one of the worst floods. Those whom we tried to help were in utter misery, looking hardly human, with their shrivelled bodies riddled through and through with disease. They had lost all courage, and wanted merely to be fed by our volunteers. It seemed almost too much for them to try even to rebuild their own huts. All desire to live had gone out of them as they clung round our rice depots, claiming relief. Our problem was to get back their inner courage and prevent the inroad of morbid despair. What the doctors call 'persistent anæmia' seemed to have set in."

"From the records," said Bruce, "I am inclined to think that the landholders in the north of India advanced in prosperity right up to the Mutiny, and even beyond it; but during the latter part of the nineteenth century other factors, such as congestion of population and excessive subdivision of the land, came in and retarded the progress already made."

"Isn't there," John asked, "something equivalent to a law of diminishing returns, which acts at once wherever the foreign ruler fails to be sensitive to the needs of the country over which he rules?"

John's phrase struck me, and I could see that it had interested Bruce also.

"You mean," I asked, "that when the first stimulating effect of foreign occupation wears off and the whole country settles down again, there is likely to come a reaction?"

"Yes," said John, "that's my point."

"I must think that out," said Bruce, "for it might mean a great deal in regard to Indian economics. These spiritual factors count for much. It isn't poverty measured in cash that is most important to register, but poverty measured in feeling."

"I can tell you one thing," said Mohanlal, "the Indian people feel now the misery from which they suffer much more than they did before."

"This matter of feeling the subjection," said Bruce, "is important. I can see it, even from the economic standpoint. A hundred years ago the British were regarded as saviours and helpers; but that character has become profoundly modified as time has gone on. That's your point, isn't it? Well, if it's true, it would make a world of difference."

II

"Mr Gandhi gives his whole case away," said Neil, suddenly changing the subject, "when he refuses to see anything good in British rule. That annoys me in him more than anything else that he does. If things were really as bad as he makes out, our rule would never have lasted all this time. It would have crumbled to pieces long ago."

"What special factors," asked Bruce, taking the Indian side of the argument, in order to test its value, "would you reckon in, while trying to make a fair estimate?"

"Surely," said Neil, "the increase of population is itself a clear proof that the conditions of life have improved." ("That's very doubtful," Bruce said in a low voice.) "Then, again, you yourself have admitted that the land area under cultivation has largely increased. Along with this, the value of the soil has gone up. Then, if you look at commerce, both exports and imports have risen in a remarkable manner, and this shows that the country is producing more, and absorbing more, than it did before. India has become one of the chief 'industrial' countries in the world."

"Aren't we really losing, rather than gaining, on our exchange of goods?" asked Anil doubtfully.

"This might have been true," said Neil, "before the Fiscal Convention came into force; for India was then bound up with the Free Trade policy of Great Britain and could not support her own growing industries. But the practice of tariff regulation during the last ten years has carried India a long way forward in the direction of financial freedom."

Anil shook his head. "I doubt it," he said. "We're only tied up afresh in other ways. There's no real freedom yet."

"Perhaps," said Neil, "the strongest argument for the recent benefit of British rule is to review the last few years and watch how India has weathered the storm. Is it possible to call a government 'satanic,' which has brought India successfully through all that crisis?"

There was much that could have been said in reply, and Neil had no first-hand knowledge of the things about which he spoke.

" Do you realise," I asked, " that India has been on the very edge of an agrarian revolution, out of sheer misery? Do you know that the indebtedness has been so great, that it has been like a mill-stone round the neck of almost every Indian peasant? We mustn't keep a blind eye, Neil, to glaring facts like these!"

III

" But what about the present situation?" Bruce asked me. " Let's stick to the main issue. You've heard my own opinion. What is your estimate?"

" My position," I told him, " as far as I have been able to think it out, is that those earlier beneficial days of British rule are now over. The good that Great Britain could do has now been accomplished. If, therefore, we still cling to power and prevent Indians, who have the capacity, from governing themselves, the good that has been done by us in the past will be turned to harm; and there are ominous signs that this is already taking place.

" No doubt," I continued, " if I'd been born in India and had passed through all these difficult years without a break, I should speak exactly as Mahatma Gandhi does. The whole vivid picture of the present evils under which

India is suffering would be thrown back into the past. But I was born in the north of England, at Newcastle-on-Tyne, and therefore I have had to keep on revising the deep-rooted traditions which were implanted in me when I was young."

"What is your opinion," Bruce asked me, "about Mr Gandhi's village programme? I've studied the theory of home-spinning very carefully, but have never been able to make up my mind about it."

"Here," I told him, "I'm wholly one with him; for his diagnosis of the disease is clearly correct."

"Do you mean," he asked, "that the villager requires a supplementary industry?"

"Yes," I replied. "But when all the blame for what has happened is laid on the Government, I'm in doubt. No! The main reason why spinning dropped out of favour in the villages was a simple one. There had come over the world a great eagerness to try the cheap articles produced by the new mills. The love of novelty is one of the deepest instincts in the human breast. A strong tide of material prosperity had swept over the world, and people thought the millennium was at hand. Another tide of thought is now needed to set the moral value of things right. Gandhi has done more than any other living soul to bring this new moral emphasis into prominence."

IV

Abdul Majid had not been at all satisfied with the course which the discussion had taken. He was eager to discuss much more radical issues along socialist lines. Gandhi's spinning programme, he said, was out of date. His insistence on non-violence as the only moral means to bring about a social revolution in India was unpractical. Thus Abdul shared the "Moscow" contempt for what he called the insignificant achievement of Khaddar in the sphere of Indian Economics. This was a time when the whole world was being turned upside down, and great things might be accomplished by rapid action.

"Not by violence," I urged.

"Why not?" asked Abdul. "What's the use of merely dealing with symptoms, when the root of the disease is left untouched?"

"That's begging the whole question," I answered. "What *is* the root of the disease? Isn't it selfishness? And isn't violence akin to selfishness? Don't we get very near to the fatal death-trap of all hasty actions, namely, that any means can be used to bring about a desired end? Do you really think that violence can drive out violence?"

"No," said Abdul; "but, all the same, Gandhi's method's far too slow. While he is touching one per cent of the population, the other ninety-nine per cent are dying of starvation and oppression."

"I'm afraid," said Bruce Martin, laughing, "that we shall remain here all night, if we get tied up in an argument concerning the use of force as a means of bringing about a social revolution."

"Force is not the Christian way," said Alan.

"The Christian nations of to-day believe in it," said Abdul Majid, "and I believe in it also."

"There we differ," said I, "and I am on the side of Gandhi, with all the simple-minded village people in India. They have suffered for centuries, but still are able to hold up their heads in the world to-day, while the militant races have gone under."

"I don't accept that," said Abdul Majid. "The only weapon that's any good to-day is a strong right arm. That's the only thing you Englishmen respect."

"Not all of us," I pleaded. "Remember how your own Prophet declared, 'Let there be no compulsion in religion.' I deeply honour that word."

"But the whole question," said Mulchand, "of Capital and Labour needs to be discussed. That's what Young India's facing. We're not merely nationalists as we were before. We're socialists—and we've got a socialist programme."

"Do you really think," said Bruce Martin, "that the doctrinaire socialism of the West can be applied unchanged to the East?"

"Not at all," said Mulchand. "We're not so foolish as that; but there are human rights which every one can claim so long as those extravagances exist which we see around us every day. Christ surely taught that lesson when He set before us the parable of Dives and Lazarus."

Bruce Martin looked at his watch. "I'm afraid," he said, "I've got a class to take in a short time. May I say one thing more before I go? The British rulers never realised the harm they were doing by encouraging the sale, in Indian villages, of cheap mill-made goods. They were confident that they were conferring a benefit; for the Manchester School was in the ascendancy and the best liberal thought paid homage to it."

"What was your own opinion," asked Anil, turning to me, "before you came out to India?"

"I was all in favour of Free Trade," I answered, "and most Englishmen of my own generation shared the same outlook. I can well remember my astonishment when I heard this doctrine being called in question by my friend Susil Rudra, who was Professor of Indian Economics. Certainly, at that time, I believed with all my heart that Free Trade had proved an immense blessing to the poor of India and that they had prospered under British rule. Only when I was brought into closest touch with Mahatma Gandhi, whose practical knowledge is quite unrivalled, was my earlier belief shaken."

"But what about Lancashire?" asked Neil. "How will Lancashire get on, if Gandhi's programme succeeds?"

"The Lancashire working men and women," I said, "whom I know well, have had a great shock. They were confident that they were helping the poor people in India. Now they are told that they are hindering them. It will take some time for them to adjust their minds to that new conception of their own industrial life. But when they know that they are hindering Indian development they will give way."

"Just one more point remains," Anil urged, "which Neil brought forward, namely, the rapid increase in the Indian population."

"That's by far the most serious danger," said Bruce Martin. "Yet no one seems to care two pins about it. Think of it—thirty-four million people added in ten years—more than three million every year! Where will it all stop?"

"Whatever blame there is for the high birth- and death-rate," said I, "must be shared between Government and people. For the evils of child-marriage can only be remedied by the people themselves."

"That's true," said Anil, "but Government's military extravagance has led to the starving of education; and illiteracy makes all reform difficult."

"We're involved there," said Bruce, "in a vicious circle, and mutual recrimination is useless.

I'm afraid, however, my time is up, and I must hurry away."

Before we parted we thanked him for giving us so much of his time.

"Not a bit of it," he answered; "the thanks are all on my side. The truth is, the problem of India's poverty is almost insoluble. Only on a world scale can facts of such magnitude be dealt with; and this question is the biggest world question of the future."

CHAPTER XII

THE CULTURAL GAIN AND LOSS

THE Summer Term at Oxford was rapidly drawing to its close, and our last meeting had come. It was one of those perfect evenings when twilight lingers and the stars come out one by one as night draws on. We were all seated in a College garden, and friendliness was the very air we breathed.

This time we had not chosen our subject. We were expecting to sum up what had gone before, when Anil broke the silence. "I'm afraid we've left out," he began, "the most important matter in the whole discussion. I can't think how we did it!"

"What's that?" I asked with some surprise.

"The cultural loss which comes from the continuance of such a foreign rule as yours. Surely this is far the greatest harm we have received, and also the hardest to repair."

"Didn't we deal with that point," Neil asked, "when we freely accepted the fact of the Indian Renaissance? Wasn't it decided at that time that there had been a real gain during last century, even in the literature of the common people."

"I was just getting to that," said Anil. "We accepted, perhaps too readily, the theory of the gain which came to India, owing to the first impact of British rule; and Safdar was intrigued by the analogy with Norman and Saxon in England. I wasn't quite so taken with that analogy as he was, because I've studied the British period in Indian history through and through, and the analogy is somewhat misleading. But I'm quite ready to grant you that, in the first instance, after British rule was established, there was a creative period in Indian literature and religious thought, with great personalities behind it. We may well call that a Renaissance. But what about the after-effects of foreign rule? What is happening to-day?"

"You're quite right in drawing our attention to that point," said I. "Don't you remember the emphasis I laid on Seeley's pronouncement, that *prolonged* subjection was harmful?"

"Yes," said Anil, "I noticed that very carefully indeed. As a matter of fact, we all did; for you made it abundantly clear. But while we worked out at length the harm that had been done in other directions, we left this cultural side almost untouched. Yet, in the long run, nothing can be of greater consequence."

"I agree," said I, "for it is written, 'Man shall not live by bread alone.' The spirit rules the body; the body ought not to rule the spirit."

"No, indeed," said Anil. "Do you remember that other sentence in Seeley about 'creating a notion that it was shameful to assist the foreigner in maintaining his dominion'? Well, we've now got to that point culturally: for we've reached a complete deadlock. The reason is, that in our heart of hearts we're all of us conscious that if this foreign rule is continued much longer, and no real power is given us to rule over ourselves, it's going to kill, not our bodies only, but our minds. The stimulating effect of the first impact with the West has worn off. The novelty has disappeared. Can't you all see here, at Oxford, where intellectual genius is worshipped, how a foreign rule of your British type must mean for us, in the long run, merely second-rate, third-rate and even fourth-rate imitation, with all its soul-deadening effects?"

"How do you account," asked Alan, "for the rapid deterioration which is clearly happening to-day?"

"Let's get right down to facts," said Anil. "When you British first came out to India, you brought with you some really great men, who met our great men on equal terms. Genius met genius, and the sparks flew. Think, for instance, of Duff and Raja Ram Mohan Roy. Look at outstanding statesmen, and men of intellect such as Munro, Metcalfe, Malcolm and Elphinstone. *They* didn't need to pass Rowlatt Acts in order to keep us quiet. We were of one mind with them, and they were of one mind with us. Again, among non-officials, remember David Hare and that strange genius Derozio. Why! Derozio, who had Indian blood in his veins, would be clapped in prison at once if he were a teacher in Bengal at the present time. But in those days there was freedom everywhere. It was like new wine. It went to the head. And even in a later generation you sent out such men of genius as Edwin Arnold, who appreciated our religion and our literature. Where is there a Macaulay or an Edwin Arnold in the Civil Service to-day? Who cares a straw for our literature and culture? Who among the civilians at Simla gives a moment's thought to the study of the Indian Renaissance about which we have just spoken? When has this Government patronised, in the slightest degree, our great men of art and letters—our poets and artists—in accordance with the immemorial custom of the East?"

"You've got to ask a more fundamental question," said Neil, with scorn. "How *can* a Secretariat patronise anything? When my uncle was out in India, District Officers lived their own independent life and were not employed in writing endless reports. They had leisure to cultivate a taste for Indian literature, and also a real love for the village people."

"Why, Neil," I said, with some bitterness—for I had groaned under the misery of it for many years—"they haven't got leisure to-day to cultivate a taste for their own literature, let alone that of India. They've dropped all the old interest that used to exist in Art and Poetry as lovable things in themselves. There's the root of the mischief. Only one who loves Art itself will take a living interest in Indian Art, and study its forms till the whole subject becomes a passionate search for new beauty. Only one who deeply loves Shelley and Keats will want to read Tagore in the original Bengali, and refuse to be content with translations. But the truth is we've reached a series of lean years even in Great Britain, especially since the War. Each day's being crowded out with motors, cinemas, wireless and other interests, while the true culture of life itself, through the Fine Arts, is falling into decay. Add to this, in India, the mass of files which the Secretariat system has introduced, and you kill the soul of poetry in the Civil Service.

"Take another point," I continued. "When I was in Delhi I made a special study of the last days of the Moghuls: for there were still living men of letters, like Munshi Zaka Ullah, who had intimate recollections of those times. I found out from Hindus and Muslims alike that there was a deep affection lingering on for that remarkable line of rulers, in spite of the decadence which had taken place. Old Bahadur Shah loved poetry up to the very last. He had his own poet's *nom de plume* like the rest of them and wrote verses. He would call every one alike to his Court within the Delhi Fort. There he held his 'Kingdom of Letters,' wherein there was no distinction of race or religion, and no Hindu-Muslim tension. But this has all died away now, with deplorable results. Think of any of our present Governors holding his court in a 'Kingdom of Letters,' and writing poetry!"

Asha had been listening intently. She too had made a study of this subject. "Haven't you noticed one thing," she asked, "which shows what has happened? The Moghul Emperors, just like the British rulers, were foreigners. They came from Central Asia, where it is bitterly cold for nearly half the year. But they went out of their way to acclimatise themselves to the habits of our country. They were true patrons of art and literature. As a result, we Hindus look upon Akbar and Jehangir and Shah Jahan as our very own. Through them we have learnt to admire Islam, as a religion of culture, which has brought new gifts to India, our Motherland. When we see the great Moghul architecture, or study the miniature paintings, or learn from our childhood to love Persian poetry, we absorb these things, and make them a part of our own religious nature. We have even taken something from the music they brought with them from Central Asia and Persia. The whole culture of Sind and the Punjab is full of these things."

"Don't you find the same great quality," I asked, "in English literature?"

"Ah, yes," said Asha, "that's the side of

your culture that we *have* absorbed. We love Shelley and Keats and Wordsworth. Our Bengali literature bears the mark of their influence on every page. But you, on your side—have any of *you* taken the trouble to study *our* literature and culture? Just one or two, perhaps, but what are they among so many?"

"Let's come back to the facts," pleaded Anil. "Let's find out what's actually happening. Take Bengal. No historian could doubt for a moment that the literature of Bengal last century showed a great advance. There was an intellectual and spiritual revival, which went on from one generation to another. You've only to read the story of the Tagore household, as it is told in Rabindranath's *Reminiscences*, or to dip into a novel like *Gora*. Then there were women, like Aru and Toru Dutt. All this was something to be proud of. But look at Bengal to-day. There's no lack of intellectual genius. Think of Aurobindo and Monomohan Ghose, and Barin, all from one family! But repression has crushed the heart out of our young people. Bengal has no means to-day of giving free expression to its deepest inner thoughts. The finest genius is being wasted—pitilessly wasted."

"Here in Oxford, at least," said John Murray, "you have perfect freedom."

"Yes," replied Anil, "that's quite true, and we're grateful for it, as Asha also will tell you. But do you realise, Alan, what awaits me when

I get home? Oh, I know," he added, as Alan touched his arm, "I know, Alan, that a great deal of it's our own fault. Don't think we don't blame ourselves. We sometimes even overdo it, and give way to despair. Think what Satyen wrote—that tenderest soul in the world, who was crushed beneath the weight of his own burden of sorrow, and died young."

Anil then recited, with intense emotion, the words of Satyendranath Datta's poem—

> Crushed are we on the cross of slavery all our lives,
> Our politics—a crown of thorns,
> Our social life—a bed of spikes,
> Which pierces us at every movement of our bodies.

Anil's eyes were filled with tears which he brushed away with haste.

Alan could hardly bear it. "Anil," he cried, "don't take it so much to heart! We're with you—we of the younger generation. We *do* understand! Oh, believe me, Anil, the heart of England is with you in your longing to be free. But can't your people drop their secret plots and murders? We love freedom. But as long as the world lasts, secret violence like that will only be met by measures of repression in return. It always gives rise to a vicious circle from which there's never any escape."

"We realise all that," said Safdar. "But what are you doing to those who practise *non*-violence? Think of a pure-hearted man like Mahatma Gandhi, forced back into prison time after time!"

"Didn't he declare," asked Neil, "that he was a rebel, and at 'war' with the British Government? How was it possible to do otherwise than imprison him?"

"Oh, they never tried to understand him," said Safdar. "They merely called out, 'Off with his head,' like the Queen in *Alice in Wonderland*. Why couldn't you see that you had to deal with the greatest spiritual genius in the world to-day? Think of him; and then think of your own politicians."

"But Lord Irwin," said Alan, "didn't misunderstand him in that manner."

"No," said Anil; "only unfortunately you cancelled Lord Irwin's policy the very first moment you could do so."

Mulchand intervened. "Let's face realities," he said. "Every one's heartily sick and tired of fighting, even by civil resistance. But every one's also sick and tired of the present Government, and would turn it out to-morrow if they got the chance."

"When you're in this state," said Asha, "all your culture goes to pieces. Even a 'war' of civil resistance absorbs all the country's energies. There's nothing left over for poetry and song. Your own poets in England, like Rupert Brooke and Siegfried Sassoon, had to dig trenches. The war atmosphere's foul with poison gas. It kills all culture."

"But we're not at 'war' with India," urged Alan.

"No," said Asha, "you're not at open war with us. We shouldn't be here, if you were. But all the same we have to resist your domination. We do it by non-violence, and that takes up all our energies. We believe our cause is just and, as Mahatma Gandhi once said, we'd almost dare to ask you to come over on to our side, so that you might fight against your worst selves."

"What can we do to help matters?" asked Neil Munro.

"There's only one thing to be done," said Anil. "You've got to learn over again to *trust* us; to meet us as equals, just as you do here in Oxford. You've got to be on our side in our longing to be free, and not to bind us, hard and fast, with safeguards and reservations which show a fatal lack of trust."

"Do go on, Anil," said Alan; "tell us all that is in your heart."

"Shall I tell you a dream I had the other night?" asked Anil, with great diffidence.

"Yes, do!" said Neil. "We want to get at the truth; and to-night we meet for the last time."

"All day long," said Anil, "some lines of Tennyson had been ringing in my head:

> In Love, if Love be Love, if Love be ours,
> Faith and unfaith can ne'er be equal powers:
> Unfaith in aught is want of faith in all.

and then the conclusion:

> So trust me not at all, or all in all.

"That night," Anil continued, his voice becoming stronger, "I went to sleep and dreamt that we were called upon by God to build a large and spacious house to live in, and all the materials were given us and put in order. There were stones already cut of different sizes. Then a dispute arose about the way of building, and in a moment everything was in terrible confusion. Each one seized the stone which was nearest to him in order to kill his brother. The noise became terrific; and then, as suddenly as it had appeared, the nightmare dream came to an end.

"After that, I lay awake half the night, wondering what the dream meant. While I lay thus, thinking, thinking, the lines of Tennyson came back to my mind:

> Faith and unfaith can ne'er be equal powers:
> Unfaith in aught is want of faith in all.

and the last line more than any other:

> So trust me not at all, or all in all.

"Then I began to go over our discussions, and I could see that behind all our arguments, on either side, was a want of faith. We were trying to score for our own side."

Alan had been listening intently, as if eager to speak, but he restrained himself, and Anil went on:

"Alan, you and I have learnt completely to trust one another, here at Oxford. We don't use arguments to throw at each other—like those stones in my dream. We can really say the words :

> So trust me not at all, or all in all.

We've learnt that great secret, haven't we ? We know that friendship can only be built upon Love and Trust. I heard, the other day, in Chapel, some splendid words,

> ' Except the Lord build the house,
> Their labour is but lost that build it,'

and they came back to me after my dream."

Neil Munro was the first to break the silence which followed. " Anil," he said, " you don't know how hard you hit me when you said that we were trying to score for our own side. I see your point about Trust. We've been wanting you to trust us all the while ; but we've not been ready to trust you."

" Shall I tell you the honest truth, Neil ? " said Anil, laughing, as his mood changed from grave to gay. " We're such an absurdly affectionate people that you could get almost anything out of us if you only showed us affection, instead of despising us and calling us cowards."

" What would you *do*, then," asked John Murray, " if you were in our shoes ? "

" I'd get rid of all those safeguards as soon as possible ; and the moment we Indians came to any agreement among ourselves, I'd register it straight away and give us ample leave to act upon it. Above all, I would insist on never for a moment making capital out of our divisions."

"You'll forgive me asking the question," said Neil, "but isn't the real object you have in view complete separation? Wouldn't you want to leave the Empire?"

"The Empire!" exclaimed Safdar Ali. "Why, the Empire wouldn't exist, if only you acted in that way. We should all be free and independent nations, as we ought to be, and you would be free as well."

"Neil!" said Anil, who had been eager to speak. "Don't you see that your very question has led you back into a vicious circle of distrust? Can't you come out of it? Can't you trust us completely?"

Neil nodded his head and smiled. Then Asha said to her brother, "Don't forget the lack of trust on our side also. When we've got so little trust in ourselves and can't trust each other, we try to throw all this distrust on other people. But that's no good at all. We've got to build up self-confidence first. Then other things will follow."

The night had drawn on and the moon had just begun to appear behind the lattice of the trees. We were all unwilling to break off, but the time had come at last, and we had to get back to our rooms. I saw Neil and Anil earnestly engaged in carrying on the argument as they walked away. Alan was with them.

CHAPTER XIII

THE WAY TO PEACE

I

HERE, then, is the conclusion of the whole matter. This volume has attempted to show, in the guise of a dialogue, that there has been a dual line of development running through the past record of Britain's connection with India. One line, which I have called the racial principle, has continually led to strife, because it has roused up racial antagonism in return, whenever it has been put into practice. The other line, which I have called the liberal principle, or the principle of political freedom, has led to reconciliation, progress and peace.

Whenever the racial principle has been uppermost in men's minds, the emphasis has been laid upon the idea of Empire, wherein the British race must at all costs and at all times be the ruling power. Indians, not being members of the ruling race, are regarded as subjects rather than citizens, and India is thought of as the "possession" of Great Britain. The imperial power in this case must always be supreme. The subject race, being inferior, has to be thankful if it receives material benefits from the superior power; but it cannot claim equality.

Along this second line of development political independence becomes impossible. Therefore it carries no moral sanction with it. Ultimately, it relies upon the passive contentment brought about in the things of the body, and leaves out of account the things of the soul. Its weapon is force.

When, on the contrary, the principle of political freedom is aimed at by the power from outside to which has been committed the direction of affairs, then the development of free institutions becomes the primary concern. Higher education is advanced as rapidly as possible with that end in view. Racial equality follows as a natural corollary, and is fostered in all the processes of government as an integral part of the liberal principle itself.

The great Victorians, from Macaulay to Gladstone, never regarded India as a conquered country. They held that the soul of India was free; to be respected in the spirit of freedom and on equal terms. They were not imperialists, in the racial sense of the term. Therefore they encouraged to the utmost freedom of education, freedom of the press, and freedom of speech. They appealed not to force, but to goodwill.

When the theme is thus divided out, it becomes luminously clear that only the second line of approach can offer a secure moral foundation for the future. As a Christian, my ardent hope is that this liberal principle will prevail; for to me there can be no question that it is more in accord with the mind and will of Christ.

But if, by some fatal mischance, under the cover of specious phrases the racial principle tends in the long run to predominate, then I can see no hope of future settlement, but only the certainty of bitter, unceasing conflict. British rule in India will then become one of the greatest tragedies of history. It will represent fair hopes raised high, but dashed to the ground owing to the fatal temptation of power to cling to possession at all cost.

For, in that case, this racial principle itself, which had already been the curse of India for centuries past, and had led to "Untouchability" and a thousand other evils, will have returned in a new form, far more deadly than before. No Christian could defend it; for it would be morally indefensible.

All around in Asia, Indians watch the nations of the East governing themselves. Afghanistan has its own independence. Persia, Turkey have theirs. But India, one of the greatest countries of the world, not only in its population but also in its literature, religion and culture, has no independence at all. Whenever some important crisis arises, the final word lies with Great Britain.

II

Beyond all this, as I have fully shown, lies the Colour Bar, from which Indians suffer in almost every part of the world, and especially within the British Dominions. The modern East, and India in particular, will not tolerate any longer insults which were patiently borne in days gone by. The temper of Asia is rising, and Europe can no longer bestride the rest of the world "like a Colossus." It is noticed by every thoughtful Indian that this evil has its centre in the Anglo-Saxon world, and has become entrenched within the Christian Church.

This brings us to the heart of the subject, which may be stated in the following terms:

"If Great Britain comes to stand for a 'White Race Empire,' wherein Indians are to be treated as racial inferiors, they will have none of it."

III

It is futile to go on framing Constitutions which have distrust at the very centre and safeguards attached to every clause: for this is to build on fear and to create suspicion in return.

If, on the other hand, we could learn from Christ that love alone can cast out the torment of fear; that true kingship consists in humble service; that by losing life we save it; then all might be well. The moral problem between the two countries would vanish, as it did among those care-free undergraduates at Oxford.

For though we may speak with the tongues of men and of angels in India; and though we may have all knowledge and understand all mysteries; and though we may be eager, in our zeal for reform, to improve the lot of India's poor: yet, if we have not got that love which is patient and forbearing; which does not vaunt itself and is not puffed up, we are nothing. What we do will not abide; for we shall be finally judged there, not by what we do, but what we are.

CHAPTER XIV

A GLEAM OF HOPE

THE sun is setting at Simla over the mountains with an amazing beauty of light and colour and shade. Yet there are ominous signs of thunder and storm, which give awe to the scene and sadness to the mind.

The symbol fits in with the theme of this volume which has tried to represent the light and shade and colour of human life in the two countries which I love most on earth—Great Britain and India. Thunder and storm are in the air to-day and sadness reigns, because there is as yet no harmony and peace. But in the end the sunshine will break forth out of the very heart of the storm-clouds themselves, if only we cling to faith and hope, and do not give way to despair.

For in spite of the atmosphere of resentment in the East against Europe, which is everywhere apparent, I have often been touched to find at Oxford and Cambridge how eagerly Indian students have sought for aid in making known among their English friends the true moral situation as it exists in India to-day, causing them such pain at heart. Their sense of justice has been hurt most of all, and the wound has gone very deep. Also, I have found a corresponding anxiety to sympathise among the British students whom I have met, and opportunities have been freely given me of explaining the facts as I have known them.

Although, therefore, the immediate prospect has its dark shadows, there are certain aspects that even now bring a gleam of light into the picture. For, looking back, it becomes abundantly clear that some of the deepest loyalties, both of the spiritual and intellectual life, have united British friends with Indian friends, as individuals, on the basis of perfect freedom. We have suffered together in our common sorrows; we have rejoiced together in our common joys. These things remain, while much that is transitory has vanished.

Memories, most sacred of all, are still fresh concerning lives laid down for one another in times of stress and peril. If there is no "greater love than this, that a man lay down his life for his friends," then truly there are noble records of that "greater love" on either side, both Indian and British, which must bind us with invisible bonds in one body and one spirit.

Furthermore, there are those who have gone forth with a high purpose from a dearly cherished family-life in Britain to make India their own home. They have had their children born to them in India. These, when they have grown up, have looked upon India as the land of their birth, and have loved it with loyal affection. Some, even, have maintained their home ties with India right up to the third and fourth generation.

It would be unthinkable that all these precious links should be destroyed in the heat of the present controversy. Rather, when the dross has been burnt away, such old intimacies and dear affections will shine out again like gold, purified seven times in the fire. Much that has happened may rightly be forgotten on both sides, but these things will always be remembered.

How strong these personal ties of affection are may be easily understood from certain things that I have witnessed in Great Britain. Indian students have told me, on the one hand, of their exceeding bitterness of heart at what is happening to-day in India, and the misery of hope so long deferred. On the other hand, their love for the ancient seats of learning in Britain, where lifelong college friendships are made, has been deeply touching. Appreciation of the kindness they have received from those with whom they stayed has been continually on their lips.

Still further, there is always some individual companion who is attached to one or other of them with a sincere devotion. There will be at least one friend to whom their confidence has been given without any reserve. These exceptions appear to me to prove the rule, that the present bitterness itself is a sign of love that has been very deeply wounded and is now passing through a strong reaction. For as Coleridge has truly said:

> . . . to be wrath with one we love
> Doth work like madness in the brain.

Yet if once full freedom, along with equal racial status, is willingly acknowledged as a matter of right and justice, then I have no doubt that the old loyalties and personal affections will return.

We may well take heart, therefore, and firmly believe that in the future, as well as in the past, men and women will be raised up from both sides, who will be able to point forward to that one human brotherhood, which is the goal of all our striving. Their united work of reconstruction, starting from a firm moral basis, will remain strongly established long after the politicians have had their say.

For the union of the human race, transcending all the narrow limitations which hamper us to-day, is the one supreme end ordained by God that lies before us. If only these storm-clouds of suspicion and mistrust can be cleared away, goodwill between India and Britain may even yet be renewed, and become a token of the final unity of mankind. Therefore, this present urgent demand in India for political justice and equal racial treatment cannot possibly be dismissed, as if it were but little concern of ours. It is the deep concern of every lover of mankind.

No one who utters sincerely the sacred name

of Christ with heart allegiance, can refuse to follow Him along these paths. None can fail to obey Him when He speaks to us in a manner which touches the future of humanity so intimately as this. For in everything we do to India, Christ Himself stands before us and speaks the word—" Ye did it unto Me."

Far more closely than we sometimes care to remember, we ourselves have had in our own hands the making of India's present condition—her poverty, her hunger, her illiteracy. We ourselves have grown rich, while India has remained one of the most poverty-stricken and illiterate countries in the world. On our heads lies the blame.

When, therefore, we turn from our own selfish striving and listen to His voice, our sympathy with India's suffering will be the first thought in our minds that will take the place of impatience and disdain. But if we are determined to hold India selfishly by force; if we yield to craven fear, sinking lower and lower, as repression follows repression, and violence leads on to further violence, then the future will be dark indeed, not only for India and Great Britain, but also for the rest of the world.

NOTES

A.—ACKNOWLEDGMENT OF THANKS

For many historical details in this volume I wish to acknowledge my indebtedness to a recent important book called *The Rise and Fulfilment of British Rule in India*, by Thompson and Garratt, published by Macmillan, which has given full value to the benefits derived from that rule, without glossing over or ignoring its defects. As a help to my wider thinking, I owe much also to Mervyn Davies's *Warren Hastings*, published by Ivor Nicholson and Watson.

My gratitude is due to many Indian and English friends who have read these pages in type and offered valuable suggestions; also to Mrs Allen and Mr Jaipal Singh of Achimota College; the Rev. S. G. Williamson of Wesley College, Kumasi, West Africa; and to Messrs Azmat Ali and Sharif of Simla, for typing and re-typing my manuscript.

B.—BENGAL IN 1769

Mervyn Davies, in his *Warren Hastings*, gives the following account of Bengal in 1769:

"The general condition of Bengal was every bit as bad as in the Carnatic. Here not war, but famine had been the deadly agent of desolation. The failure of the rains of 1769 throughout the greater part of the province had deprived the people of their supply of food for the following year. The result was one of the most appalling disasters in the recorded history of India. Nearly the whole of the two provinces of Bengal and Bihar was devastated. We read in the official reports of the Resident at Murshidebad that the living were feeding on the dead, and the streets were choked with corpses. Scenes of like horror were witnessed in every town and village. No less than one-third of the population, according to the best estimates, perished; according to others, it was a half. Whole districts were left entirely depopulated and returned to jungle.

"If this had been the only misfortune to overtake Bengal in these seven years, the story would have been tragic enough, but, as though an avenging deity had determined to ruin the country almost beyond hope of redemption, it had been accompanied by a complete collapse of government. The Company was not responsible for the famine; but it, and its agents, were largely to blame for the second disaster. The heavy hand of Clive had fallen for the space of two years on the English officials, and he had striven manfully to curb the abuses and reintroduce a sense of decency and discipline. But though the reforms that he made in the service were valuable, he had not touched the real root of the trouble; so far from improving the state of the province and the lot of the hapless peasants, he had in a measure made them worse" (p. 72).

In an earlier passage the same author writes:

"One thing only had brought these Englishmen to India, one thing only held them there. Money. Their object was to make enough money so that they could return to England, there to live in ease and comfort for the rest of their days. And they wished to make it quickly. Not only because they found no pleasure in their exile, but because for most of them life in India was a race against death, the climate being such that for a white man to live there for long at a time when the laws of health were little understood and still less observed was not a little hazardous" (p. 20).

C.—WARREN HASTINGS ON THE GITA

In Mervyn Davies's recently published volume on *Warren Hastings*, the following letter to his wife is quoted:

"My friend Wilkins, has lately made me a present of a most wonderful work of antiquity, and I am going to present it to the public. Among many precepts of fine morality I am particularly delighted with the following because it has been the invariable rule of my later life, and often applied to the earlier state of it, before I had myself reduced it to the form of a maxim in writing. It is this: '*Let the motive be in the deed, and not in the event.* Be not one whose motive for action is the hope of reward. Let not thy life be spent in inaction. Depend upon application'—that is, as is afterwards explained, the application of the rule of moral right to its consonant practice, without care for the event as it may respect ourselves. 'Perform thy duty, abandon all thought of the consequence, and make the event equal whether it terminate in good or evil; for such an equality is called application.'"

D.—LIONEL CURTIS ON FOREIGN RULE

The following passage from Lionel Curtis's *Civitas Dei* (p. 117) gives a picture of what is likely to happen under foreign rule:

"In countries ruled by foreigners whose views are in fundamental conflict with those of their subjects, political factions tend to develop on similar lines. The rulers enter into relations with such of the native race as are willing to act as their agents. They naturally endeavour to make this section feel that its interests are identical with their own, and, with this object in view, often entrust them with extensive powers. The people at large view with disfavour those of their race who are helping the foreigner to rule them. The native agents themselves regard with suppressed dislike the foreigners whose authority it is their interest to maintain. The best friends of the foreign authority are usually to be found in the classes more interested in business than politics. They fear disorders, which any attempt to eject the foreigner will necessitate. On the other hand, they are chafed by the failures and abuses from which no government is exempt. They seek reforms without revolution, but are seldom satisfied with such reforms as are actually made. There is, also, the party mainly drawn from the young and the poorer classes, who, with little to lose but their lives and with no experience of administrative problems, mistrust all measures for reform which are not based on physical force."

E.—THE "SAHIB" ATTITUDE

The Rev. Dr D. J. Fleming has given the following picture of the difficulties of the "Sahib" attitude which confront the young missionary when he comes out to India for the first time:

"In any field it is hard enough for missionaries to free themselves from a domineering and autocratic attitude which seems—even when falsely based—to be a natural characteristic of western races. But missionaries in India especially are played upon by innumerable social forces, that tell upon the life, moulding it in spite of principle and reason. In India the white man is a 'Sahib'; every one makes way for the wearer of the sun-hat; people salaam; policemen salute; the many little symbols of a submissive attitude, instilled by decades of British rule, are exhibited toward the missionary without the asking. All the more does he find himself surrounded by suggestions of superiority when he mingles with those classes from whom converts have come. Small wonder it is, that with the passing of the years, unless it has been consciously and prayerfully resisted, little ways of arrogance and patronising manifest themselves."

F.—"CHRISTMAS DAY"

[I have been often asked for a full translation of Satyendranath Datta's poem on "Christmas Day," which I quoted briefly in *Christ and Labour*. I owe to my friend, K. M. Sarkar, of St Stephen's College, Delhi, the translation given below. He writes: "Satyendranath Datta (1881-1922) is a well-known figure of the literary world of Bengal. Like Shelley and Keats, though only allowed to sing for a few brief years, he has left a volume of lyric poetry remarkable for its sweetness, simplicity, pathos and idealism. His life was a counterpart of his poetry—full of gracious deeds. His heart was full of love for his country and his people, especially the down-trodden. This poem was written after the War (1920) on Christmas Day,—the Day of peace and goodwill."]

"Though they do not call me Christian, I bow to you on your day of birth, O Christ! the beloved Son of God—the saintliest of Saints.

"Worshipped by wise men, O Shepherd! O poorest of the poor! the world owns its great debt of love to you.

"With your heart-strings you bound this world to God and called him 'Father' in gladness like a child. The world looked up in wonder at this new name. The men of religion were enraged and the wicked conspired. The sceptics laughed at what they thought was but a hollow claim; but the blood shed on the Cross made that claim secure.

"Light came from beyond the darkness of death. The song of victory arose. Your death gave everlasting life to men. You bridged the gulf between heaven and earth and glorified the world by your advent. The baptism that conquered death is not touched by loss or gain, by failure or success.

"Therefore do we call Christmas 'the Great Day,' the very thought of which expands the heart and kills all selfishness. We love and revere you, though not called Christians. Asia claims you—her blood flows in your veins. We, little men of a great land, lift up our tired eyes to you in wonder, crushed as we are under the cross of multiform servitude all our lives. Our politics—our crown of thorns; our society—a bed of spikes, which pierces us at every movement.

"We drift, like rudderless ships, on the ocean of life,—and our miseries multiply. The tyranny of might levels us to the ground. The heartless and the wicked vie with each other in the work of destruction. The cynic laughs, as hypocrisy strangles the throat of truth. The roar of the howitzers drowns the voice of prayer. Humanity bleeds, while Thugs flourish. The innocent suffer. These agonise your heart and with fresh nails crucify you every day.

"By persecuting you and abusing her power, Rome lost her glory and was reduced to dust. In their perversity, men have forgotten the lesson of history; they build a house of cards and are proud of their achievement. Their chariots in mad fury crush mankind under their wheels and raise clouds of dust. Christianity is lip-worship and too feeble to withstand the doctrine of Nietzsche. The world stands aghast and speechless at Europe's endless lust of power. Civilisation gives way as avarice grows. Reverence evaporates and culture faints. Imperialism and materialism hold high carnival. On Europe's bleeding breast dance the three witches—War Lust, Race Lust, Gold Lust.

"That is no place for you, my Lord. Come away to this Asia—this land of Buddha, Janak, Kabir, Nanak, Nitai, Shuk and Shanak. Bring your new message to this ancient home of idealism. Reign supreme in Hind and be the brightest jewel in her diadem. Our heavy-laden hearts will find comfort in you. Teach us the lesson of humility, service and truth. Sound the trumpet of a new awakening. Teach us patience and courage; remove all fear. Give us the strength to accept all suffering, O glorious first of *Satyagrahis*![1] Let us not be faint-hearted when persecution comes. May your light guide us in the

[1] Passive resisters.

pursuit of life eternal. Teach us sympathy, O Teacher of love. Come and fill our hearts. Give us the love that fulfils itself in service among the poor, the lowly and lost.

"Our hearts aspire for that ideal, but if we falter, extend your loving arms to help us. Give us the strength 'to die to live.' O Helper of the helpless! nourish our feeble desires. Touch our paralysed hearts. Hold our hands and guide us to the true life. Give us the faith that brings never-failing strength. O Comforter! lead us to the feet of the Father. When sorrow and suffering make us faint, let us remember your cry at Calvary—

"'Forsake me not my Father, O my Father!'"

G.—BIOGRAPHICAL NOTE ON PAGE 84

Macaulay wrote of Bentinck, who was Governor-General from 1827 to 1835: "He inspired oriental despotism with the spirit of Britain and Freedom." Roy co-operated with him in the suppression of widow-burning. Keshub inspired the Marriage Act of 1872 which opened the way to inter-caste and civil marriage. Ramkrishna and Vivekananda inspired the Ramkrishna Mission, which carries on dispensaries, orphanages, schools, etc. (EDITOR.)

INDEX